DETAILING AND MODIFYING READY-TO-RUN LOCOMOTIVES IN OO GAUGE

VOLUME 2

British Steam Locomotives, 1948–1968

DETAILING AND MODIFYING READY-TO-RUN LOCOMOTIVES IN OO GAUGE

VOLUME 2

British Steam Locomotives, 1948–1968

GEORGE DENT

THE CROWOOD PRESS

First published in 2009 by
The Crowood Press Ltd
Ramsbury, Marlborough
Wiltshire SN8 2HR

www.crowood.com

British Library Cataloguing-in-Publication Data
A catalogue record for this book is available from the British Library.

ISBN 978 1 84797 145 6

Typeset by Servis Filmsetting Ltd, Stockport, Cheshire
Printed and bound in Singapore by Craft Print International Ltd

Contents

Acknowledgements

In the first instance, I must extend my gratitude to Simon Kohler (Hornby) and Dennis Lovett (Bachmann) for generously providing the models contained in this book. John Bristow (Deluxe Materials), Alex Medwell (The Airbrush Company), Dave Alexander (Alexander Models), Ken Bridger (Genesis Kits) and John Peck (Precision Labels) have also provided kind assistance over the past few years.

For support, help and advice I'd like to thank my colleagues at *Model Rail*, Ben Jones, Chris Leigh, Dave Lowery and Richard Foster. Thank you also to the many readers and contributors who have taken the time to share their opinions, tips and recommendations through the magazine. Thanks also to Nick Brodrick (*Steam Railway*), Mike Wild (*Hornby Magazine*) and the staff at The Crowood Press.

Various (some now former) members of staff at the NRM went out of their way to help improve my understanding and appreciation for both the steam locomotive and 1980s Nissan Micras: thank you to Roy Boulton, Stan Knowles and David Wright. Thank you, Dad, for your persistence in trying to ensure a rounded knowledge and appreciation of railways and, along with Mum, for encouraging my creative and practical skills.

As much of this manuscript was written on location in Settle, I must thank Jeanne Carr for the use of her idyllic cottage and to the local bakers for keeping me in sustenance. The understanding of my 'in-laws', Ma and Pa Strange, is appreciated and I'm also grateful to Lily-Rose for humouring my train obsession. And thank you, little Joey, for reminding me of just how wonderful it is to see a real, working steam engine.

May I wish much love to Maude for her devotion, even in the face of a beleaguered guardian and, finally, to Julie-Marie: I shall be eternally grateful for too many things to mention here. Thank you.

Preface

My first railway memory involves watching a scruffy blue Class 25 diesel trundling past Donkey's Hill en route to Liverpool's northern docks, sometime in the late 1970s. I can easily picture the sight of the locomotive with its solitary brake van and, although it may be embellished by nostalgia, I seem to remember that the driver created a jaunty tune with several toots of his horn. The guard waved heartily and shouted something witty to my indulgent mother who had agreed to wait patiently with her two boys on this summer's afternoon, just in case any trains should pass.

Living so close to an increasingly moribund freight line was not the most exciting baptism for a budding trainspotter, especially when set against tales of folk with homes alongside the East Coast Main Line in the days of Gresley's 'Streaks' and 'A3' Pacifics. However, it had me hooked and, with a fellow enthusiast for a father, it seemed impossible that railways would not form a significant part of my life.

My family later left Liverpool, heading for a small village near Warrington and, while this was initially a bit of a culture shock, Arpley marshalling yard and the West Coast Main Line came within cycling distance, as did three of the Liverpool–Manchester routes. Obviously, this being the 1980s, diesel and electric traction prevailed and so, for someone raised solely in the 'modern' railway era, steam traction was inevitably viewed as something related to museums and preserved lines.

Dad's tales of his spotting days at Edge Hill – of 'Black Fives', '8Fs', 'Duchesses' and 'Princesses' – seemed like they belonged in a far distant past. Excursions orchestrated by my Dad to Steamport Museum in Southport and the odd fling across the Pennines to the National Railway Museum (NRM) were enjoyed as a form of induction into the joys of steam. However, I must admit that I was a bit slow on the uptake as contemporary forms of traction still held my imagination; those trips to York were remembered more for the anticipation of seeing HSTs on the East Coast 'racetrack'. It was probably my first taste of a preserved railway that did the trick, a charabanc tour to Haworth for the (tedious) Brontë experience that was enlivened by an unofficial tour of the Keighley & Worth Valley Railway's motive power depot. That we didn't ride on the line was not important, as walking amongst various BR 'Standards', a Midland '4F' and a 'Jinty' was good enough for me. Additionally, seeing Bullied 'West Country' Pacific *City of Wells* coming on-shed, at dusk, will live long in my memory.

Despite my modelling interests remaining rooted in the 1980s BR scene for a while, things changed as I got older and could afford to expand my collection of stock to incorporate more of the 1960s period. The final deciding factor was taking a job at the National Railway Museum as a conservator and any job where you spend your first day reassembling the freshly burnished coupling rods of a Great Western 'Star' class 4-6-0 is going to grab your imagination. My time at York also led me to take a deeper interest in Britain's railways, looking further back in time to the pre-Grouping (pre-1922) companies and, in particular, the Midland Railway.

Eventually, I was entrusted with conserving many items from the NRM's collection of models and other small objects and, having now been an active railway modeller for more than twenty years, this led me in 2004 to become the model-maker in residence at *Model Rail* magazine, one of Britain's foremost hobby titles. Having always preferred to model in OO gauge, my professional work has nevertheless meant the odd dalliance with both the larger and smaller scales. In this book, however, I will be concentrating solely on OO gauge.

The author takes the opportunity to examine the frames of the new-build 'A1' Pacific *Tornado* at Darlington in July 2007. George modified a Bachmann OO gauge model to represent this unique locomotive and an auction for the finished model raised hundreds of pounds for the A1 Steam Trust. Photo: Ben Jones

Introduction

The suffix to the title of this work, *British Steam Locomotives 1948–1968*, sets out explicitly the subject matter contained herein, this period of railway history still remaining by far the most popular with modellers. Concentrating on the 1948–68 period may encompass the lifetime of British Railways (BR) steam, but that does not mean that only BR-designed machines are featured. Indeed, as the newly nationalized railway inherited a staggering array of motive power, of some weird and wonderful designs, many dated well into the previous century. That is why the likes of Hornby and Bachmann are now delving into pre-Grouping (pre-1922) designs without committing commercial suicide: many of these engines were in everyday service into the 1960s. Besides, the recent appearances of the London & North Western Railway (LNWR) 'Super D' 0-8-0 in the Bachmann range and Hornby's London & South Western (LSWR) 'T9' 4-4-0 and 'M7' 0-4-4T reflect the fact that many of the pre-nationalization and subsequent BR designs have already been covered.

On the topic of prototype treatment, I've endeavoured to include as broad a range of period and geographical area as possible within the remit of this book's subject. Spreading the coverage evenly has not been so easy, however, and the modelling press is constantly awash with 'wish lists' for what many of us consumers want to see offered in the red or blue boxes of our two main manufacturers of steam models. While London, Midland & Scottish (LMS) and Southern Railway (SR) fans are well served, the Great Western (GWR) and London & North

Eastern (LNER) lag behind in terms of models offered, especially to contemporary 'high-spec' standards.

What I must point out is that with a good many of the suggested projects contained herein, the actual techniques are not specific to the particular locomotive model featured. The object of this book is to encourage readers to take a look at their models, assess what improvements can be made, then choose a suitable method and material to do the job. The greatest assets to any modeller are confidence and experience and, while mistakes are almost inevitable, neither of the above can be obtained without practice. It might, therefore, be an idea to start with an older product, perhaps purchased second-hand, on which various techniques, tools and adhesives can be trialled without the worry of ruining a £100-plus model. I still make mistakes, but knowing how to remedy or disguise them can be very handy!

Throughout the book, we shall look primarily at how to refine certain details, correct errors, add missing equipment and customize models to create items that are not only more authentic, but are also unique to your collection. It's rare that any ready-to-run (r-t-r) maker will offer every permutation of number, name, livery and condition so, if a particular engine would be more appropriate for you, it helps to know how to go about changing the running numbers, names and tweaking a few details here and there.

The advantage of studying a book on locomotive detailing over a magazine article is that there is more space to devote to demonstrating and explaining each technique. This is often difficult in a monthly publication where a specific number of pages have been allotted to reveal how a model was created; a model that may have taken a few months to build. Readers sometimes complain that a certain amount of prior knowledge is assumed, but this is often essential as it's unrealistic to be able to explain the basics in every feature. Therefore, only a handful of full projects are included here; seeing a particular model through from beginning to end, over a number of chapters. Much of the other demonstrations, especially in the early chapters, are included to offer something of a foundation course in the core skills as well as showing how to go about specific tasks, such as replacing a chimney or making your own cylinder drainpipes.

Deciding on a cut-off point in terms of required ability and the extent of modification to a model was not an easy decision. This book is intended to appeal to as broad a range of modellers as possible, regardless of their favoured region, period or their level of practical experience, but a line had to be drawn somewhere. It had been my intention to include a chapter on building a replacement chassis, complete with new motor, gearbox, wheels, coupling rods and valve gear. However, after giving the matter serious thought and with the intention of explaining the various intricate processes properly, it seemed likely that this facet of locomotive enhancement would need far more space than was available. Indeed, another volume could easily be filled with such advanced techniques.

As the chapters progress, so too does the difficulty rating of most of the techniques. By working through the book, beginners can build their practical skills, while the more experienced may like to 'dip in' and find some inspiration. As my own fluency in model detailing increased, I became aware that buying off-the-shelf components was not always necessary and, certainly, not the most cost-effective way to work. Therefore, I've demonstrated a number of ways to 'scratch-build' some parts using various materials and techniques that drastically reduce the cost of a detailing project.

I've endeavoured not to duplicate too much information that appeared in Volume One of this series (*Detailing & Modifying Ready-to-Run*

This LNER 'B17' 4-6-0, although based around a Hornby model, only retains the original boiler and cab. Etched brass replacement chassis kits are available from firms such as Comet Models. These kits require new wheels, motors, gearboxes and power collection to be assembled, as well as the complex working valve gear and coupling rods. Can this be classed as a detailing or modifying project, or is it an advanced kit-building exercise? Unfortunately, when using the only OO gauge 'B17' model available at the time, such a protracted exercise was the only way to achieve an accurate rendition of the real thing. Not long after I finished this lengthy project, Hornby announced that it was planning a new, high-specification 'B17' in the near future.

Locomotives in OO Gauge: British Diesel and Electric Locomotives 1955–2008 [The Crowood Press, 2009]), but I'm also aware that not everyone reading these pages will have an interest in diesel and electric locomotives. Therefore, both titles aim to stand alone, while also complementing each other, so please bear with me if you've heard some things before, although I shall be expanding on certain topics that were mentioned only briefly in the previous book and there are aspects of other subjects that demand a slightly different slant when talking about steam traction.

Modifying and detailing r-t-r locomotives can be one of the most rewarding aspects of the model railway hobby and achieving a refined, personalized finish to your humble yard pilot shunter or 'top link' Pacific can provide an endless amount of satisfaction. Be warned, however, as it can be addictive!

GETTING TO KNOW YOUR STEAM LOCOMOTIVE

As the ensuing chapters contain many references to the various components and equipment found on steam locomotives, it seemed prudent to include a visual reference to explain these terms. Here are a few images of a BR Standard Class 4, 76079, standing in the locomotive works yard of the East Lancashire Railway at Bury in October 2007. Also included is a shot of LMS 'Royal Scot' 46115 *Scots Guardsman* at Carnforth in July 2008, just prior to its repaint following extensive restoration.

1: smokebox; 2: chimney; 3: boiler water feed; 4: dome; 5: boiler barrel; 6: safety valves; 7: whistle; 8: regulator coupling; 9: speedometer; 10: coupling rods; 11: reversing rod; 12: motion bracket; 13: crosshead and piston rod; 14: slide bars; 15: ejector; 16: steam pipe; 17: valve chest; 18: cylinders; 19: valve cylinder drains; 20: pony truck.

1: firebox; 2: wash-out plugs; 3: sandbox filler; 4: mechanical lubricator; 5: sanding pipes; 6: frames; 7: brake shoes; 8: injectors; 9: water feed from tender tank; 10: cab; 11: cab doors.

1: smoke deflectors; 2: smokebox door; 3: strap hinges; 4: smokebox door handle; 5: inside cylinder cover; 6: bufferbeam; 7: vacuum brake pipe; 8: lifting eye; 9: lamp bracket; 10: screw coupling; 11: buffer; 12: AWS protector plate; 13: guard irons; 14: cylinder relief valve; 15: front footsteps.

1: water filler hatch; 2: water scoop inlet dome; 3: coal bunker; 4: bulkhead; 5: rear view spectacle; 6: water tank; 7: water sieve box; 8: axle box and spring assembly; 9: rear guard irons; 10: train heating pipe; 11: brake pipes; 12: access ladder; 13: lifting eyes.

CHAPTER 1

Doing Your Homework

'Think what you're going to do before you do it' was a motto that my old football coach used to shout at me, both repeatedly and with little effect. His constant berating was brought about by my seemingly random ball play, which left my team mates in a state of confusion. Although claiming that you're working purely on instinct sounds romantic, it also smacks of being pretentious, especially when you're a skinny full back playing only for Crosfield Chemicals.

Coach Terry Mac was not surprised when I quit the team to go away to Art College. In fact, he was very supportive. But I soon learned that even Jackson Pollock usually had a very good idea of what he was aiming to achieve before he opened his tins of paint. In modelling terms, doing your homework is an essential part of the process, whether you're working on scenic, architectural or rolling stock subjects.

If you're aiming to enhance a model, then you need to know: a) what it is you want to change or add; b) what you are going to use; and c) is it available, or will you have to make it yourself? While the solutions to b) and c) should be answered in the ensuing chapters, a) must be derived from delving into the history of that particular class of locomotive. Photographs are an obvious source of visual information, although they may not tell the full story. I've lost count of the times I've resolved to model a specific locomotive, but, after many hours spent trawling the Internet and library shelves, every image that arises seems to be of the same side of the machine, or does not show the one part I'm interested in. Therefore, for example, if you need

to know whether 'Terrier' No.32670 had lost its Westinghouse pump by 1950, some further digging may be necessary.

History cards were kept by railway companies and formed something of a log book, detailing build dates, repair and overhaul information, shed allocations and disposal details and we are lucky that some of these have survived from BR ownership to enter personal or national archives. General arrangement (GA) drawings are also useful for overall dimensions and specifications, although many details shown can differ wildly from what was carried by each actual engine during a long service life. How likely was it that a fitter at Edgeley depot would shape a replacement copper pipe, during running repairs to an '8F', exactly as it was shown on the GA plans?

The NRM's new Search Engine facility is aimed at making what archives it has more readily available and, in addition, a new reading room has been commissioned overlooking the Great Hall exhibits. The British Library and Public Record Office (both in London) also hold an enormous amount of primary railway sources, as do most local Record Offices and smaller transport museums.

Modellers with specific regional or company interests may be well served by joining one of the numerous railway societies. For example, I've been a member of the Midland Railway Society for some years and the quarterly journal and newsletters offer up lots of interesting and useful titbits. There are similar groups catering for many of the pre-Grouping companies as well as each of the 'Big Four': LMS, LNER, GWR and SR.

Books with more of a technical aspect contain much information relevant to modellers. Some, such as these 'Locomotive Profiles' concentrating on LMS prototypes, include detailed plans and diagrams, as well as extensive statistics.

Railway publishing has proved popular for generations and, in recent times of cheaper production costs, the number of new titles released every year is considerable. Album-style photographic collections are perfect for modellers, especially those containing colour images.

Regular lecture meetings, study centres and their own archives are usually freely available to other members. Many model railway societies also offer their own archives and/or libraries and it can certainly be worthwhile joining your local club.

ARMCHAIR RESEARCH

Serious researchers and railway historians may have the time to spend in archives collating information from such sources, but what about us 'regular' modellers who have but a few evenings or weekends set aside to spruce up our latest locomotive acquisitions? Happily, there are countless books on the market (new and out of print) that contain much of the required information. However, be warned that some contain errors and, having read a few titles on the same subject matter, you may notice the odd contradictory remark. If authenticity is important to you, the best recommendation I can make is to obtain written and visual material from as many sources as possible before committing knife to plastic. Some people gain as much pleasure from the research element as from the actual practical work and, if the time is available, I do enjoy the challenge of searching for an elusive snippet of information.

The Internet has undoubtedly made research easier, but it pays to be discerning before trusting anything as pure fact. There are, none the less, some excellent resources and forums where opinions and advice can be exchanged with other modellers (see the 'Sources of Information' section of the Appendix for some sample website addresses).

A browse across the shelves of a decent newsagent will reveal the popularity of railway-themed magazine titles intended for modellers or general enthusiasts. Many of these publications are aimed solely at steam fans, the nostalgia business being especially buoyant at the moment. Titles such as *British Railways Illustrated*, *Steam World*, *BackTrack* and *Railway Bylines* offer a photography-rich glimpse of what used to be. *Heritage Railway* and *Steam Railway* do likewise, but with a definite slant towards what's happening in the steam preservation movement today. The long-running partwork, *Locomotives Illustrated*, has now left steam subjects behind in favour of 'modern' traction, but over the years it covered a plethora of locomotive types, each issue concentrating on a sole class, or a closely related family of engine types. Back copies of *Locomotives Illustrated* can still be found in transport bookshops, or direct from Ian Allan ltd (see the 'Reference Material Sources' section of the Appendix for the address).

Old copies of classic titles such as *Trains Illustrated* or *Modern Railways* can also be picked

There are plenty of railway magazine titles that cater purely for steam enthusiasts. *BackTrack* is a journal that charts all areas of railway history, from the beginnings to the very recent past, while others like *Steam Railway* concentrate on being the 'clarion' of the worldwide preservation movement. Looking at magazines contemporary to the days of working steam can provide a goldmine of information, just as today's issues are indispensable for 'modern image' modellers.

up at specialist retailers, or perhaps in 'junk' shops. I've been lucky enough to gather nearly a full set of the above titles (the former changed its name to the latter in the late 1960s) from 1959 to 1970 without paying more than 50 pence per copy. Indeed, I found a bag of six years' worth in a charity shop priced at £2. As well as being an enjoyable read, they are packed with contemporary facts and figures such as engine allocations, repair and withdrawal statistics, plus a good assortment of photographs. Some public libraries have these titles in store and the NRM has its collection of journals available for reference.

In terms of modelling magazine titles there is, again, plenty of choice. The four main monthly titles – *Railway Modeller*, *Model Rail*, *British Railway Modelling* and *Hornby Magazine* – are joined by *Model Railway Journal*, a more specialized bimonthly publication aimed at 'finescale' modelling. The four main magazines all cover a broad range of subjects in terms of period, region and ability.

Other than looking at printed, archive or Internet-based sources for reference, there's also the possibility of visiting a preserved railway or museum and viewing the real thing – that's if an example of your subject type has made it into preservation. It must be remembered that the condition of a preserved locomotive will be different to when it ran fifty or sixty years ago, although most heritage movements take the issue of authenticity very seriously. Main-line registered steam traction will differ even further, as these engines must be fitted with modern safety features and air-braking equipment, although, where possible, operating groups strive to keep most of this gear out of view.

Museums and preserved railways are customer-focused organizations and, if you ask nicely, they will more than likely help out with whatever information you may require; if it's possible, they may also provide access to a certain locomotive. If a visit is planned, be sure to take a camera, notebook and tape measure to record as many details as possible. Throughout the following chapters, the sort of detail modifications and additions that will be suggested should give an idea of what to look for on the prototype. Piping runs, size and location of equipment, livery variations and so on could be unique to individual machines within a specific timeframe, regardless of whether they were part of a large or small fleet.

In summary, the key to finding the right information lies in knowing where to look and, luckily enough for us, much of the hard work has already been done by numerous authors. There are so many books and magazine articles out there containing even the most trivial of information or statistics, as to render much of the legwork avoidable. Equipped with the necessary information, we can start to think about the practical part of railway modelling.

A broad choice also befalls the railway modeller, with four 'big name' brands. Of these, *Railway Modeller* is by far the longer standing, having run for fifty years, while *Model Rail* probably covers the widest remit in terms of subject, period, ability and area.

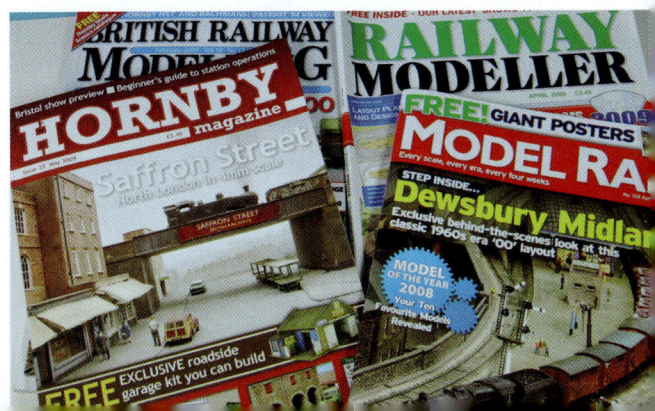

ABOVE: Choosing not only an individual locomotive, but also a specific period in which to portray it, is an important part of the research process. This 1930s view of an LMS 'Black Five' shows a number of era-specific features, not least in the application of the livery. The piston rod's crosshead shows some unusual features that would not be present on a post-war example (evidence of the former crosshead-operated vacuum pump that some machines were fitted with) and the cab side tablet-catching equipment places the loco in Scotland.

ABOVE: Compare this late 1960s view of a 'Black Five' to the earlier image. It's not the same engine, but look out for the detail differences: a flush-sided tender; different pattern of boiler with a separate dome and top feed; Automatic Warning System (AWS) fittings; and a repositioned pair of central lamp brackets.

RIGHT: Being able to look around a real steam prototype is not always possible, especially if an example of a particular class did not make it into preservation. Of those that live on, most are accessible to the polite individual, although some may be in bits awaiting restoration. Luckily, I timed this visit to see 46115 Scots Guardsman after she had been put back together!

BELOW: Caution must be exercised when using a preserved example as a source of research. This box sitting on the running plate of 'Black Five' 45407 looks just like the typical battery box fitted to BR engines as part of the AWS system installed throughout the 1960s. However, it actually contains modern equipment that allows the machine to meet Network Rail specifications. For an authentic AWS-fitted 'Black Five', a cylindrical air tank should be fitted in this location.

BELOW: LMS 'Jubilee' class No.5690 Leander currently wears LMS Crimson Lake livery, although many of her fittings and modifications render this inaccurate. But, who cares – she looks splendid!

ABOVE: This view of *Leander*'s tender shows the pronounced rivet detail, handrails, footsteps, works and water-capacity plates, as well as the attractive lining that extends to bufferbeams and frames.

LEFT: Another sop to modern-day practice is this air pump fitted beneath the cab on BR 'Standard Four' 76079. Air-braked rolling stock is mandatory on the main line these days, so some provision for this has to be made.

RIGHT: As with many pre-BR livery schemes, the GWR lining style also extended below the running plate. Here, the front bogie of *City of Truro* is about to be stripped for refurbishment at the National Railway Museum in 2003. Note the wide bands of polished brass incorporated into the lining pattern and look at the delicate spokes of each wheel; much finer than those on most r-t-r models.

BELOW: Mechanical lubricators, driven by a link from the engine's valve gear, kept all of the locomotive's important working surfaces supplied with oil. On this 'Black Five', two units are fitted and the various copper pipe runs can be seen disappearing beneath the boiler (*see* Chapter 8 for a guide to recreating this). Note also the difference in appearance between the glossy boiler and the dusty matt of the running plate.

BELOW: By arming yourself with plenty of detail photographs as well as technical and historical information – such as shed allocation, AWS fitment, livery details and tender type – a truly authentic model can be achieved. Although not as easy to come by, obtaining a copy of an engine's history card can be a very useful source of information.

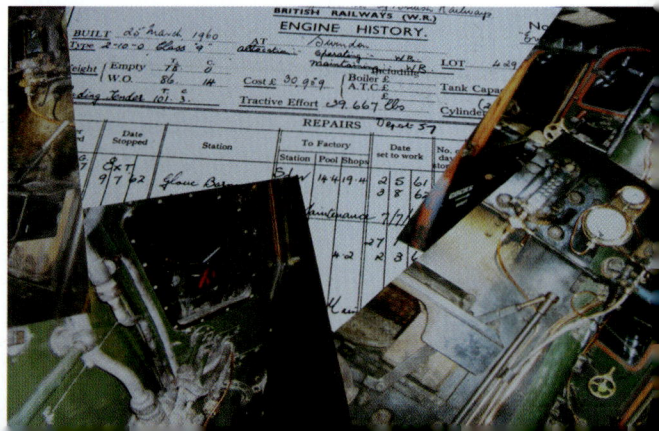

CHAPTER 2

Making a Start

It was from a relatively early age – about twelve years old – that I began to detail and modify my own model locomotives and if, at that time, someone had shown me one of today's Hornby or Bachmann OO gauge steam locomotives I would not have believed that any further detailing could be deemed necessary. Back then, many modellers were resigned to the fact that even the best offerings from Hornby, Mainline, Lima or Airfix were purchased in the knowledge that around half of the purchase price again would have to be set aside for a pack of detailing parts. A full or partial repaint may also have been required.

To be fair, steam outline products were not half as bad as some of the diesel and electrics on the market in the early 1980s and I remember looking on enviously as my brother received an Airfix 'Royal Scot' in honour of his winning the School Cup for merit. With little chance of me repeating the feat when I reached his age, I made do with scrimping my pocket money to assemble an almost exclusively second-hand collection of motive power. 'Why waste money on new stuff if I only have to take it apart and repaint it' was my mantra. Besides, the motors were rubbish even when they were new!

That model of the ex-LMS 'Scot', wearing a decent rendition of BR-lined green, looked light years ahead of anything in my collection, although the level of finish and simplified valve gear now seem primitive in comparison with today's high-specification products. Countless separately applied detail components, the finest lining, smooth and powerful mechanisms and refined wheel profiles are all things I used to dream about being offered as standard. Mind you, saving around £100 for some of today's models would have been out of my reach, although, in real terms, the cost hasn't increased over the past twenty years by much at all.

ABOVE: When taking one of Hornby's recent 'King Arthur' locomotives from its box it becomes immediately clear that this is a thing of real beauty, even before any 'improvements' are made.

BELOW: Even with such attention to detail inside the cab, the 'King Arthur' would still benefit from the addition of a realistic footplate crew.

Fitting Hornby's supplied detailing parts as well as adding a driver, fireman and a pile of coal in the tender transforms a great r-t-r product into something approaching a scale model. Some light weathering also helps – see Chapter 14 for further details.

Who'd have thought that a drive unit in the locomotive (as opposed to the tender) would now be standard, with all-wheel power collection and fully detailed cab interiors? While we should be appreciative of the great efforts that r-t-r manufacturers put into their new products, as customers there's no reason why we still can't be a little choosy. As I write this chapter, the new Bachmann LMS un-rebuilt 'Patriot' has just been released and, while it's an exceptional product, there is no representation of the prominent injector and ejector valves beneath the cabs; something that has almost become standard issue for new models in the past couple of years.

Other small issues still crop up on a good many new models, such as unflattering chimney mouldings, the odd incorrect detail that's unsuitable for a particular livery or period, the omission of footsteps to cope with tight curves and the

Another impressive model straight from the box is the Bachmann Ivatt '4MT' 2-6-0. A wealth of pipework adorns the boiler and chassis, but all this good work is let down by something so simple as this heavy moulding seam along the boiler and chimney.

understandable economy of using a common chassis under a few different locomotive classes when not wholly appropriate. Maybe these things are just part of the compromise necessary for a mass-production model: a little corner must be snipped here or there in order to bring the project under a certain cost threshold, or to fit within the production foibles of a Chinese factory. I don't know if this is true, as I'm not running a large, international company with shareholders to keep happy and production targets to meet, but what I do know is that the number of railway modellers who care about the more minor compromises is relatively small. What most people care about is whether or not the new Hornby model looks like a GWR 'Grange'. Well, yes it does. Some of us, however, find it harder to overlook certain defects, especially those that spoil the character of a model. For instance, a poorly rendered chimney, although only a small part of the overall picture, can have a dramatic 'make or break' effect. Other discrepancies such as 'modern' fittings on older liveried variants or incorrect apparel on Western or Southern Region allocated machines, for example, can stick in the craw a little.

It's not just errors that may need addressing. Taking the Bachmann Ivatt '4MT' for instance, this splendid model is almost perfect as it comes out of the box, except for the unsightly moulding line that runs the length of the boiler top, encompassing the chimney, top feed and dome. Just a few minutes work with a needle

43154

file and fine abrasive paper and the locomotive takes a step up in the world of realism. As these machines were usually less than spotless, a bit of weathering will complete the job and the model can sit nicely amongst miniature scenery without looking like an expertly produced assemblage of plastic mouldings.

This, then, is the crux of the matter. If you are aiming to make your locomotive collection look more like real, working machines rather than just plastic models, then please read on.

CREATING A TOOL KIT

No matter how far you may be thinking of going down the road of modifying your r-t-r locomotives, some basic tools and implements are a necessity. Even simply adding the supplied detailing parts that now come with most new models requires a pair of tweezers to handle them, a scalpel to trim away excess plastic and, in some cases, a set of miniature drill bits to open out the hole in the engine's bufferbeam or cylinders to allow the extra parts to fit.

Illustrated here is what I'd term a kit of essential tools for everyday modelling. As I explained in depth in Volume One of this series, it's surprising how many modellers or craftsmen tend to use only a small selection of 'core' tools for all but the more specialized undertakings. The comfortable, familiar feel of an old knife handle or tweezers may see newer, fancy items gathering dust in a toolbox somewhere. As this book progresses, some further devices and modelling aids will be introduced and their benefits explained.

As well as having the right tools to hand, a suitable working area is also very important, not only for safety and comfort but also to ensure that a high quality of workmanship can be achieved. A small area of a table or desk is all that is required for most projects and the provision of a good amount of light is a must, be it natural (near a window) or artificial. For the sake of your eyes, use a good reading or craft lamp, preferably with a daylight-simulating bulb. Regular table lamps tend to cast light in all directions and can create dense shadows, even in daylight, that confuse the eye and cause headaches. Modelling should be an enjoyable hobby, so comfort is a big issue.

The other thing to think seriously about is a good supply of fresh air, particularly when

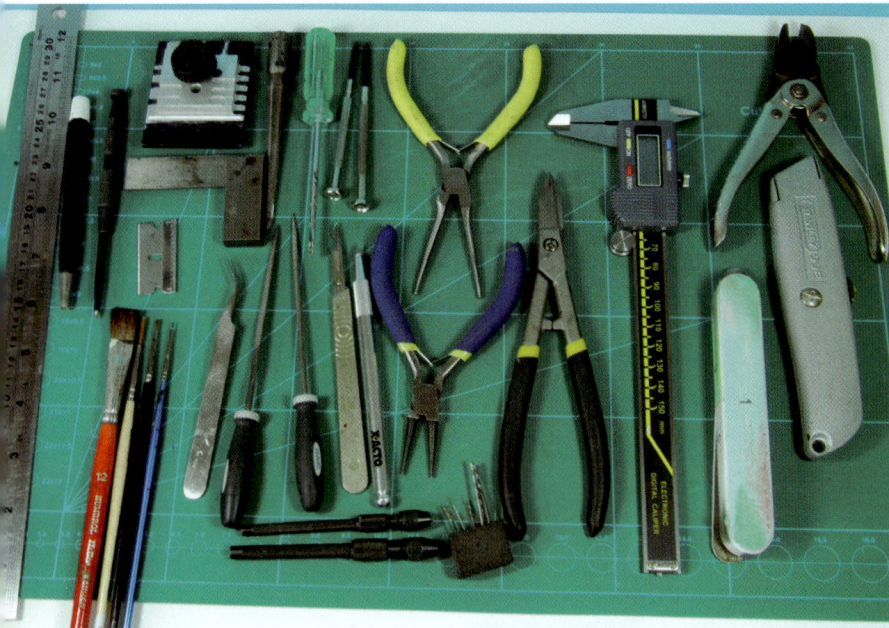

A basic tool kit for the budding locomotive detailer: a good quality knife handle and blades are a must, along with a miniature hand drill and a selection of bits. Files, ruler and set square, calipers, a scriber and/or punch, glass-fibre brush, fine abrasive paper, screwdrivers, tweezers, pliers, end-cutters, tin snips and a cutting mat are all relatively inexpensive and easy to source from craft tool suppliers such as the Hobbycraft chain, Squires or Axminster (see Appendix for the latter two). Various brushes for paints and glue, plus cocktail sticks and cotton buds will also serve you well.

A suitable workspace is just as important as having the right tools. Safety and comfort come with a tidy and well-ventilated space, while a good source of lighting is vital.

working with solvent-based adhesives and paints. Without wanting to sound like I'm obsessed with health and safety issues, having spent the last decade working with smelly substances, I'm aware of how lightly some people tend to treat these hazards. The person working away in a small shed or spare bedroom may be oblivious to the concentration of fumes that have been building up. It's only when a spouse or offspring enters the room and quickly turns a shade of green that you realize what you've been inhaling for the past few hours. So, take sensible precautions and read the hazard information on the packaging of glues, fillers and paints.

Working with sharp tools is also something that should be done with a certain amount of responsibility. Tools should always be sharp, otherwise they're useless. When not in use, place knives or other pointy things out of harm's way. I say this because I can boast an impressive scar obtained by simply wiping dust from my workbench; an absent-minded flourish with one hand across the table top and, oh look, there's a Stanley knife sticking out of the back of my hand. Be warned.

FIRST PROJECTS

It seems logical for us to start by looking at some of the 'modern' crop of high-specification model steam locomotives and to see how we can go about adding some simple improvements that, nevertheless, will make a big impact. According to the type of engine, many new models now come supplied with a small plastic bag filled with a selection of plastic mouldings for the customer to fit. These are usually offered as separate items because some modellers may prefer not to have them ready fitted – many of us with limited space have layouts with tightly curved rails and this has an impact on what details can be offered on a locomotive as it comes straight from the box. Obvious examples include front footsteps and cylinder drainpipes that can hinder a leading pony truck or bogie as the engine trundles around corners. Other items such as brake pipes and cosmetic screw couplings can only be incorporated if the factory-fitted tension-lock couplings are removed from one end. This isn't always convenient, so manufacturers kindly leave such decisions to their customers.

Choosing the Right Adhesive

Glue should be viewed as a tool in its own right and deciding the most appropriate adhesive to suit a particular task is an important factor in all aspects of model-making. Some adhesives, for instance, can cause damage to certain plastics or paint finishes, while others are produced to bond only one specific material. It pays, therefore, to have a small selection at hand and to understand the properties of each in order to achieve a successful and tidy bond.

What we all know best as 'superglue', cyanoacrylate is one of the most versatile adhesives and is available in a variety of formulas. Thick, gel-type solutions are offered with slightly longer curing times – between ten to twenty seconds – for when a component may need some degree of repositioning to ensure a perfect fit. Ultra-viscous fluids, on the other hand, will set almost instantly and this can be of great advantage if a part is going to be awkward to hold in place while the fixative sets. Because they are so thin, however, the fluid requires great care in application to avoid making a mess.

It's important to note that the strong solvents present in virtually all cyanoacrylate-type glues can damage paint finishes and clear plastic if used in excessive amounts. A white, cloudy appearance will form around the joint where the solvent fumes react with the surrounding materials and this can be very difficult to remedy. Odourless formulas, such as that offered in the Deluxe Materials range, are a way round this problem, especially when required in proximity to glazed areas. Indeed, I tend to use this formula whenever working on a particularly precious model, or when undertaking conservation work, just in case.

Hopefully it shouldn't be needed, but it may be beneficial to keep a jar of cyano debonder around. This thin liquid will soften any superglue joint, whether on a model or between your fingers! Take care with these agents as they can also react adversely with certain plastics and fine model finishes.

Epoxy-based glues are also indispensable to modellers, especially when working with more substantial components such as brass and white-metal. Some brands and formulas of superglue can produce strong but somewhat 'brittle' joints that can fail with the odd knock or bump (although there are brands that offer a slightly more flexible cure such as Roket Poly). Epoxy, meanwhile, offers a supple yet durable bond, although there are some limitations: the adhesive is much more

Cyanoacrylate – or superglue – is available in various grades to suit different tasks. Separate accelerating fluids can also be used to make bonds instant, while micro-tips and tube applicators help the glue to reach into awkward corners of a model without making a mess. Roket Powder filler is a useful tool that, when combined with cyanoacrylate glue, sets rock-hard within seconds and can be filed or sanded smooth.

Other adhesives essential to the locomotive detailer include twin-pack epoxy formulas (again of various grades according to setting time) that will fix most materials. Slower-setting, PVA-based glues are perfect for adding coal to an engine's tender as well as other applications such as fitting glazing and cab interior details, while Tacky Wax provides a temporary bond suitable for lamps and headboards that can be swapped between locomotives without damaging the model's paintwork.

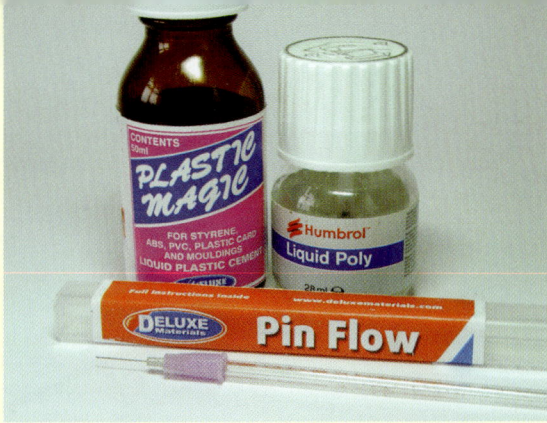

Liquid plastic cements are perfect for plastic-to-plastic joints and the thin nature of the liquid means it can be applied – by brush or needle-point applicator – with accuracy. Setting times vary, but are longer than superglues, as the solvents work to 'weld' the plastic surfaces together, leaving a very strong bond.

solvent concoction such as Plastic Weld or Deluxe Materials' Plastic Magic.

Avoid using the tubes of polystyrene cement that many model shops offer with plastic construction kits, as this simply can't be applied with anything like enough care to delicate detailing components. Jars of liquid cement, such as the two already mentioned and Humbrol's Liquid Poly, are much more appropriate and can be applied to the joint using a fine paintbrush. All plastic cements can destroy a model's paintwork if used excessively, so take care and apply only the minimum amount of glue, then set aside to cure completely, usually overnight.

viscous than superglue, so joining very small items or achieving an invisible joint can be a bit tricky. Even the fastest-setting epoxies take around four minutes to 'go off' and, while this doesn't sound very long, wait until you've sat holding a set of miniature footsteps under a locomotive – four minutes can seem like an eternity! Again, there are many different brands and specifications of epoxy, with curing times of up to an hour, and it will join almost anything to anything.

Whereas epoxy and cyanoacrylate adhesives work by forming a chemical bond between two materials, liquid plastic cements actually 'fuse' the parts together by temporarily softening the materials' structure. This, naturally, is only good for bonding plastics to other plastics and various brands cater for differing grades of material. For example, the tougher industrial grades of plastic, such as ABS (Acrylonitrile Butadiene Styrene) – as used on some locomotive underframes – require a more potent

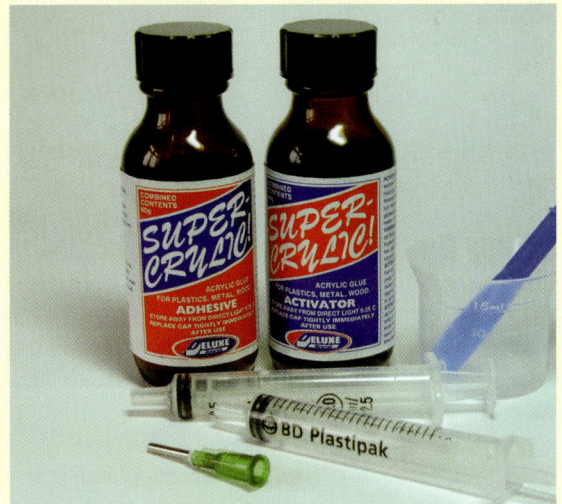

When nothing else will work, there's always Super-Crylic from Deluxe Materials, which will stick virtually anything, even oily underframe parts. It consists of a two-pack solvent, a mixing bowl, a spatula and a pair of needle-point syringes to aid application.

Fitting these extra bits and pieces, if appropriate, is a fairly simple task and virtually all models are accompanied by an exploded diagram illustrating where each item should be placed. However, what these instructions fail to relay is what type of adhesive to use or how best to go about the task. Holding the model is the primary problem, especially if adding things below the running plate. In this case, it's much easier to work with the engine upside-down, but that

leaves only one hand free as a steam locomotive won't stay inverted on its own.

With any model, I'd usually recommend handling it as little as possible to avoid the risk of damaging the delicate components or inadvertently spreading gluey fingerprints along the paintwork. Locomotive 'cradles' are available from a number of sources such as Sarik Vacform (see Appendix); these consist of a foam-padded holder that allows work to be done on the

A good many of today's generation of r-t-r OO gauge locomotives now come supplied with a small bag of separate components for the customer to fit, usually consisting of dummy couplings, footsteps, cylinder drains, steam and vacuum pipes, plus maybe an optional wheel set for a trailing axle, as offered with some of Hornby's Pacifics. Fitting some of these parts is not as simple as you may think.

undercarriage, such as regular mechanical servicing and wheel cleaning, in relative safety.

I mentioned earlier about the possible need for drilling out mounting holes provided on a locomotive's chassis before the supplied plastic pipes or couplings can be fitted. This is easy enough and by using a set of calipers to gauge the size of the component's mounting lug, the correct drill bit can be chosen. Some of these parts are designed to be a tight, friction fit to negate the need for glue. This is a good idea if you don't fancy making these fittings permanent.

However, I've found that trying to push a plastic part into a tight hole in a steel chassis usually results in the plastic breaking. It's a far better proposition to open out the hole for a comfortable – but not sloppy – fit and to add the faintest drop of glue to keep it in place.

As far as choosing an appropriate adhesive is concerned, the notes above should indicate which are the more suitable. I tend to use various grades of cyanoacrylate (superglue) for virtually all of the little bits that come with Hornby and Bachmann models, not least as this invariably

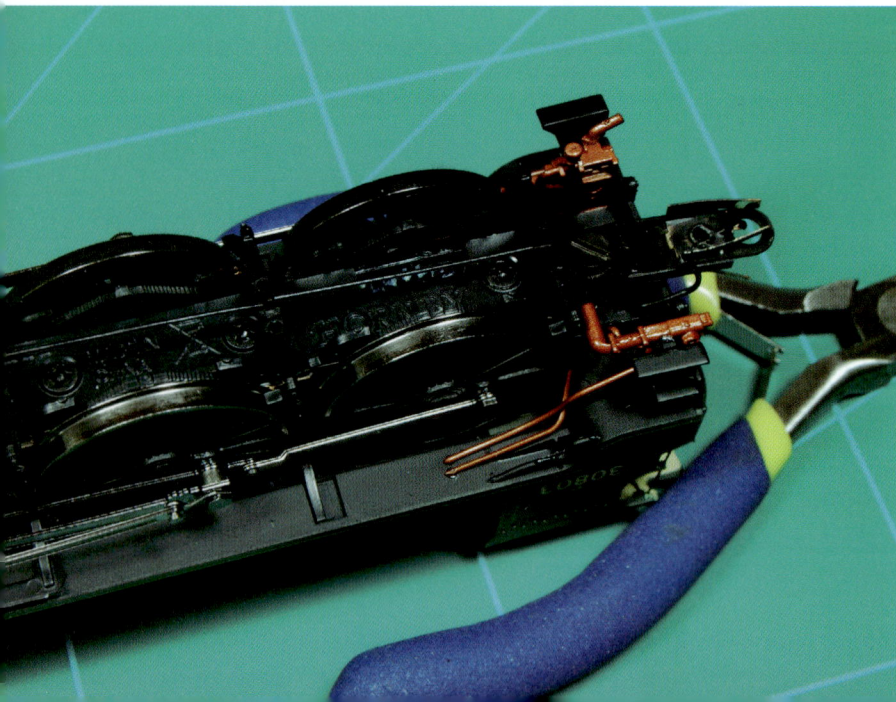

While purpose-built foam-lined locomotive 'cradles' are available for holding your precious model while you work on the underneath, a cheaper trick is to balance the cab roof on a rubber cutting mat, between the handles of a pair of pliers. As long as care is taken, this should suffice for the gentle action of fixing new components.

Choosing the right glue for each job is helpful in terms of both achieving a reliable bond and making the process quicker. Avoid applying any glue directly to a model or component from the tube or bottle. Instead, decant a little onto some scrap and use a cocktail stick to dab a little adhesive to the surface. This way, cleaning up messy glue seepage is avoided.

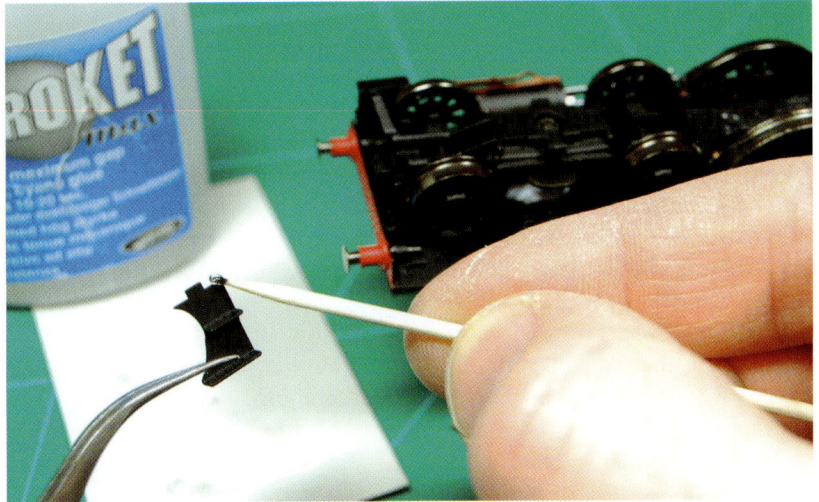

Using a thicker, slower-setting cyanoacrylate such as Roket Max will allow for adjustments to be made before the part is stuck fast, usually about ten seconds or so. This is important when making sure a set of footsteps are mounted straight and square.

For parts where adjustments shouldn't be necessary, a faster-setting formula can be used as this will reduce the time needed to hold the part in place before the glue 'grabs'. Often, a preformed mounting hole may have to be opened out slightly with a drill and measuring the pipe's mounting lug with a set of calipers makes choosing the correct drill bit easier. Do a dry run first, without glue, to make sure everything's okay, then add just a drop of adhesive with the cocktail stick.

involves attaching plastic to metal. If a plastic-to-plastic joint is to be done, however, such as adding cylinder drains or brake parts, I use liquid poly cement such as Plastic Magic, although superglue would do the job just as well. While epoxy glue has its uses, it is not really appropriate here as these small components need a neat, if not invisible, joint and while epoxy can be cleaned up with a damp cotton swab before it sets, it can still be more hassle than it is worth.

Talking of cleaning up excess glue, this is something that can be difficult with superglue. That's why it's important not to apply it straight from the bottle. Micro-tip applicators and fine tubing are available from Deluxe Materials to make application more controllable, but I do prefer to use a nice sharp cocktail stick, having deposited a small blob of glue onto a scrap of card. That way, you are completely in control of how much adhesive finds its way onto the component. With just a couple of practice runs on scraps of plastic, it can quickly be discerned how much is needed to form a strong joint without excess oozing out.

If the unthinkable does happen and we end up with a large glue stain, a cyano debonder may be used but *only* with extreme care. The debonder offered in the Deluxe Materials range (Glue Buster) certainly works well, but, as it's a very runny liquid, it should preferably be applied with an old, small paintbrush. I got caught out when using it for the first time and duly smothered the front of a model diesel loco with the stuff, which then went on to soften all of the paint, leaving a real mess. In the case of glue smudges, it's sometimes preferable to let the glue harden completely, then rub the area down with fine abrasive paper and try and resurrect the paint finish with T-Cut or by patch-painting. This will be covered in more depth in Chapter 13.

POPULATING THE FOOTPLATE

No railway locomotive is complete without a footplate crew of driver and fireman, unless the machine is intended for static display in a siding or engine shed. Although the odd r-t-r model may come with a pack of plastic figures (unpainted in Hornby's case), the majority do not, making this an obvious area where we can have an improving effect. On the whole, the cab of a steam engine is easy to access for this purpose, with little or no dismantling necessary; the opposite is true with many diesel or electric models.

A most simple but effective enhancement to factory-fitted glazing is to reduce the prismatic effect of the thick clear plastic by running a little matt black paint around the edges of each window using a fine paintbrush. This is being done here to the tender from a Hornby 'Britannia' and makes a vast difference.

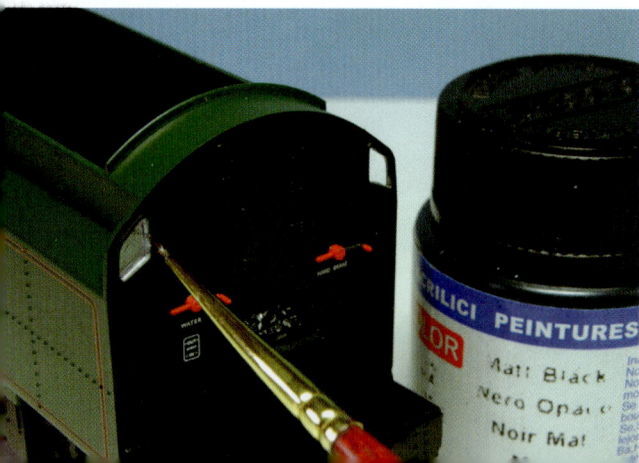

Although there are some packs of pre-painted footplate crew, they can be expensive compared to unpainted sets. Besides, painting your own people can be rewarding and allows for more individuality, especially when using figures such as these from the Aidan Campbell range. Undercoated first with an aerosol car primer (from Halfords), Lifecolor and Humbrol acrylics follow, varying the uniform shades slightly to prevent everyone from looking the same. Finishing with a wash of Tensocrom paint, wiped away with a cotton bud, highlights the relief in the castings and adds a suitably dirty sheen to the overalls.

The figures to front of this view are by Dart Castings. Painting figures can be made easier by gluing them to a scrap of wood with just a tiny blob of superglue. As the figures are cast metal, they can easily be snapped off when ready to fit and the feet tidied up with a flat file if necessary.

A wide choice of footplate crew figures is available in ready-painted or unpainted form, although the cost of the former is higher. Painting your own can be an enjoyable exercise and, depending on your skill with a paintbrush, a high degree of detail can be achieved. Miniature figure sculptors such as Aidan Campbell and Inkerman

When adding heavy white-metal figures, a strong cyano-type glue should be used. In theory, epoxy would be well suited to this task as it would protect against the bond failing under mild knocks or impacts, but holding a figure in place for five minutes while the glue sets is not much fun. Instead, I use a flexible formula of superglue, Roket Poly, which offers faster curing and a resilient joint. If your model does not come with the cab controls ready picked-out in paint, why not take the opportunity to add a little colour using metallic enamel shades such as Humbrol No.12 Copper, No.54 Brass and No.27003 Metal Cote Polished Steel.

Castings offer a broad selection of poses and figure types to suit different time periods; even, in Aidan's case, going back to Victorian times when drivers wore large top hats! Other makers include Langley Models and Dart Castings, both of whom also cater for BR-era men as well as slightly earlier periods.

All of the above sources offer their wares in cast white-metal, so priming is essential before painting. It adds to the realism to 'weather' these little chaps with Tensocrom acrylic pigments, from the Lifecolor range. I'll talk more about these useful pigments in Chapter 14, but an overall wash with the dilute liquid, followed by rubbing down with a cotton bud, will leave mucky deposits within the creases of their work clothes and impart a suitable oily look to them.

COALING UP

Not only does every steam engine need a driver and fireman, but it also requires a supply of coal in its bunker. No matter how well models are produced, a believable mound of plastic coal has yet to be invented, so it falls to us to add a sprinkling of the black stuff. By and large, this can usually be applied on top of the moulded mound, secured with a carefully applied layer of a PVA (polyvinyl acetate)-type glue. Always spread the glue on first, before dropping the coal on – working in the opposite way, as is often the case when fixing scenic ballast to model railway track, will give the coal chippings a 'glazed' appearance.

Choose your 'coal' carefully, as there are many options available. By far the most realistic material to use is real coal (for obvious reasons) and, to add an extra hint of authenticity, why not ask the train crew for a single lump next time you visit a preserved railway? I'm sure they'd oblige. By pulverizing the lump with a hammer, while it's wrapped in an old tea towel, a suitable array of chippings and dust can be created. I've filled nearly one hundred model bunkers from one lump of steam coal (taken from *Green Arrow*, no less) and I've still enough to fill twice that amount. It's helpful to sort the broken-up coal into two

Many model tenders feature a removable moulded coal load to permit either an almost empty bunker or one filled to whatever level is desired. For a full load, the moulded coal can be used as a base for the real chippings, otherwise cut your own former from packaging foam or similar material and carve the top to form a suitably shaped mound. Don't worry about gluing the foam in place as the fixing of the coal will hold it all together.

Apply a thin layer of glue, using a paintbrush and keeping it away from the vertical sides of the bunker. This formula of craft glue (Deluxe) is very tacky and sets perfectly clear. Remove any spillage with a damp swab.

Sprinkle the coal onto the wet glue, covering the whole bunker. Don't worry about adding too much, as whatever fails to stick can be shaken off later. Lightly push down with a finger or the back of a teaspoon, if necessary, to persuade the chippings into any nooks and crannies.

It can be a good idea to ensure all of the glue is covered by sprinkling on a little fine coal dust. Leave overnight for the glue to set completely, then upturn the model onto some scrap paper, collect and reuse any loose coal.

Small coal chippings and a little dust can also be added to the shelf on the bunker's bulkhead as this is where the fireman would be shovelling the fuel from. A small amount of spillage on the floor can also be a nice touch, although train crews were usually very good at keeping the footplate clean and, therefore, safe – so don't overdo this. Just brush a dab of glue onto the shelf and floor and sprinkle on the coal and dust as before. I'm sure this fireman will attend to that coal spillage once he's finished mopping his brow!

separate jars for safe-keeping, the 'lumps' in one and the dust and finer chips in another.

A look at period images of steam locomotives, freshly filled with coal, will reveal some seemingly enormous chunks sitting in the bunkers. This is why firemen were issued with coal hammers, so that anything too large to shovel into the firebox could be shattered into a more manageable size. With this in mind, it's important to add a mix of coal chippings to a model's bunker, followed by a sprinkling of dust, which also works to hide any gaps and stop the glue showing through.

Bags of coal chippings are available from model shops and suppliers, but, as noted above, you should choose your brand carefully, as some can look very peculiar – not many of these packs actually use real coal. Some are also graded too consistently, which is fine if modelling a coal merchant's yard with separate bins for various types of coal, but not for the typical engine load.

Another thing to consider is the amount of fuel to add. Do you want a bunker that's full to bursting point? That would mean the engine has just come 'off-shed' rather than having been at work for a few hours. If coming to the end of its turn, the bunker may be looking a bit on the empty side. Engines with smaller coal spaces would naturally run down their supply quicker (although they'd be used on shorter journeys accordingly) and a bit of variation amongst a locomotive fleet can be attractive.

These first steps in improving r-t-r locomotives form a useful introduction into gaining a working knowledge of adhesives and a small selection of tools. They also allow us to develop a confidence in our practical abilities and allow us to go forward towards the next stage.

With the small, separately supplied details added (front footsteps, cylinder drainpipes, cosmetic coupling, hoses and, in the case of this Bachmann model, etched nameplates – *see* following Chapter), a footplate crew in place and a load of real coal in the tender, BR '9F' *Evening Star* has already progressed from an impressive r-t-r model, straight from the box, to looking more authentic. But, we can go much further still ...

CHAPTER 3

Aiming Higher

Other than those extra details already provided with r-t-r locomotives, what other simple adornments can we add without too much effort being expended? Engines with nameplates can almost instantly be enhanced by replacing the factory-printed nameplates with etched brass or stainless steel sets. Firms such as Fox Transfers, 247 Developments and Modelmaster Decals (*see* Appendix) produce a vast range of nameplates, ready painted with the correct backing colour and these require only to be cut from the metal fret before fixing in place.

Handling these replacement nameplates requires an amount of care as, if bent or twisted, they are very difficult to repair. Cutting with a sharp pair of tin snips will make for a good, clean edge, but using a blade or a punch can often cause the plate to disfigure, especially if working on a soft surface such as a rubber cutting mat. If a blade is to be used, it's far better to lay the fret on a scrap of plywood while cutting the retaining tangs and I'd recommend leaving a fraction of waste material to be filed away rather than aiming for a cut against the very edge of the nameplate.

The size of the retaining tang employed tends

Although carrying a similar nameplate pattern to the other named 'Black Fives', 45407 *The Lancashire Fusilier* was named after being preserved. Most r-t-r models that carry names have them printed onto plastic mouldings that can look over-scale in section and a little flat in relief when compared to the real thing. Etched replacements are available, however, and are often easy to fit.

Whether the nameplates are etched in brass or stainless steel, cutting them from the fret and preparing them for fitting is a delicate task, as any damage is hard to repair. Invest in a good pair of tin snips (Xuron offers a pair designed specifically for such tasks and are available from Mainly Trains [*see* Appendix]) and leave just a little waste tang to be filed away.

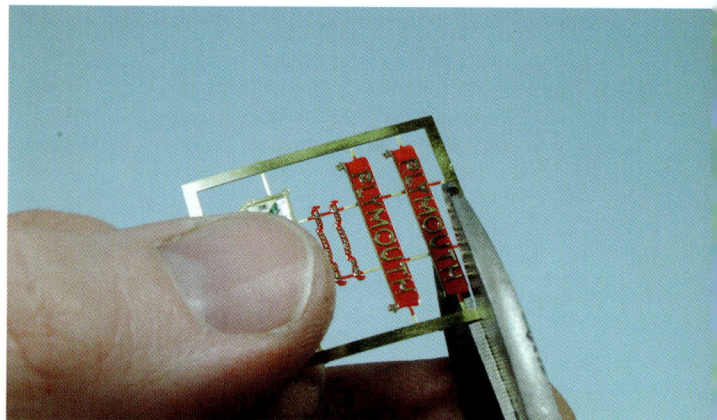

Clamping the nameplate in something like this Hold 'n' Fold tool will keep it safe from distortion while the edges are dressed with a fine flat file. A slip of paper between the top side of the plate and the tool will prevent damage to the painted surface. Finish with a rub of fine abrasive paper to polish out any scratches.

also distort it. Using something such as a Hold 'n' Fold tool will enable the plate to be clamped tightly while remaining completely flat. We'll see more of these handy devices in later chapters.

A flat needle file will remove any excess material and, once the visible edges are smooth, you can always finish with a little abrasive such as 1,000grit wet & dry paper. There are two ways of fitting replacement nameplates, either just by covering the originals, or by first removing the moulded plate. Unless we're dealing with factory-printed plates, such as those applied to smoke deflectors, prior removal of the originals is not always necessary as long as the new parts cover the printed names fully; indeed, the original can act as a convenient guide for aligning the new etched name.

By covering the moulded plates, however, you will naturally increase the thickness of the names further; these being already over-scale. This can be especially noticeable on the sides of a boiler such as when fitted to an LMS 'Duchess' or SR 'Light Pacific'. Removal of factory-fitted plates is not always easy, as there is a risk of damaging the paintwork beyond what will be covered by the new parts. In some cases, the glue used at the factory is so keen that the moulded plate may

to differ among manufacturers and plate design, the smaller ones obviously being easier to snip through. Once the plate has been freed, the edges will invariably need tidying with a file and/or abrasive paper. Again, be very careful here as clamping and working on the part may

This Hornby 'West Country' has received a new nameplate and mounting bracket, the latter requiring priming and painting before fitting.

simply disintegrate around the joints, leaving a tricky clean-up job and this was the case with a Bachmann 'B1' that I recently denamed, as illustrated in Chapter 7.

Hornby's 2008 releases of the rebuilt LMS 'Patriot' and 'Royal Scot' 4-6-0s have proved to be awkward customers when it comes to swapping the nameplates that are wrapped elegantly around the wheel splashers. As the nameplate is cast integrally to the front of the metal splasher, it is almost impossible to modify *in situ*. Instead, the splasher must be pulled from the running plate with a pair of pliers and then cut and filed in a vice before refitting. Inevitably, the paint finish will have been damaged to some degree and some careful retouching will be needed, which may include the fine orange-red lining. Luckily, Modelmaster Decals have introduced packs of inexpensive etched brass splasher covers that form a convenient backing for their accompanying range of nameplates and are quite simple to fit. Etched in 0.020in (0.5mm) thick brass, the covers are a direct fit into the locating hole on the Hornby chassis and are available either unpainted or ready-finished in BR green. Three small brackets support replacement etched names, allowing the model to show off some authentically slim nameplates.

Something to bear in mind is that many nameplates incorporated a section of the livery scheme applied to part of the casting. The Great Western was especially partial to doing this and,

as was the case when upgrading the names of my 'Patriot', a section of BR green had to be applied to the new plates, complete with a dash of lining to the edges. Lining is covered in Chapter 13, but the finished articles can be seen in the photograph overleaf along with the Modelmaster splasher covers.

We've already mentioned the fitting of small components to locomotives; nameplates are no different. Smear only the faintest amount of superglue to the rear of the plate and carefully fix it in place. A surfeit of glue will only be squeezed out from between the two materials and make a mess. If the nameplate is straight and is to sit on a flat surface, a strip of masking tape can act as a useful guide to applying it accurately. Using a slower-setting formula of superglue will give you a short window of opportunity to make any adjustments before it sets hard.

Works plates and builders plates are another area where etched replacements can make a positive impact and these can usually be placed over the printed originals (if there are any). Distinctive plate styles such as those fitted at the works of Armstrong Whitworth or the North British Locomotive Company make for attractive features and Fox Transfers, Modelmaster and 247 Developments all offer a broad range of etches to suit various engine types. It pays to choose the correct type, so research your prototype before placing your order as, for example, North British fitted both diagonal- and oval-style plates to different classes at different times.

Etched plates have been added to this Hornby GWR 'Grange' and, when mounted in place of the originals, are significantly more realistic. The moulded plates can be 'snapped' off easily and, with the model's small mounting bracket retained, the rear of the new brass parts is given sufficient support.

Some nameplates incorporate a lined livery panel such as can be seen here on GWR 'King' 4-6-0 *King George V*. This feature is not always provided by etched nameplate makers and will have to be filled in by hand.

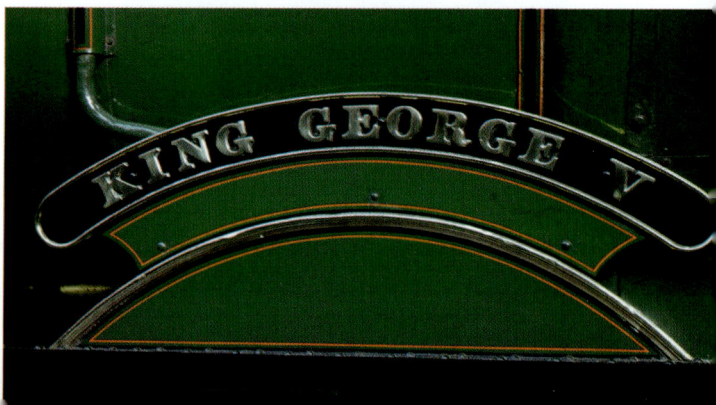

Hornby's rebuilt 'Royal Scot' and 'Patriot' models have the names cast integrally with the steel splasher front and this can make replacement difficult, although the originals can be pulled from the chassis with a gentle tug by a pair of pliers. Either the Hornby nameplates can be cut and filed away before refitting the splashers, or replacements can be obtained from Modelmaster Decals. Etched in brass, these new covers are a slot-in fit and come either in bare metal or ready painted. Small brackets provide a suitable surface for new nameplates to be added.

Other plates that are equally as important and still freely available include those fitted to the rear of tenders or bunkers, displaying build numbers and water capacity. Shed plates, attached to smokebox doors, were also cast and these can place an engine to a certain location and period in time. All BR sheds were allotted

Distinctive builder's plates were fitted to all steam locomotives, no matter how humble. Works of the major railway companies usually offered quite sober plates, with just the date and place of manufacture, while some outside builders, such as Armstrong Whitworth & Co., had their own style.

Adding new nameplates to flat surfaces, such as smoke deflectors, poses much fewer problems, as the originals have probably been printed. Just ensure that the new plates cover the old ones properly. If not, see Chapter 7 for how to remove factory-printed detail.

specific codes consisting of a number and letter (following LMS practice) and, as locomotives could move regularly between sheds, the shed plates were duly changed. Ensuring these small details are correct for your layout's chosen time-frame adds an extra degree of realism.

Again, there are miniature etched versions of most patterns of builder's plates. This highly distinctive, diamond-pattern plate shows that this LNER 'B1' was one of a batch built by the North British Locomotive Co. in Glasgow.

HEADBOARDS AND OTHER ADORNMENTS

Locomotive headboards owe their origins to the North British Railway and, when this company was absorbed at the Grouping of 1922 into the LNER, the new company continued the practice. Moreover, the famous 'Flying Scotsman' service between London King's Cross and Edinburgh began to carry headboards from 1928. BR subsequently continued the practice, introducing new and existing titles to various 'top link' services across the regions.

Various model nameplate manufacturers also produce a range of BR-era headboards for most of the express services of the 1950s and 1960s. Names such as 'The Talisman', 'Thames–Clyde Express', 'The Merseyside Express' or 'The

Miniature etched headboards are available from sources such as Fox Transfers or 247 Developments and all require careful handling, in the same manner as nameplates. If a permanent fix is required, simply add a tiny blob of glue onto the top lamp bracket and set the board in place. Alternatively, try a small amount of Tacky Wax, which will hold it fairly securely but allow for easy removal.

Locomotive headboards became common under BR from the early 1950s in an attempt to 'brand' its prestige express passenger and freight services, although the origins of such boards can be traced much further back. This preserved 'Black Five' is calling at Stockport before heading off to the Keighley and Worth Valley Railway for its fortieth anniversary celebrations. Note the appropriate London Midland Region shade of maroon on the headboard.

Cheltenham Spa Express' all conjure visions of a more romantic age and various background colours are available to suit different regions. Black was, at first, the standard colour, but gradually other shades took over such as green for the Southern Region, red for the London Midland and blue for the Eastern. As many of the long-distance services would see several changes of traction along the way, relieving engines would appear with their own headboards in appropriate regional colours.

Other attractive adornments for specific prestige services include those added to engines rostered to work the 'Golden Arrow' boat trains on the Southern Region. Consisting of a dramatic smokebox-mounted headboard, large cast arrows were also attached to the sides of the Southern's finest express locomotives. Different-sized arrows were used, depending on the type of engine in use: large for the original, air-smoothed 'Light Pacifics', while a smaller pair sat on the

ABOVE: A substitute for etched headboards is one of these packs of printed headboards from Precision Labels (see Appendix). Sitting on a reflective backing, they give the impression of polished steel. However, cutting them out neatly can be difficult, as the complex curves require much care, in addition to a very sharp, pointed blade.

BELOW: Chris Leigh's etched brass adornments for Southern Region 'Golden Arrow' services include all the necessary arrows, headboard, flags and carriage boards. A coat of primer is needed before painting, but remember to mask the arrows and other details that must remain with a polished brass finish.

After applying the correct paint to each part (BR green to the large circular emblem, white to the headcode discs and red, white and blue to the British and French flags), rub the raised detail with 1,000-grade wet & dry abrasive paper to reveal the brass lettering once again. Ensure that only the raised detail is abraded by cutting a strip of wet & dry and fixing to a flat material such as thick plastic card. Touch in any imperfections and, if the abrasive won't reach some of the paint, use a sharp blade to scrape it clear.

smoke deflectors of rebuilt variants. A pack of etched brass parts, including coach boards for the Pullman cars, is produced by Chris Leigh (see Appendix), although these require priming and painting before fitting. A more expensive, but fully finished, set is offered in the Fox Transfers range (ref. FEP HB350).

Each of the aforementioned tasks has required no great degree of skill or experience, only a little patience and care. So far, we've avoided having to dismantle our new models in any way, but, in the next chapter, we shall start to look a little closer to see where a few improvements can be made to the actual fabric of the locomotive.

The twin flags will look better if folded a little to look like they're fluttering about. Finish by coating everything with a clear varnish, which will also stop the bare brass parts from tarnishing. To help fix the large emblem to the smokebox front, I cut a couple of pieces of plastic strip to form a pair of brackets. Once painted black, along with the rear of the logo, they are not noticeable.

Steam Locomotive Headcodes

In the days before computerized train-reporting systems, a visual description of a train's 'type' was effected by a display of oil lamps on the leading end of a locomotive. By train 'type', we mean express or stopping, passenger or freight, and so on. Such an arrangement was aimed at helping railway personnel such as signalmen, station staff and those working about the tracks to identify particular workings.

The use of headlamps on locomotives dates from the very beginnings of railways, ostensibly to warn of a train's approach. However, as railway traffic increased towards the end of the nineteenth century, some form of train description was deemed necessary and the many individual railway companies adopted lamp codes, that is, lamps in various positions on an engine's front. Some used different-coloured lights to signify train types, but, by 1905, the Railway Clearing House (a sort of 'standards watchdog' for the railways) insisted on a standard code being employed nationwide. This was not adopted as stringently as intended, with plenty of local variations, and it was not until the advent of nationalization in 1948 that a common code was strictly enforced. Even then, though, the Southern Region managed to maintain its own idiosyncratic system to cope with the enormous amount of commuter and freight traffic around London and the South East.

In the standard code system, four lamp brackets were fitted to both the front and rear

In the standardized BR system of train description, this lamp code display refers to single or multiple 'light' engines, hauling no more than two brake vans and termed as Class 0.

This display of lamps describes a Class 1 train, being either an express passenger or newspaper train. The same code could also mean a breakdown train, snow-plough, a light engine on its way to assist a disabled train or an officer's special that is not booked to stop within the section.

This single light in the raised position shows a Class 2 working, meaning an ordinary passenger, branch passenger or mixed train. A breakdown or snow-plough train also carried this code if 'off duty'.

Both Classes 3 and 4 were represented by the same pattern of lamps: empty passenger stock, parcels or perishable loads such as fish, fruit, livestock or milk, were classed as Class 3, as long as all vehicles conformed to coaching-stock specification; Class 4 meant an express freight train fitted with automatic brakes on not less than 90 per cent of vehicles ('fully-fitted').

This Bachmann 'B1' carries a Class 5 lamp code, describing an express freight train with automatic brakes operative on at least half of the wagons. Although many LNER locomotives were fitted with electric lights, oil lamps were still carried in daylight hours to aid sighting of the code.

Typical of the type of traffic hauled by engines such as this Hornby GWR 'Grange', is the Class 6 express freight train with automatic brakes operative on not less than 20 per cent of wagons.

Slower Class 7 express unfitted freight trains would show this lamp code. This weathered Bachmann 'Super D' carries a pair of typical LMS-pattern oil lamps.

Class 8 freight trains were unfitted throughout and this Bachmann 'J39' carries a BR-standard pattern lamp on the upper bracket, but an LNER-style unit in the lower position. Such a mix of lamps was a common sight, especially in the 1960s.

of locomotives, three along the running plate and a single central bracket in a raised position. This pattern allowed for ten different codes to be displayed and descriptions were set into a range of classifications in order of speed or importance. Class 1 denoted an express passenger service, while Class 9 referred to the humble pick-up branch freight; Class 0 was used for light engine movements. Moreover, there were variations in each of these ten classifications, so it could still be difficult to ascertain exactly what service was being witnessed by simply looking at the headlamps.

A single lamp on the right-hand bracket signifies the Class 9 pick-up branch freight. It was also shown on officer's specials or ballast trains due to stop within the section.

The Southern Region's code system was inherited from the Southern Railway and its own predecessors, which had attempted to make train identification more explicit. A choice of six different lamp positions was available and, in daylight hours, large white metal discs would be carried instead of oil lamps. This allowed only a limited number of permutations, so most codes related to different services according to individual sections of track, thus allowing for duplication. As this meant that codes would differ over relatively short distances, a driver might have to change the display on his charge before entering a different section, although the great many short-haul suburban services would not be affected by this. Although I've illustrated the various standard lamp positions on these pages, giving a full (or even partial) account of the Southern's system would fill a book on its own, so I'd recommend obtaining a copy of *The Southern Railway Handbook*, as mentioned in the Bibliography, as this covers the subject in a little more depth.

Miniature headlamps are available from various makers such as Springside and these are obtainable from most model shops. Cast in metal, they come ready painted in white or black, where appropriate, and contain small glass 'jewels' to represent the glow of the oil lamp. Tail lights, to be carried at the rear of the train (or loco if running light) are also included in most packs with red-jewelled aspects. As various railway companies had their own design of lamp, regional variations persisted well into BR days and, although BR did issue its own pattern, this only became standard issue by the 1970s, once steam power had gone. GWR and Western Region headlamps fitted onto a different pattern of bracket than seen on the three other BR regions, the bracket slotting into the side of Western Region (WR) pattern lamps rather than at the back of the others. Springside caters for these various lamp patterns and it was not uncommon for engines to carry a mix of lamps in terms of colour and regional patterns.

Engines at work on shunting or station pilot duties carried two lamps (over each buffer), one showing a red aspect and the other a white light. This was repeated at both ends, although the BR rules were not explicit as to which side the coloured light should sit. This engine is fitted with working lamps that take their power from the running rails and are produced by First Class Trains (see Appendix). Although they're not easy to fit, they do look good when lit!

Whether fitting lamps or discs, they can either be fixed permanently with a minuscule drop of superglue, or temporarily with Tacky Wax to allow repositioning at will.

Some Southern Region services saw the white discs displayed with various reporting numbers applied to one of the discs themselves. This can easily be portrayed using a draughtsman's fine ink pen. Working from photographs helps with accuracy and this BR 'Standard Five' is displaying the headcode of a Bournemouth–Birkenhead express as seen in June 1962.

As diesels and electrics came on stream, they initially followed the same principles of lamp placement, but with folding white discs. This then gave way to a system of four character headcodes that better described not only the class of train but where it was heading and the stopping nature of the service. The London Midland Region of BR had actually pioneered the use of the four-character scheme on steam traction, while the Western Region employed a similar three-digit system and these were usually displayed on a board hanging from the front of the engine, usually the smokebox handrail, although their application was often confined only to special services or summer Saturday 'extras'. The specifics of the four-character scheme were described in full in Volume One of this series.

London Midland Region four-character headcodes appeared in the early 1960s, although they were primarily used on 'extras' such as excursions or summer Saturday workings. This pack from Precision Labels includes an etched brass board that, after bending the brackets to form loops, will hang from the smokebox handrail without the need for glue. A range of self-adhesive digits are supplied to recreate a specific working. With this four-character scheme, the first digit described the class of train, the second described the destination, while the final two related to the specific service. They always followed the number–letter, number–number pattern.

CHAPTER 4

Basic Customizing

Taking the plunge into modifying model locomotives can at first seem a daunting prospect, especially given that some of them are not cheap. However, if a course of action has been planned before work commences, there should be no reason to feel unduly worried. In this section, a few minor titivations are suggested that offer big advantages in terms of realism, but also demonstrate some of the core skills required before going further.

Correcting minor flaws in the product, refining a few over-scale details, adding the odd embellishment and even introducing a bit of scratch-building are outlined below and each task is well within the grasp of all but the terminally cack-handed. Mind you, even if you do have a history of making the odd hash, why not relax and try again? Turn off the TV or the radio, find a quiet space where you won't be disturbed and just take your time.

WHAT'S TO BE DONE

The first thing to ascertain is not how many fancy new parts can be added, but what features of the existing model can be improved with a little attention, especially if it concerns production issues. Is there a dodgy bit of paintwork, a wonky lamp bracket or, more commonly, any moulding 'pips' or seam lines along plastic components? Anyone who has built a few plastic model kits will know about cutting or filing away excess plastic, or 'flash', from parts before gluing them together. Well, today's r-t-r locomotives still employ plenty of injection-moulded components and, like those

kits, there are sometimes areas where a bit too much plastic has materialized.

With recent advances in tool-making, this is becoming a rarer occurrence, although it does still happen, even on new releases. Whereas diesel-outline models have now been designed around this problem by incorporating separately fitted roof panels to cover the point of injection (the 'pip'), the top of a steam engine's boiler, however, is not so accommodating. Illustrated here is the Bachmann Ivatt '4MT', a sublime model that yet has a detracting seam running not only the length of the boiler top, but also up and over the chimney and dome. Now, some prototypes did indeed have a longitudinal line running along the boiler cladding but never along the smokebox, which was always formed of a solid sheet of metal. The chimney and dome certainly didn't have such lines either, so this really does need to be removed.

Cleaning the excess away is simple enough, but care should be taken, especially on the concave surfaces of the chimney as we don't want to alter the shape of it. A couple of flat and round files will do the job and any rough marks these may leave behind can be removed with abrasive paper and a polishing stick. However, if the plastic has been removed, then so too will the model's paintwork and retouching this can be very tricky to do well on such a highly visible surface. Just concentrating on the chimney and smokebox allows for these areas simply to be recoated in black, but the boiler itself is not so easy. Weathering conceals many sins and is especially useful here as just a fine deposit of

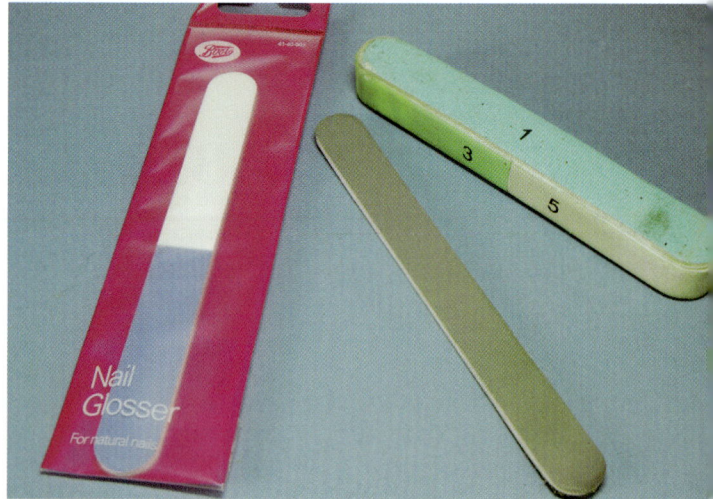

There are a few contemporary model locomotives around that are spoilt a little by the heavy moulding seams along boiler tops and chimneys. While these aren't difficult to remove, repairing the paint finish is not so easy. A flat, fine file has been used to tidy up the boiler and smokebox of this Bachmann Ivatt '4MT', while a round file is shown attending to the chimney. Work gently here as we don't want to spoil the actual shape of the mouldings and follow the file by rubbing away tool marks with a small strip of 1,000-grade wet & dry paper.

Cosmetic sanding sticks are aimed at manicurists, but can also be invaluable aids to the model-maker. On the right is a sanding stick with six different grades of abrasive, ranging from fairly coarse to super-smooth. The other sticks are for polishing nails to a high sheen, each with three grades of burnishing surfaces. It's possible, using both of these tools, to rub away unwanted raised detail or imperfections and then gradually polish the plastic surface back to a near-perfect finish. As these are cheap, cutting up a few to reach into narrow or awkward corners improves their versatility.

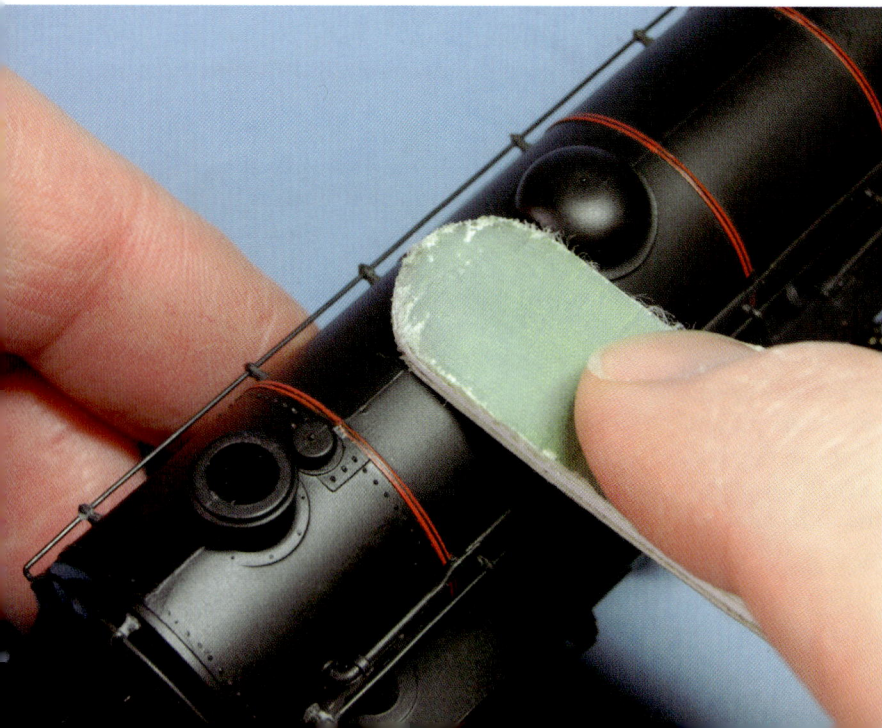

After removing the moulded seam, a nail polishing stick is seen here burnishing the plastic of any remaining file or sandpaper marks. Paint is invariably lost during this process and this will be especially noticeable on engines with a coloured livery, that is, not black. While polishing produces a blemish-free surface, it can't reinstate the paint and therefore the only realistic cure is either to repaint the boiler, or to add a little soot weathering over the top of the boiler (see Chapter 14 for more details).

soot from the chimney will disguise the modified area, either sprayed from an airbrush or lightly dusted by weathering powders (*see* Chapter 14 for further details).

For those wanting a pristine engine, only repainting the boiler is guaranteed to give a perfect finish, but this will be time-consuming, especially if any lining needs to be reapplied. Like virtually all detailing exercises, you must weigh up what the implications are for each step and whether they are deemed to be worthwhile.

STILL A BUOYANT MARKET

Even though r-t-r models now offer such high degrees of detail specification, the aftermarket enhancement products offered by the likes of Comet, Alan Gibson, Brassmasters and Markits (*see* Appendix) remain popular. Moreover, new detailing packs and components are still being tailored for even the latest Hornby or Bachmann products. The common stereotype of railway modellers being a fussy bunch is not without basis and I'm sure some people will never be truly satisfied with any mass-produced model. None the less, by reading magazines from other disciplines, such as military, aviation and automotive modelling, it would seem that this attitude is not exclusive to train buffs. It is, after all, part of what keeps the hobby interesting.

Many of the specialist parts makers have built up enviable reputations over several decades and offer either full project kits for specific models (such as the Brassmasters detailing kit for the Hornby 'Black Five' as featured in Chapter 9), or individual components such as chimneys, safety valves, whistles and so on. Depending on the maker and type of fitment, white-metal or brass castings may be utilized, while, in other cases, brass parts may have been turned on a miniature lathe, as is the case with replacement whistles, buffers, smokebox door handles and such like.

It's clear, then, that if we deem there to be something missing or if some facets of the model could benefit from being replaced, there are plenty of sources from which to obtain the required parts. Other than direct replacements, there are also generic items that may be appro-priate for a whole raft of prototypes, particularly those fleets with standardized features. The packs of etched brass lamp brackets, brake gear and cab fittings offered by Mainly Trains (*see* Appendix) spring to mind here, along with the extensive ranges of cast metal or wire steam and vacuum pipes that will enhance any engine's bufferbeam. Additionally, there are also packs of detailing material such as sheets of etched brass chequer plate that are perfect for creating the distinctive small footsteps fitted atop buffer shanks as well as some parts of a locomotive's running plate.

ENTER THE SCALPEL

Whichever locomotive type is being treated, for me the project usually begins by getting the 'face' of the engine looking right. Hornby may offer a handful of steam-outline models with a full representation of the common twin-handled smokebox door handle, but these products are in the minority, with most others having at least the lower handle moulded into the door face. Adding a replacement, ideally a turned-brass set, is probably the best way of achieving a true representation of the real thing.

Check your prototype carefully before ordering a replacement as designers will have chosen from among a variety of smokebox fastenings. Period is also a consideration as, for example, the 'Super Ds' originally wore a circular handle that screwed the locking mechanism tight, but these were eventually superseded with the twin handle – or clock face – arrangement. Variations still existed on the twin handles, however, with plain or flanged shafts (or a mixture of both) and lengths also differing. Luckily, all these permutations are catered for by suppliers such as Markits, Alan Gibson and Mainly Trains. Returning to the subject of circular handles, these too can be replaced if necessary with an etched wheel, if it is deemed necessary to replace the provided moulding.

When adding a new set of door handles, it should be remembered that the lower of the two always points straight downwards. On the real thing, a horizontal bar sits across the middle of the smokebox aperture, with a rectangular hole

As the 'face' of an engine is one of the most important aspects, refining some moulded details is key to improving r-t-r steam locomotives. Other than a few recent offerings, most models carry over-scale smokebox door handles, but these can easily be replaced with superior turned-brass components, once the originals have been cut away. Use a sharp scalpel blade and slice away the plastic gradually. Don't rush this, as trying to cut the whole thing off at once will end in tears. Cut away the central boss too, then finish with abrasive paper and a burnishing stick.

at the central point. The boss of the door handle consists of a T-shaped rod, which, when the door is shut, fits through the hole in the horizontal bar and is then turned through 90 degrees, thus locking against the rear of the rectangular hole. The outer door handle then turns along a screw thread, drawing the door and the locking bar together for an absolutely tight seal that is essential for efficient steaming.

I once received a fairly terse comment after I'd portrayed a loco with the lower handle set at about 7 o'clock instead of the usual vertical position (6 o'clock). However, that's how the real engine appeared in the photograph I'd used for reference. In this image, the engine was at the head of an East Coast service in the 1950s and it seemed to be working okay. This does highlight the fact that there can often be the odd exception to seemingly hard and fast rules; maybe the anomaly in this case was down to a twisted rod or shoddy work by the shed staff.

This may be a good point at which to introduce the subject of model fillers, just in case a first venture into hacking away moulded detail has seen a minor mishap. Alternatively, other details may also have been removed and holes may need plugging before new parts can be fixed

in place. Various types of filler are available from model shops and craft supply stores, each with their own advantages and foibles. Milliput two-part epoxy filler is one of the most widely used mediums and a choice of grades can be obtained, the Superfine white being the best of the bunch. The filler must be mixed before use, equal amounts of each stick being kneaded together until a uniform colour is reached.

Other, rapid-setting formulas are available that do not require mixing and, thus, can speed a project along. Tubes of Squadron filler are available in green or white putties and both produce excellent results, although they rarely prove as durable as epoxy filler, nor can they be drilled-into as readily. Knifing Putty, as sold in automotive stores, can also prove useful, as it offers a fast drying time and the ability to be burnished to a very smooth finish. Interestingly, Tipp-Ex correction fluid can also be used as a handy filling solution for small blemishes as, once it has set, it can be lightly sanded.

Whatever type of filler is used, it can simply be applied with a small, flat screwdriver or a scrap of plastic and left to harden completely before sanding flush with the surrounding surface. Always build up the filler above the surface as

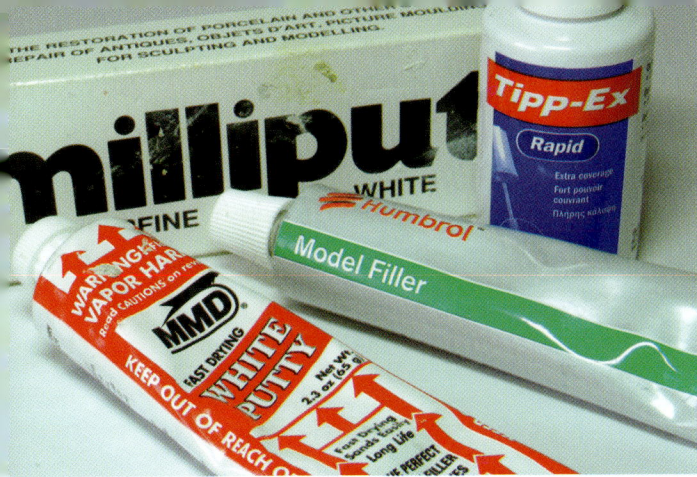

Should other parts be in need of replacement, or if you've been a bit over-eager with the knife blade, use of some model filler may be necessary. Various types are available and their merits are described in the text of this chapter. For our purposes, either Milliput two-part epoxy filler or some modeller's putty, such as the tube seen here produced by American firm Squadron, will be just the job. Both fillers set hard and can be sanded and buffed completely smooth.

Fix the central boss in place with a drop of superglue, the larger-diameter projection being the mounting lug. The two handles can then be threaded onto the boss, taking a note of whether a flanged or plain handle should sit in the lower or upper position. Secure with a blob of superglue, applied with a cocktail stick, then leave until set. Remember to have the lower handle pointing straight downwards, although the other one can face any direction. When the glue has set, use a pair of sharp end-cutters to trim the boss just ahead of the top handle and then tidy with a flat file. Aim for a nice flat surface, while being careful not to weaken the glue joint.

An inferior lamp bracket and unnecessary smokebox door knob have been removed from this Bachmann BR Class 5 and the resultant holes plugged with modeller's putty. While this hardens, the centre of the smokebox door can be marked and centre-punched to guide the drill. Measure the mounting lug of your replacement door handle and choose a suitable bit, fitted in a mini hand drill or needle vice. Avoid power drills for tasks such as this as it's impossible to retain as much control over them and, when accuracy is paramount, the risk is not worth it. Even on a slow speed setting, a power drill will create heat, leading to the bit melting its way through and leaving a sloppy or inaccurate hole. Drilling into plastic by hand is so easy that just a dozen or so turns of a sharp bit will be enough to cut right through.

This view inside the smokebox of Great Eastern Railway 0-6-0T No.87 illustrates the T-shaped locking mechanism of the door and why the lower of the twin handles should be facing 'due south'.

it will usually shrink as it sets. Use a fine file, followed by different grades of abrasive papers (400-, 800- and 1,000-grade wet & dry) to blend the material into the surrounding surface, taking care not to breathe in any of the harmful dust.

Humbrol Model Filler is an unusual substance and is suitable mainly for use on plastics. The formula works chemically to 'melt' the material around a blemish or joint, closing any small gaps. Applying too much will reduce the plastic to a puddle and will dissolve most paint finishes, so be careful! While this brand of filler is not really appropriate for much of the tasks outlined in the following chapters, it does have its uses, especially if scratch-building various plastic components, as will be demonstrated in Chapter 10.

In addition to upgrading the smokebox door handle, a proper set of lamp brackets will also improve both the front and rear aspect of a locomotive. Most models now have some representation of these brackets, but they can sometimes simply be moulded onto a bunker, or, in some cases, be in the wrong place. Modellers of the late 1960s London Midland Region may also want to replicate the moving of the central pair of brackets to allow for safe working under electrified lines and this – and all other bracket replacement jobs – requires the originals to be either cut or pulled away with pliers and the holes plugged with filler.

Mainly Trains offers a kit of etched brass lamp brackets that caters for a variety of different loco types. These, on the whole, are good, although some of the parts are slightly over-scale; however, a little work with a file can address this. What is a nice feature of the pack is that some bracket types feature rivets, which can be gently pushed out with a sharp scriber/punch before cutting the parts from the fret. Assembly consists purely of folding each bracket to the correct shape before gluing in position. With such small parts, bending accurately is difficult if using pliers – a Hold 'n' Fold tool certainly comes into its own here. Consisting of a heavy flat base and a clamp with variously shaped and sized faces, the tool holds an etched component firmly while a knife blade is used to create a beautifully sharp bend. Available in a variety of sizes, one of these tools

will soon repay the investment with consistently perfect folds. As this book progresses, you'll see the tool in use as we add more complex etched metal parts.

An alternative to the Mainly Trains set of lamp brackets is the pack of brass strips offered by Shawplan (see Appendix) that serve to form the raw material for creating your own components. These are much finer strips (being 0.75mm wide) and are perfect for forming the common plain patterns, although creating brackets of a curved shape is more difficult; ditto the characteristic GWR/Western Region style of lamp iron, thus making the previously mentioned Mainly Trains set an attractive proposition. It's not impossible to make your own, of course, and strips of 0.0005in or 0.0010in thick brass or nickel silver, 1mm wide, are cheap and easy to obtain. Folding to shape is easy enough, but ensuring that each is of a uniform length and pattern is important, so making up a small folding jig might be a good idea.

Each of the tasks illustrated in this chapter can be completed by touching in the new components with the appropriate paint shades to match their surroundings, carefully brushing on some acrylic or enamel primer beforehand. While any discrepancy between the original paint finish and the new additions can be disguised with a touch of weathering, a pristine appearance will require the odd dab of satin varnish to match the sheen of the factory finish.

Although quite minor in comparison to some of the detailing undertakings in later chapters, the adding of such small refinements as lamp brackets and fire irons and improving smokebox door handles can make a tangible improvement to the overall appearance of a model locomotive. Also, some important techniques have been learnt and we've even made a small foray into scratch-building. Outlined in the following chapter are some further processes and, by consolidating each of these new skills, there should then be no stopping you. Even progressing to superdetailing is simply a development of these core skills – cutting, making good a surface, marking, drilling and adding new parts neatly and accurately.

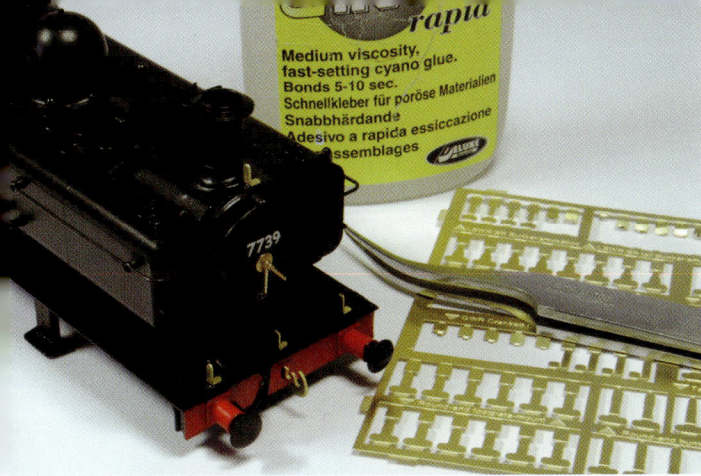

ABOVE: Mainly Trains offers a handy set of replacement etched brass lamp brackets to suit a wide range of loco types across the regions, including the distinctive Western Region pattern. This Bachmann GWR 57xx lacks any representation of the lamp brackets at the smokebox end, so adding some of these new brass details is an essential task.

BELOW: Many steam locomotives, especially those on the LMR, had their two central lamp brackets repositioned during the 1960s. This was to allow the upper position to be lowered, thus reducing the risk to enginemen working under electrified lines. Obviously, with the door handle being in the way, it had to sit to one side of the smokebox; the corresponding lower bracket was also moved to the right in order to maintain the symmetry of the lamp codes when displayed. This preserved LMS '8F' has such an arrangement, but has also regained an upper lamp bracket (although still lower than the original location) in order to carry commemorative headboards when working main-line rail tours.

ABOVE: While the Mainly Trains etched bracket set is a great resource, some of the patterns are slightly over-scale. For ultra-authentic brackets, using some strips from a Shawplan pack is the way forward. A set of sharp tin snips is useful to cut the delicate strip to length without distorting it.

ABOVE: Forming the bracket's shape is easy when using a Hold 'n' Fold tool. Clamp the strip under one of the fingers, then bend the brass upwards using a flat blade such as a scraper (seen here), or Stanley knife blade. Perfectly consistent knife-edge folds result and, by clamping on one of the outer edges, the distinctive S- or C-shaped brackets can be formed.

BELOW: Returning to the BR Class 5, after marking out where the new brackets should sit, fix them in place with a drop of superglue. Being a Southern Region-allocated engine, this Class 5 requires two extra U-shaped brackets on either side of the smokebox door handle.

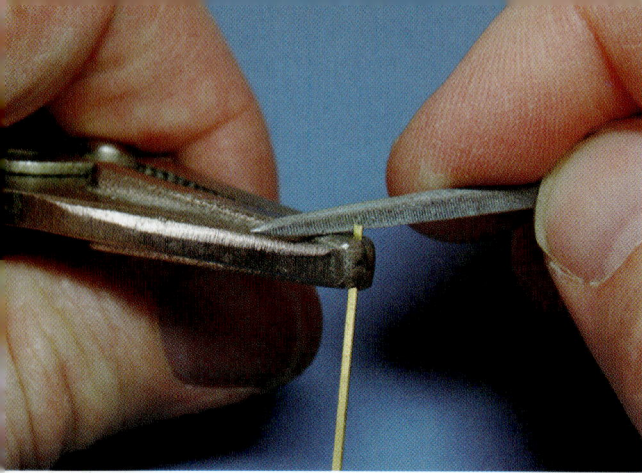

ABOVE: Another small improvement to make to the smokebox of the BR Class 5 (and other BR and LMS designs) is to add the distinctive door latch. Some models already have this well represented, the Hornby '8F' and 'Black Five' in particular, but, on others, it is either missing or only crudely represented. Using a strip of 1mm wide, 0.010in (0.25mm) brass strip, available in short lengths from Mainly Trains, a square-section needle file is drawn along one side, aiming to create a shallow cut out about 1mm × 0.5mm. Clamping the brass in a miniature spring clamp makes life easier.

BELOW: This view of LMS 'Black Five', 45407, clearly shows the distinctive smokebox door latch.

ABOVE: Trim the strip to a length of 2mm (0.080in) with a pair of tin snips, then fix in place. Make sure that the surface is suitably prepared beforehand.

ABOVE: Cutting small squares or rectangles, according to prototype, of etched brass chequer plate is an economical and effective way of adding footsteps to the top of buffer shanks; this is a ubiquitous prototype detail seldom copied by r-t-r makers. Available from both Mainly Trains and Shawplan, each sheet of material will provide enough for dozens of models. The steps added to this BR Class 5 measure 2mm × 1.75mm.

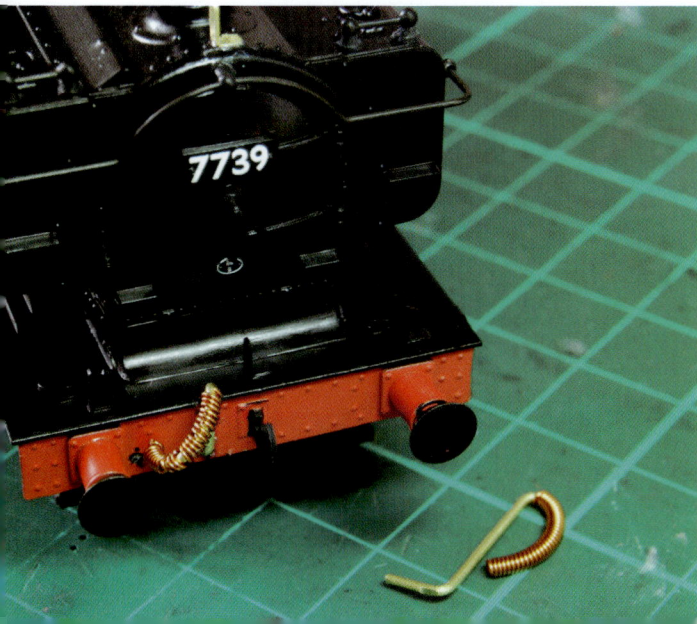

ABOVE: Hopefully, readers may by now be developing something of a critical eye (if they didn't have one already) and be looking at various models to see where improvements can be made, however minor. I love Bachmann's little GWR '57xx' tank engines, but one small detail that jars is the plastic brake pipe fitted to the front end. As the pipe is a distinctive shape, unless an exact match is available, a new part must be scratch-built or modified. These brass and wound-wire brake pipes are from Harburn Hobbies and, being formed of soft metal, can easily be altered to suit. Round-nose pliers are the perfect tool for this.

ABOVE: The same etched chequer plate material can also be utilized for details such as the tread plates atop the inside cylinder covers of GWR 'Castle' and 'King' 4-6-0s, as visible here on King George V.

BELOW: At the other end of the '57xx', Mainly Trains lamp brackets have replaced the moulded representations on the bunker rear. This time, however, a white-metal brake pipe has been fitted (this pack is from Comet Models). As the bufferbeam has part of the pipe moulded quite nicely, the white-metal part was trimmed to sit above it and any small gaps disguised with filler.

BELOW: After bending, checking and trimming to length, the Harburn pipe was fitted into a newly drilled mounting hole. Any remaining traces of the original plastic pipe were covered with model filler and touched-in with appropriate paints.

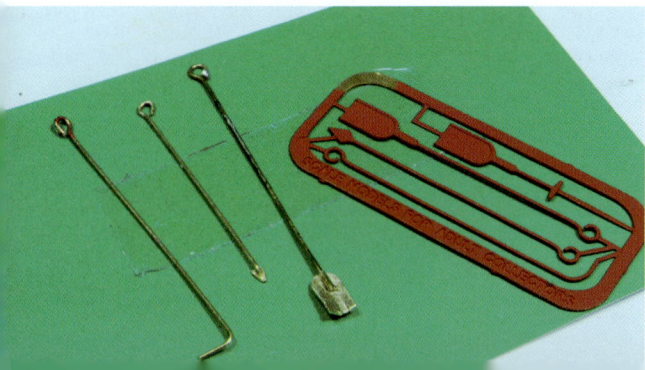

ABOVE: A nice finishing touch to all steam locomotives is the addition of a set of fire irons to the tender. A selection of these tools would be provided on all main-line engines to assist the fireman in keeping his fire burning to full capacity. This set, fixed to the delicate brackets provided on Bachmann's rendition of the LNWR 'Super D', is in the Springside range, being a choice of white-metal castings that must be primed and painted various shades of 'rust' before fitting. Not all engines boasted such an organized storage arrangement, others simply having the long irons stacked atop the coal in the bunker, although can you imagine having to retrieve one of these 8ft long irons into such an enclosed cab while plodding along on a bumpy footplate? On tender cab-fitted engines such as this, some enginemen would leave one of the rear spectacle plates open and simply thread the tools through it, rather than having to reach outside while on the move; this would be an interesting detail to capture in miniature.

BELOW: Although the cast Springside fire iron set is attractive, using an etched brass set (such as this pack from 247 Developments) offers a superior degree of realism. Furthermore, making your own set is not difficult, plus can prove both a cost-saving exercise and be more accurate, not least as different regions employed slightly different equipment. Using some 0.7mm diameter (22SWG) brass wire, round-nose pliers will help to form the distinctive swan-neck handle, while the flat end is achieved by either filing it flat, or, for wider implements, soldering a length of strip brass to the wire and forming to a suitable shape.

ABOVE: Tank locomotives would often see a stack of tools and irons mounted above the side tanks, although some types did have sets of brackets to keep them tidy and safe from falling onto the track. Oil cans and spare lamps were also common. Note the empty bucket wrapped around the far ventilation pipe of this ex-Midland Johnson '2441' tank, converted from a Bachmann 'Jinty'.

BELOW: The GWR showed a commendable attention to detail with much of its locomotive design. An example is the provision of tool brackets on the bunker of this '57xx', enabling the fireman to stow his irons and bucket. This is an exquisite handmade set of GWR-pattern tools made for me by a reader of *Model Rail* magazine, following exactly the type of equipment issued to GWR and BR/WR footplate crews. As the fireman on a GWR/WR engine worked on the left-hand side (opposite to the other British regions), the tools would be stowed from his side – a small but important detail to get right.

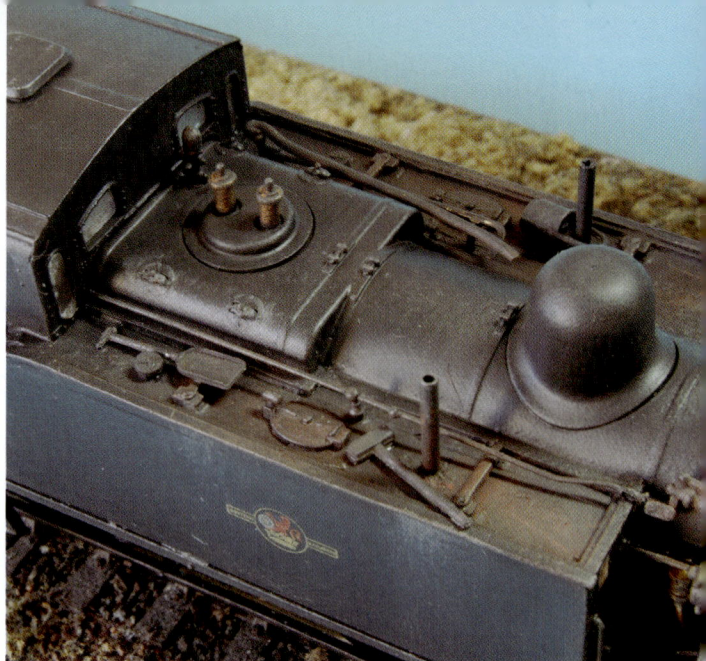

CHAPTER 5

Further Customizing

Accurate measuring, marking and drilling are some of the more fundamental practices to be found in all branches of modelling work and dealing with different materials often requires alternative approaches. Drilling into plastic is relatively easy and has been described already, but cutting an accurate hole in metal requires a good deal more care. In order to accommodate more mass in a miniature locomotive, designers have been producing a greater number of cast-metal components in addition to filling any voids in the bodyshell with separate steel weights. A heavier loco (within reason) will usually be a better runner, delivering more tractive effort to the rails and negotiating complex curves without derailing. A more consistent level of electrical connection will also be achieved if there is a greater mass sitting on the rails.

With this in mind, any modification below the boiler becomes less straightforward, as unwanted details cannot simply be sliced away with a sharp blade. Nothing is impossible, however, and work simply has to progress in a different way and with alternative tools. Mentioned in Chapter 4 was my distrust of using powered mini-drills to cut holes into plastic and the same consequences of less control and excess heat still apply for drilling into a steel chassis. Then again, the alternative of using a hand-operated drill is not only time-consuming, but can also lead to blisters! By taking a few precautions, power-drilling can be done without causing too much damage.

THE EYES HAVE IT

Perhaps a good place to start is in the drilling out of the distinctive lifting eyes that are commonly found on the two frame extension brackets fixed to the running plate, forward of the smokebox. All steam engines incorporated some form of lifting points and the locations of these varied between engine types; a quick glance at a prototype photograph will reveal their location. Such fixtures enabled repairs or re-railing to be effected with the minimum of fuss, using an overhead or rail-borne crane that would simply attach a couple of hooks to one or both ends before lifting. Only a few r-t-r models have these details included in full relief, so drilling a couple of holes is a simple way of representing an important detail. Mark the locations carefully, ensuring an exact match on both sides, and create a small indentation at the centre of the hole with a fine punch, tapped lightly by a pin hammer. This is an important step as, with the harder material, the drill is more likely to wander off course if it cannot get an accurate and sure foothold into the metal.

Use good-quality, sharp drill bits for tasks like this and apply only gentle pressure. A lot of heat will be generated by the tool, so work gradually, withdrawing the bit on occasion to clear away the swarf and to let the tool and surface cool a little before proceeding. Keep a close eye on the bit's progress through the metal, as once it nears the other side, the tool is likely to run away if excess pressure is being applied. You can see on the photograph here that some of the lining on the running plate has been damaged as my

Take care when drilling through a steel chassis, such as when adding the distinctive lifting eyes in a locomotive's frames. A lack of concentration can result in a loss of control and the tool may damage the surrounding paintwork, as has happened here.

concentration wavered; the drill popped through the metal without me expecting the sudden loss of resistance and the edge of the chuck duly ground into the paintwork. At least this wasn't a plastic running plate, or it would have made much more of a mess.

Tidy up the area with needle files and abrasive paper, being careful to remove all metal filings; if any of these were to get into the motor mechanism or any bearings and gears, damage could result. Take care also not to disturb details such as builder's plates and Overhead Warning symbols if sited nearby, although these can always be reinstated with transfers or etched plates if necessary. Touching in the bare metal with some suitable enamel or acrylic paint finishes the job.

LANCES, VALVES AND PIPING

Another distinctive front-end fixture found on numerous loco types is the lance valve, usually sited on the side of the smokebox. These valves drew steam directly from the boiler and powered a long hand-held lance inserted into the various boiler tubes. The high-pressure jet would flush out any scale and soot deposits during routine servicing. Certain Hornby and Bachmann products now feature plastic or metal lance valves, where appropriate, but some of these are not

perfect, while others are missing altogether. Something else to consider is that certain engines had their valves moved to different positions, especially some LMS types such as '8F's and 'Black Fives'. So, if your chosen engine warrants its inclusion, adding or moving a lance valve can be done with little fuss.

Brass handrail knobs are perfect for forming improvised valves and in cases of engines wearing external pipework, making use of fine copper wire makes any painting of new parts unnecessary. Such wire, along with reels of brass, nickel or lead wire, is readily available from craft stores dealing with jewellery-making. Indeed, some railway modelling suppliers sell small packs of various grades of copper wire, but I've found that a selection of 10m jewellery reels (which is the same material) can be had for only a few pounds each. Keeping a stock of 0.3mm (30SWG), 0.5mm (24SWG) and 0.9mm (20SWG) copper wire will prove useful for a multitude of tasks.

Turned-brass handrail knobs are offered by various makers of detail parts, produced in varying lengths to suit different applications; it's not unusual for one engine to carry three different-length knobs along just one side of the boiler, especially if the barrel is tapered. It also pays to keep a bag of N gauge knobs to hand, as,

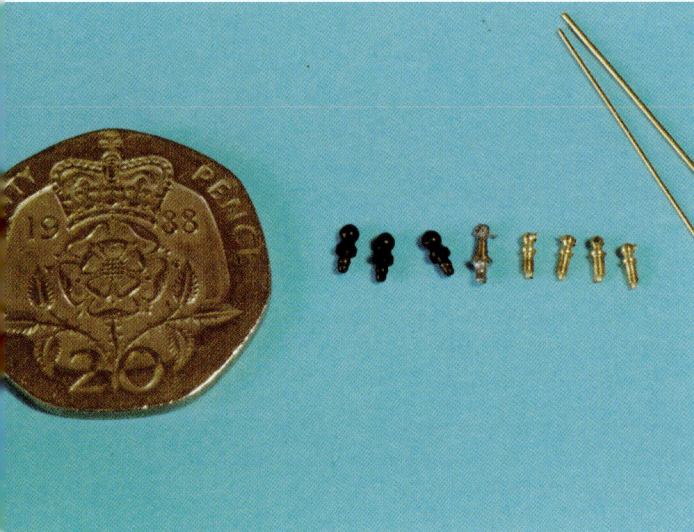

Turned-brass handrail knobs come in different shapes and sizes and can offer an improvement over some r-t-r fittings. They can prove handy for improvising other components, while having a stock of N gauge units will also come in useful.

Using both 2mm and 4mm scale handrail knobs (both of the shorter variety) and some lengths of 0.3mm (30SWG) copper wire, a steam lance valve arrangement can be added to the side of a loco's smokebox. Not all engine types wore such piping externally, while others could differ due to modifications, so check photographs carefully. This is the pattern on a BR Class 5 and a number of LMS '8F's had a similar layout, although without the vertical pipe carrying on to the running plate. A few tiny drops of superglue will hold everything in place, the wire having been shaped with a pair of round-nose pliers.

being much smaller than the OO gauge versions, they can be utilized for pipe brackets and other fittings. All of these knobs come with a suitable hole ready-drilled through the boss, allowing fine wire to be threaded through and just a dab of superglue, applied with a cocktail stick, will hold everything together.

HANDRAILS

Most steam-outline models now come with separate wire handrails as standard issue and there are only a handful of products that still retain solid plastic fittings. Some of those that do boast separate rails may have over-sized mounting knobs or heavy gauge wire that can easily be replaced. Furthermore, modifications and minor variations to individual or small batches of locomotives could mean that the odd extra handrail was added or relocated. Like-for-like replacement is certainly straightforward as the old knobs and wire can be pulled away from the model with a set of pliers and new parts simply glued in their

place. Packs of stiff, straight brass handrail wire are offered in varying diameters by Alan Gibson and the 0.3mm certainly looks good. Although I've mentioned the economy of using reels of jewellery wire for piping, this softer material is no good for making handrails as it is impossible to form into straight lengths.

If a model carries moulded handrails, cutting them away is not a difficult task, but it is one that should be undertaken with care to prevent damaging other details and to produce a good, smooth finish. Don't forget that even once the new wire rails are in place, the modified surface will be clearly visible, so take the time to cut the plastic away gradually and don't scrimp on the abrading to remove any scratches or tool marks.

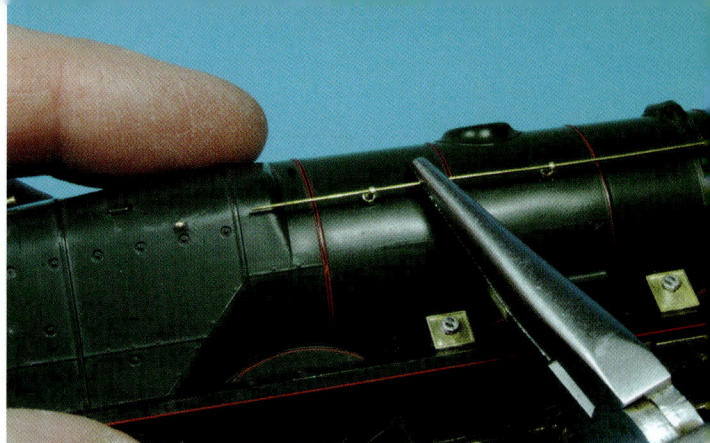

ABOVE: Although most r-t-r steam outline models have, for some years now, offered wire handrails as standard fittings, some of them can still benefit from replacement with fine wire and mounting knobs. This Hornby 'Duchess' is having new Comet handrail knobs fitted into the holes vacated by the originals (pulled out with pliers). Choose the right-length knob for each part of the boiler to keep the handrails straight; usually short-pattern knobs sit at the firebox end, with longer ones fitted along a tapering boiler barrel. By holding each knob with the tweezer prongs inserted through the hole, correct alignment can be made.

RIGHT: There are still some products in current production that lack even an over-scale complement of wire handrails and the Hornby LNER 'J83' 0-6-0T is one of them. Although updated in terms of finish and a few improved fittings in the mid-1990s, the main fabric of the model dates back to 1976 and it shows in the moulded plastic handrails around the smokebox. Cutting these away is not difficult, using a sharp blade to slice away a bit at a time, working until flush with the surface and following with abrasive paper to give a smooth finish. Take care not to damage any other moulded detail.

ABOVE: If the knobs have been fixed with the holes aligned properly, the new 0.3mm brass wire can be threaded through. Use only stiff, straight wire for long handrails such as these as, although the packs are slightly more expensive, straightening-out coils of softer wire is impossible. When threaded fully, dab a little superglue at each knob and, when set, use a set of end-cutters to trim the wire.

LEFT: Mark out the locations of the new handrail knobs, drill holes to suit, then thread on the handrail wire. Using a tailor's chalk pencil, whittled to a very sharp edge, will help when marking out onto a dark surface. When faced with handrails that encircle the smokebox front, shape the wire using round-nose pliers, then thread the knobs onto the wire before fixing to the model. Check that the rails run straight and level in relation to the boiler and other fittings before securing with glue.

BRIDGING THE GAP

With nearly all r-t-r products, the necessity for each model to cope with tight layout curves leads to a number of compromises in appearance and there are few more visible than the gap between the engine and tender. Recently, some novel designs have been incorporated to allow modellers a choice of gap that can be altered to suit the vagaries of their layouts. However, older models lack this feature and the space between cab and tender can be vast, leaving one wondering how on earth the fireman can reach the coal. Closing the gap, in a literal sense, is discussed in Chapter 12, but here we shall look at how to disguise the space by adding cab doors and a fallplate.

A fallplate is fitted to virtually all tender engines and consists of either single or multiple panels, hinged from the rear edge of the cab and sitting on top of the tender's running plate. This allows the gap to be safely bridged for the train crew without hindering the articulated nature of the engine and tender. These plates were often formed of heavy-gauge steel with a tread panel cast into the top face to provide a non-slip surface. Some detailing-part sources offer etched fallplates, some with integral cab floorboards, but making your own from etched brass chequer plate sheet is far cheaper and each plate can be tailored to fit a particular model.

Rolling a slight curvature into the plate not only adds a little extra realism to the part, but also allows it to 'float' over the tender footplate without actually touching it. This way, the model can still negotiate corners without the new piece of brass getting in the way. Rounding-off the corners will also help. Forming a curve in brass is not as difficult as many people think and can be achieved without any specialist tools; I simply use the rear of a computer mouse mat and a length of scrap steel rod. The diameter of the rod dictates the amount of curvature that will be produced, so for tight curves choose a small rod, while a larger tool will produce a more gentle camber. Copper piping will also do the trick and I've used the plain shank of a drill bit and a screwdriver's shaft with good results. The soft mat is crucial as it absorbs the pressure from the rod and distributes it evenly across the brass. A few layers of soft tissue paper will work just as well.

Cab doors can equally be cut from strip brass, or a set of off-the-shelf etched parts can be obtained. Mainly Trains, Comet, Brassmasters and others all offer etched doors in a variety of patterns and sizes and these can have a slight edge over simple strips of plain brass, not least as they often include beading strips and hinge detail where appropriate. Engines often featured folding cab doors, allowing them to be stored out of the way when open. There's nothing to say that scratch-built doors could not incorporate such features if a little extra work is put in, but, as etched sets are fairly cheap, it's not always worth the extra effort.

With nearly all r-t-r products, the necessity for models to cope with tight curves leads to a number of compromises in appearance, none more visible than the large gap between engine and tender. On older models, this can sometimes look like a chasm and is typified by this side view of a Bachmann LNER 'B1', a former Replica product dating back to 1987. Without closing this gap, there are still ways of disguising it.

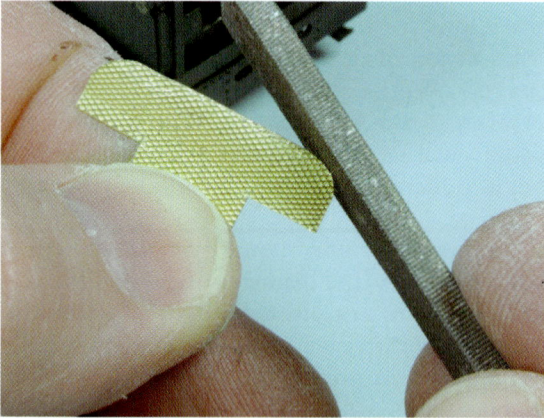

ABOVE: By cutting a rectangular piece of etched chequer plate to approx 28mm × 12mm, a realistic fallplate can be created. File the corners of one end to a rounded profile as this will let the tender turn freely on the track; the more material removed from the corners, the more freedom the tender will have.

BELOW: To enable the plate to fix to the cab floor, a flat section must be reinstated after rolling the curve. Here, the Hold 'n' Fold tool proves its worth again as, by clamping part of the brass into the device and using the rod again, a slight fold can be formed while the clamp also flattens the material.

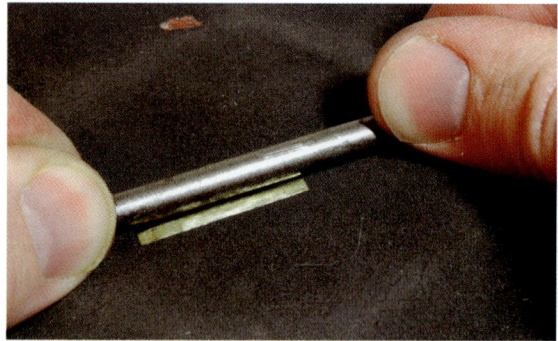

ABOVE: Fallplates sometimes possessed a slight curvature, sloping down towards the tender. A curved profile is achieved by placing the brass face down on the back of a computer mouse mat and rolling a solid metal rod (about 6mm diameter) over it, just as if rolling out pastry. Keep the rod square to the workpiece and apply firm pressure. Very soon, the brass will start to take on a rounded form and the amount of pressure will dictate the degree of curvature achieved.

BELOW: Test-fit the fallplate into the cab, checking that it doesn't interfere with the tender before fixing in place with superglue; the finished profile of the plate can be appreciated in this view. Thin, plain brass strip (say 0.0030in thick) can also be used for creating your own cab doors, being cut into squares or rectangles and glued inside the cab and/or tender sides. Check how much your engine needs in the way of free movement to cope with the tightest curves on your layout. Adding undersized doors, along with a fallplate, will make a dramatic improvement. These doors measure 4mm × 10mm for the cab and 3mm × 10mm for the tender.

Once painted, the new doors and fallplate look well at home and help to disguise the enormous gap between cab and tender.

This Bachman 'Jubilee' (of the older ex-Mainline pattern) has been similarly treated, although using an etched set of cab doors from a Mainly Trains detailing pack (ref. MT256), including a pleasing representation of the beading along the top edge and a small locking handle. You can see how the fallplate hovers just a millimetre or so above the tender footplate, so not impeding the movement of the engine or tender around curves.

IS SCRATCH-BUILDING WORTH THE EXTRA EFFORT?

Making your own detailing parts may not always be quicker than opening a packet of purpose-made etches or castings, but it does have a couple of points weighed firmly in its favour. The first is cost, so long as suitable materials are at hand; it may not be as cheap if only embarking on one or two projects. The second factor is convenience: not having to sift through suppliers' price lists and catalogues, then placing an order and waiting for the parts to arrive by post, can see the job done and dusted much more quickly. Model railways are still my hobby as well as my livelihood and, when I know I've got some spare time to devote to a project of my own, the last thing I want is to waste that window of opportunity searching through online parts lists and amassing a stockpile of bits to linger in a box until a free evening comes around.

Creating bespoke components also allows for extra flexibility, as many off-the-shelf parts are designed for modellers with more of a finescale leaning than I have, such as those optimized for engines converted to either EM or P4 gauge (a more accurate scale/gauge ratio for 4mm scale than OO, which is actually under-scale as far as the track is concerned). This can often mean paying for new parts and then having to fettle them to fit with your own running specifications. Mind you, before I make myself out to

be a martyr to scratch-building, I do limit this activity to the more basic items and make use of numerous castings and detail kits. Combining the two disciplines, however, can be rewarding and, as your experience develops, it's possible to make an informed choice as to what is and isn't possible to do yourself.

A quick and effective upgrade for a set of front footsteps is to fold up some rear strengthening brackets from strip brass, twisting the top edge through 90 degrees to fix behind the bufferbeam. Many engines had these diagonal braces fitted. Make sure the brackets are identical for both sides and fix in place with superglue. Buying strip brass is not always necessary for jobs like this as parts can often be improvised using the scrap fret material from packs of etched detailing parts.

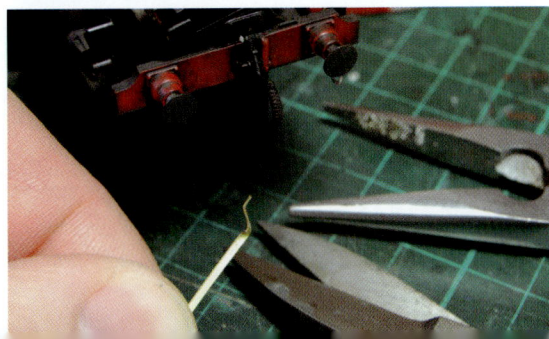

The Coupling Quandary

Within the previous volume of this series, dealing with diesel and electric trains, a whole chapter was devoted to the subject of alternative coupling options and, while I'm loathe simply to repeat the information again here, I'm also more conservative with what I stick onto the ends of my steam engines.

Although I can forgive contemporary locos for carrying American-style Kadee buckeye couplings, as many modern diesels do these days, seeing them on a 'steamer' just doesn't do it for me. However, I readily accept that they offer many advantages, not least in remote coupling and uncoupling without the need to hang over the trains with a wire hook. What's more, a set of tension locks is just as unprototypical as a pair of Kadees,

although we shouldn't forget that the tenders of certain express passenger engines did carry retractable 'buckeyes' for connecting to coaching stock. The tension-lock system dates back nearly fifty years and can always be retained with a few refinements, such as keeping the proprietary couplings fitted to the rolling stock but improvising a stiff wire drawbar on the locomotive, so arranged as to work reliably when hauling and propelling a train.

The introduction of NEM (*Normen Europäischer Modellbahnen*) pockets was meant to standardize the specification of couplings in terms of height and compatibility, but it hasn't worked out to be 100 per cent effective as yet. However, the convenience of plug-in alternatives means that other systems can be trialled with little or no

The tension-lock form of coupling has long been associated with British-outline OO gauge railways and, although the design has been tinkered with over the decades, it can still prove troublesome, as the standard mounting height can vary between models, never mind across brands. The advent of NEM-type mounting pockets does mean that replacement for other compliant units is a simple push-fit and there are numerous types that can be substituted.

This Roco-type coupling, now available under the Hornby brand, simply clips into the NEM pocket although it doesn't always offer the same degree of close-coupling as modern tension lock systems (as seen in the background). With nearly all r-t-r coaching stock now offering sprung, close-coupling units that increase the distance between vehicles as they encounter bends in the track, operating with finer tolerances is now within the grasp of most modellers.

The US brand Kadee has been producing a range of excellent buckeye-style couplings for decades and, if fitted and operated correctly, they offer a reliable and versatile system, including the facility for remote operation using hidden magnets. However, British steam traction didn't carry such fittings and the miniature units were designed for use on American stock without buffers, so they must protrude slightly further than intended, thus losing some of their close-coupling characteristics. Various fitting arrangements are available including NEM-compatible Kadees, as fitted here to the standard socket on a Hornby Stanier 2-6-4T.

If the Kadee couplings are going to work properly, they need to be set to the correct working height as specified in the detailed instructions supplied with every pack. Investing in one of these height gauges will speed up the installation.

modifications necessary to loco or stock. A number of European-style couplings, some of which follow the same basic principle of the tension lock, do offer improved close-coupling performance and reliability in operation.

Kadee couplings come ready assembled as far as the buckeye or 'knuckle' are concerned, with just the method of mounting being left to resolve. Various sizes and mounting styles can be chosen to suit the vagaries of the model at hand and the

instructions supplied are extensive. A full low-down of this system was explained in Volume One, but a more in-depth study can be made by viewing the Kadee website (see Appendix).

As we have seen in Chapter 2, dummy scale couplings are offered in the packs of extra bits and pieces with some r-t-r releases and, while these look nice, they can't be used to haul a rake of carriages or wagons. Working-scale couplings are available in various forms, both assembled or as kits, and offer fully prototypical operation. The big drawback to these is that the makers don't also offer 4mm scale shunting staff to operate them, especially in hard to reach corners of a layout. Another point against them is the effort needed – and problems encountered – in the fitting of each unit. Sadly, it's seldom just a case of drilling a hole in the bufferbeam and adding the sprung drawbar. Many models now have cast beams, usually with a big lump of metal behind them, a locating bolt for the chassis, or a swinging pony truck – all of which will be in the way. Devising bespoke remedies for various engines can be a drag and the system is in no way suited to layouts with tight curves and short radius turnouts; but all of these negatives have to be weighed against the unbeatable scale appearance.

A more practical solution to a desire for authenticity lies in the Sprat & Winkle coupling system, which offers magnetically controlled operation and a near-scale appearance – in effect combining the attributes of scale couplings with the convenience of the Kadee set-up. Again, hidden magnets set into the track bed will activate the moving parts to allow instant or delayed uncoupling, thus making shunting a far easier prospect. Locomotives only require a fine horizontal wire stretched between buffers, while rolling stock carries a similar bar with a double hook protruding at a slight angle from the bufferbeam. Propelling and hauling is achieved without the vehicles' buffers coming into contact and this means a more dependable operation, free from the risk of buffer-lock and subsequent derailments.

Working-scale couplings are probably the most faithful to the real thing, although operating them requires good eyesight, a steady hand and easy access. There's certainly no option of automatic coupling/uncoupling in far-flung sidings or fiddle yards, although a handy coupling tool can be improvised using a small torch and a length of stiff magnetized wire. Consisting of a drawhook, spring and split pin, accompanied by either a screw-adjusted or three-link chain, the use of the spring allows the couplings to slacken a little when faced with a curve in the track. It will help enormously if similarly sprung drawhooks are fitted to each item of rolling stock, as well as to the locomotive.

Fitting scale couplings is not always easy as many r-t-r models are simply not designed with these couplings in mind. Take, for instance, the Bachmann Ivatt '4MT' with its solid metal chassis. There's no way that a sprung drawbar can be accommodated amongst this mass. Not without a serious amount of work, anyway.

A compromise solution to awkward situations is to add a fixed drawbar into the bufferbeam, drilling a mounting hole as deep as possible and trimming the mounting tang to suit. Try to get as much material into the hole as possible to form a strong bond and fix in place with epoxy glue. These etched drawhooks from Mainly Trains (ref. MT356) are nicely shaped to make coupling-up that bit easier.

Whatever considerations are at play, choice of coupling system is entirely up to you and it should be tailored to your own operating requirements and aesthetic sensibilities. Running stock and locomotives in fixed rakes virtually solves any problems, as the couplings won't readily be seen, although choosing types with closer-coupling properties does make a difference. If plenty of shunting happens on your layout, however, will you be happy to spend the time and effort in attaching miniature chain links onto hooks and will such arrangements suit the curvature of the track? Or, would you rather sit back and let the invisible

magnets do the work for you? There are certainly enough options out there to help you make a decision. I've included an image of a wagon rake captured on one of my favourite exhibition layouts, Dewsbury Midland, which employs dedicated rakes of stock for certain purposes: those that are commonly shunted about the yard and sidings are fitted with DG couplings, which work in a similar way to the Sprat & Winkle, while the rakes of goods and passenger trains that simply pass through the station feature all manner of coupling systems that go unnoticed: 'horses for courses', as the saying goes.

Tenders can also prove frustrating when adding scale couplings, as there's often something in the way behind the bufferbeam. On this Hornby Stanier tender, a hole has been bored through the former coupling mount and the drawbar passed inside. As the other side of the chassis is open, the spring and (shortened) split pin can be added, although the latter must be folded tightly to allow the assembly to move within its 'trench'. Reinforcing the rear of a plastic bufferbeam can be a good idea, especially if a large mounting hole has to be cut, leaving only a little material around the coupling.

The Spratt & Winkle coupling system aims to combine the authentic appearance of scale couplings with the convenience and automation of Kadees, and a trial pack contains all the parts needed to make a start with this system. The double hooks allow for pushing and pulling without the buffers coming into contact and also permit cosmetic couplings to be hung. Adding full bufferbeam detail to locomotives and rolling stock is not hindered, either. Magnets, hidden under the track, allow for remote coupling and uncoupling that saves the back pain associated with leaning over stock with scale couplings.

A similar system to the Sprat & Winkle is the DG coupling, as fitted to these wagons on the Dewsbury Midland layout of the Manchester Model Railway Society. These couplings offer a lower-profile appearance to tension locks with automated coupling/uncoupling and a high degree of reliability in use.

There's a wide choice of replacement buffers should your model need them. Choose from turned-brass or cast-white-metal fixed units, or the more expensive but more attractive sprung sets with turned-brass shanks and steel heads. Various mounting methods are employed according to manufacturer, with some sprung sets coming ready assembled. Shawplan and A1 Models both offer etched square backplates to sit behind new turned-brass buffers that may lack this important detail.

BUFFERS

In Chapter 4 we talked about maximizing the potential of a locomotive's 'face' and the buffers can also play a critical part in this aspect. By and large, models now feature either good or very good sets of buffers, the majority being sprung units. However, some products still linger in the Hornby catalogue, for instance, that carry somewhat crude fixed units. There are certainly plenty of replacements to choose from in the form of white-metal or brass castings, turned-brass sets, or high-quality sprung buffers and virtually all prototypes are catered for, certainly in terms of post-Grouping designs. Besides, many railway companies adopted common designs across large parts of their fleets, so the same packs can be used on several different models.

The size and shape of buffers worn by locomotives could vary according to duties and design.

Many loco buffers can simply be pulled out of their mounts with a pair of pliers, but others, usually older models, are moulded integrally to the bufferbeams and must be cut away. Depending on the replacements to be fitted, the loco's square backplates must also be cut back flush with the surface of the buffer beam. Take care, especially if there is rivet detail around.

Some shunting locomotives boasted large round heads, especially those employed at dock or industrial sites and expected to traverse very tight curves; the larger heads prevented locking with the buffers of rolling stock. Certain express engines, on the other hand, could carry surprisingly small heads, for instance the London & South Western Railway's 'T9' 4-4-0s.

Larger engines, such as LMS Pacifics, wore oval buffer heads at the front of the engine and smaller, round pattern units at the tender end. Traversing curves or crossings, whilst propelling a vehicle from the front end, the degree with which the body might swing necessitated a wider contact surface, again to avoid locking-up with the stock's buffers. The same situation also applied to the larger tank locomotives, such as LMS and BR 2-6-4Ts. Such a pattern was certainly more of an attractive feature for a main-line loco than large round units, which would have provided the correct amount of lateral surface area.

Working sprung buffers are a nice feature to have on a model, although, if utilizing tension-lock, Kadee or other such coupling methods, they are more or less decorative features. If using scale couplings, incorporating sprung buffers is almost a compulsory requirement, as they will provide for more reliable shunting operations and allow some degree of compensation when traversing curves, taking pressure off a strained coupling. There can be a problem with fitting sprung oval buffers, however, as the round shanks tend to rotate and leave the elliptical heads facing any which way. Most r-t-r models fitted with 'ovals' feature square section shanks that keep the heads (almost) constantly aligned, but not many replacement units offer the same facility.

A new set of buffers, whether fixed or sprung, is not usually a difficult proposition to fit, once the originals have been removed and the buffer-beam prepared. The mounting holes will almost certainly need opening out, which can offer the odd peril, depending on the brand to be fitted. Slater's sprung buffers (*see* Appendix) are usually my preferred choice, but they do need large holes drilling to accommodate the shanks and, on occasion, this has led to the bufferbeam buckling under the stress, with only a fraction of material being left around the edges. Even cast-metal beams have disintegrated on occasion as I've gently reamed the hole to its final size, forcing me to resort to reconstruction using epoxy putty. Once in place, though, they do look terrific, as long as they are aligned properly whilst being glued in position.

The sprung buffers in the Alan Gibson range are equally impressive, but can also be a little difficult to assemble. Unlike the Slater's packs, the Gibson shanks need to be built up from two separate parts. Either glue or solder can be used for this, but care must be taken not to clog the small inner channel through which the buffer rod and spring are to pass. Instead of a bolt, the Gibson heads are retained by folding over the end of the rod.

Having decided on a suitable coupling method, refined our drilling technique and dallied with a little more scratch-building, we can look ahead to introducing soldering to our array of skills and considering various other opportunities that may arise.

Cut away the moulded buffer shanks with a razor saw or end-cutters, leaving a little waste and working back flush with the bufferbeam. Be careful of any raised rivet detail.

Fitting new solid buffers usually means drilling or opening out an existing hole to accommodate the lug of the new part. Fix the new buffers with either epoxy or a strong superglue, such as Roket Poly, which will give a durable joint to these exposed details. Check that the buffers are aligned by looking from the front, side and above before the glue sets.

Fitting sprung buffers is a little more involved, not least as the mounting holes need to be bigger. Slater's buffers, in particular, require large holes and this can sometimes prove difficult on some models. Open out the holes gradually, working up through the drill sizes in 1mm increments to prevent the holes from becoming distorted. This can be extra tiresome when drilling into a steel chassis. Indeed, on this Bachmann Ivatt '4MT', the new hole left so little material around it that the metal broke away on one side of the bufferbeam, necessitating the use of some epoxy putty.

The Slater's sprung buffer heads are retained by a small nut, after inserting into the shank, along with the spring. Press the head inwards and add the nut, using tweezers or fine pliers to hold it still while the head is turned. The amount that the head protrudes from the shank depends on how far the nut is screwed on. Ensure the pair is set equally, then add a drop of Loctite thread sealant to stop the nut working loose.

Sprung oval buffers are available but these tend to roll around in their shanks, so keeping the heads aligned is difficult. Instead, fixed turned-brass buffers have been fitted to this Bachmann Fairburn 2-6-4T as superior replacements to the originals that looked a bit 'leggy'. Etched square backplates, from Shawplan, have been added to the bufferbeams before the buffers were fixed in place.

CHAPTER 6

Superdetailing: Part 1

Superdetailing, while not a term that can be found in the English dictionary, crops up regularly in modelling magazines and alludes to the act of adding as much prototypically correct detail to a replica as possible. This may include trying to get the best from older models, bringing them in line with twenty-first century specifications and expectations, or taking one of the best r-t-r products and seeing how much further it can be pushed towards ultra-authenticity.

There's no reason why such lofty ambitions cannot be within everyone's reach, especially if the techniques already outlined are developed, pushing yourself to go a little further with each new project. Moreover, superdetailing is a logical step forward from the art of customizing, in which, thus far, the aim has been to add appropriate fixtures and fittings to enable a model to stand apart from other out-of-the-box products.

AWS FITTINGS

One of the most ubiquitous modifications made to BR steam locomotives, across the regions, was the installation of Automatic Warning System (AWS) equipment, primarily to express passenger engines, but also to many mixed traffic and freight types. Not all were fitted, by any means, but from 1956 onwards it became a common feature on those engines that survived into the last decade of steam.

The system owed its origins to an electronic warning device introduced by the GWR that worked in tandem with traditional mechanical signalling equipment, acting as a secondary warning to engine drivers as a train approached a signal. Equipment fitted beneath a ramp, sited between the rails, would be automatically magnetized when its accompanying signal was set at danger, then a receiving 'shoe', located between the frames of the locomotive, would detect the magnetic presence and sound a siren in the engine's cab. If the signal was 'off' (that is, the road was clear), the ramp would be demagnetized and thus no warning would sound. Installation of the system began on GWR main lines from 1906 and, by 1912, was developed further to include an automatic brake application and was termed Automatic Train Control (ATC).

BR refined the ATC system during the 1950s, changing the track-mounted ramps to permanent magnets and adding a visual display as well as an audible warning that sounded whenever a signal was approached, regardless of it being at danger or not. The driver had a few seconds to acknowledge the warning by pressing a plunger in the cab, otherwise the brakes would come on and this could not be over-ridden until the train had come to a stand. As the system had now become more of a vigilance-checking device than a control method, the equipment became known as the Automatic Warning System and its installation spread across the network until, by 1990, it covered more than 70 per cent of BR lines.

Depending on the engine type, a number of common fittings were necessary to the exterior of a locomotive to allow the AWS system to function. Most important was the magnet set in front of the leading axle and this is something seldom seen on model locomotives, not least

AWS equipment was fitted to numerous engines from the late 1950s. This kit of AWS parts is by Comet and includes the style of battery box and cylinders as fitted to ex-LMS and some ex-LNER locos. Drilling out the centre of the cylinders to accept short lengths of 0.3mm wire (30SWG) adds a little extra finesse; the piping extends from one end only, heading towards the cab.

as a coupling mount is usually located in this area. However, if dispensing with tension-lock or similar couplings from the front end, there is no reason why a magnet cannot be scratch-built from plastic rod, being that the real things were simple affairs. A steel plate sat beneath the bufferbeam to protect the delicate magnet from the swinging coupling and suitable plastic mouldings are now becoming a familiar sight in the small bags of detailing goodies offered with certain new Hornby models. If that's not the case, then etched brass plates can be had from

detailing suppliers, or, again, making your own is simple enough.

Other adornments that went with AWS fittings included a battery box and one or two cylinders, all of which would be sited wherever was deemed convenient, depending on the class of loco involved. The pattern of these components could also differ according to region and some were tailored particularly to fit into certain nooks and crannies of running plates or frames. Later BR Standard designs managed to conceal most of the fittings within the frames and cabs, but the front coupling plate would be the tell-tale sign of being AWS-equipped. Looking at period photographs is therefore crucial to getting these things correct, not least to find out whether your chosen loco was ever fitted with the gear at all!

INTRODUCING SOLDERING

Cyano- and epoxy-type adhesives will serve us well in many modelling applications, but there are instances when using a soldered joint between two metals is preferred. Solder is an alloy, made up of various metals with low melting points. Various types of solder exist, fine-tuned to suit different circumstances and operating temperatures; these dictate exactly what ingredients are contained in each formula. In the main, metals such as tin, lead, antimony and zinc make up a large proportion of solders and the material should be treated with respect as these elements can be harmful to our health.

Other than mending any loose wiring or poor electrical connections, solder is especially

Once painted and blended in with their surroundings, the new AWS parts look convincing, helped by the addition of the pipe runs. The Comet AWS kit does not include a front coupling guard, however.

useful when assembling brass components. This might consist of just a small, scratch-built part, a set of etched smoke deflectors, or even a new tender chassis. Either way, soldering will provide strength in the joints far superior to even the most sophisticated adhesives.

Creating reliable solder joints relies on a number of factors:

- clean, grease-free surfaces
- an adequate supply of heat
- a clean iron tip
- the addition of a suitable chemical flux
- the correct grade of solder to suit materials and the iron temperature
- a close bonding of the materials to be joined – solder cannot bridge large gaps
- avoidance of 'dry' solder joints.

Before joining metals, it is always best to give each surface a light rub-down with fine abrasive paper to remove any oil, grease or other residues that may hinder the forming of a joint. Incidentally, this can also be beneficial when gluing metals, as some formulas struggle to adhere to a greasy surface. Etched detailing parts always should be treated in this way, as the chemical etching process is bound to leave some residual traces behind. If part of the metal carries a paint covering, be aware that, even by clearing to a bare surface, the surrounding area will also get hot and this may result in blistering paint and more noxious fumes being emitted.

Choosing the right iron for the job is also important, as an underpowered tool with a micro-tip will not generate enough heat to deal with a large joint. Conversely, too powerful an iron may cause thin material to buckle under excess heat. For most detail work and general brass kit-building in OO gauge, an iron of between 15–18watt output is more than enough. A 25watt iron can also be handy for larger components or thicker-gauge material, although such things are seldom used in the majority of detailing tasks. Regardless of the stated wattage of a tool, the iron bit temperature is often universally set to around 200–240°C; the higher power output refers to how quickly the tool can transmit all of that potential heat to the workpiece.

Choose a good-quality iron, such as those offered in the Antex or Weller ranges, as these are reliable and are backed-up with available spares and interchangeable tips of varying shapes and sizes. Keeping the bit clean while in use is paramount, so as to avoid impurities being mixed into the joint. Many general-purpose solders contain a resin core to help the molten material's flow characteristics and, in addition to the

Soldering irons come in a range of power outputs as well as mains-powered and butane gas-fired, cordless form. Brands such as Antex, Weller and Dremel are well established and it's worth investing in a decent tool if presentable and reliable results are to be achieved. Irons with interchangeable bits can also be an advantage in case of damage or to suit different applications. A temperature-controlled tool is needed for soldering white-metal, but these can be expensive. A cheaper option is an Antex power regulator that replaces the mains plug on any corded iron. A range of clamps, a tool rest and a heat-resistant work surface are also useful.

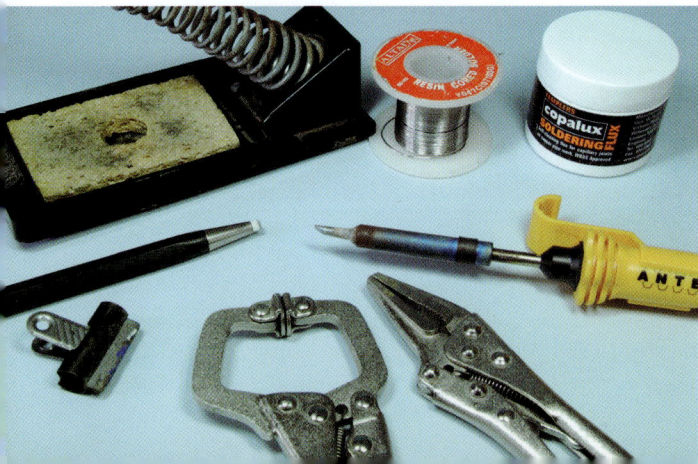

Assorted grades of solder are available to suit different tasks and materials and choosing an appropriate liquid or paste flux will help to form sound joints.

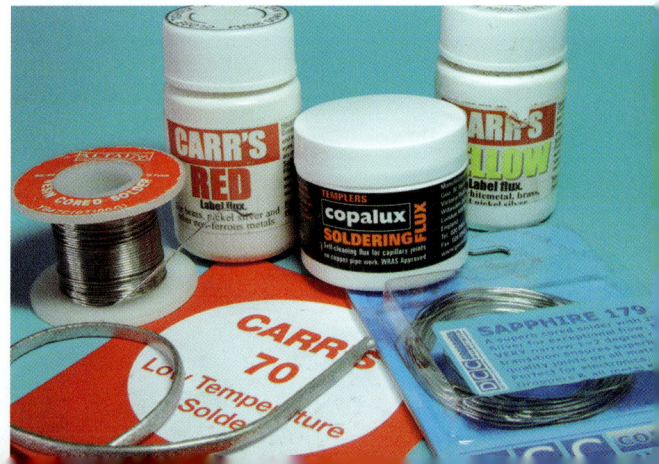

use of chemical fluxes, will result in the iron tip quickly becoming soiled with unpleasant deposits. A quick wipe over a damp sponge before and after every application is a good habit to get into and will not only improve your work, but also prolong the life of the bit.

Using a chemical flux, available either as a liquid or paste, is an essential part of soldering, as it allows the molten solder to penetrate more quickly and further into a joint. This has benefits in the reduced amount of time that an iron needs to be in contact with the metal and so removes much of the risk of heat distortion. Fluxes consist of chemicals such as zinc chloride or phosphoric acid and can be extremely dangerous, so it is essential to wash your hands afterwards and to avoid any vapours. Carr's Modelling Products offers a range of liquid fluxes, each tailored to suit particular metals and these are available from model shops or craft supply outlets such as Squires (see Appendix). Paste fluxes can sometimes be easier to apply as they tend to stay still and the Templer's range of Copalux flux can be recommended, although Bakers and Fluxite products are equally suitable. After soldering, it is vital to remove all traces of flux from the workpiece with clean water and a suitable detergent, otherwise the chemical residues will spoil any consequent paint finishes.

Fastening components into a spring clamp, mounted in a table vice, allows both hands to remain free during soldering. Adding a little flux to each surface before applying the hot iron will encourage the solder to flow into the joint and avoids the need to heat the workpiece excessively. Continuing the AWS topic, this is a scratch-built coupling guard plate being assembled from various pieces of scrap 0.0010in thick brass sheet and strip, mostly offcuts from etched detailing frets.

The most common brands of what we may term 'DIY solders', such as those sold in hardware stores for making general electrical or plumbing repairs, are perfectly appropriate for most modelling applications and can be used in conjunction with regular soldering irons. For more specialized work, including bonding white-metal, a low temperature solder is necessary along with an iron with an adjustable power output. High-performance solders, such as those produced by DCC Concepts of Australia, offer solders containing a small amount of silver that enhances the material's molten flow and adhesion properties and are primarily designed for use on sensitive electrical work, or for working with delicate kit components (see www.dccconcepts. com for more details).

As the soldered joint is being made, the metal parts should be crafted to be as close a fit as possible; relying on solder to cure any imperfections or to cut corners is not really acceptable, not least as it has limited use as a filling agent. Aim to clamp the parts to be soldered wherever possible to prevent movement while the heat is applied and this will also guard against creating 'dry' solder joints that can compromise the integrity of a bond and adversely affect electrical continuity. If the joint is disturbed, the solder will take on a hazy appearance as it cools, instead of being a nice shiny blob. In my days of building bespoke electric guitars, poor-quality soldering was seen as shoddy workmanship that could be

Two mounting brackets of strip brass, folded to shape, fix the plate to the rear of the engine's bufferbeam, while smaller strips, folded over and linked with a further strip, form the pocket for the couplings' lower link to sit into. Soldering this collection of parts creates a far more durable component than would be the case if glued.

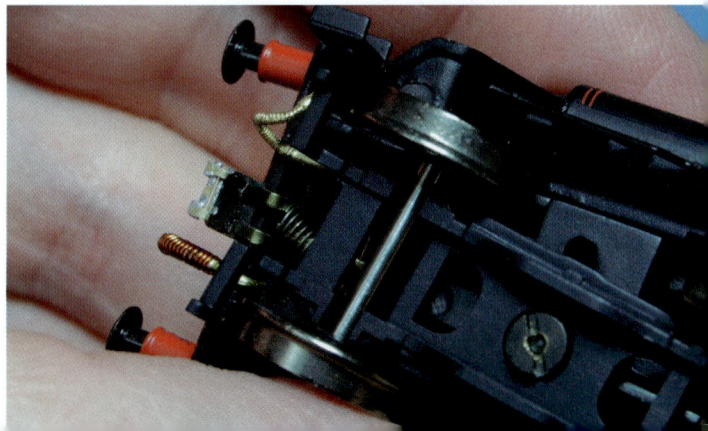

The AWS coupling plate is clear in this view of a preserved BR Class 4 2-6-0, with a modern magnet assembly visible behind it.

A traditional-style AWS magnet is simple to construct from plastic rod and a short length of wire, as long as the loco's front coupling has been removed. Wire conduit along the side of the running plate was another distinctive feature of many AWS-fitted engines.

of detriment to the instrument's audio output, as well as risking future failure as the joint can become brittle over time.

FURTHER DETAILING STEPS

Pardon the pun, but constructing etched metal footsteps is a logical next rung up the detailing ladder and a good means by which to practise the art of soldering. Typically, packs of replacement steps are available for specific engine types as well as generic sets that can cater for a variety of locomotives with or without some degree of modification. Nearly all follow the same assembly procedure where the step treads are folded to shape and fixed into half-etched locating ridges on the main component. According to type, some rivet detail may also be provided, usually required to be punched-out from behind with a sharp point.

Soldering small parts like this illustrates the usefulness of liquid or paste flux compounds as, by spreading a little onto the joint before touching with the tip of the iron (with a blob of molten solder loaded onto it), the solder will flow quickly into the joint. With practice, it can be discerned how much solder to load onto the iron's tip without flooding the parts and covering any fine detail. Any excess can be filed away gently after a few seconds of cooling.

Adding solder to the inside edge of any folds, such as the right-angled bends required with these footsteps, adds rigidity to the new components and extra strength, while realism can be had by soldering a diagonal brace behind the steps using some 1mm wide (0.0010in thick) brass strip, in a similar manner to that applied in Chapter 5.

Not only are these packs of etched footsteps handy for refining overly thick moulded plastic units, but they also permit alternative patterns to be substituted according to locomotive batch variations and to instate any missing steps omitted from an r-t-r engine. The Bachmann Fairburn 2-6-4T is a good example to include when discussing the latter, as the prototype carried three separate pairs of footsteps, while the model only boasts a single pair serving the cab. Front-end steps allowed access to the top of the bufferbeam and the smokebox, while an alternative pattern of steps was fixed behind the bufferbeam at the bunker end to help staff to trim the coal load and to attach oil lamps on the rear brackets. The latter steps can only be fitted if dispensing with the NEM-mounted couplings and the front steps may interfere with the movement of the leading axle around tight corners – presumably factors that led Bachmann to omit these features from its model.

Etched brass or nickel silver footsteps are available in numerous patterns to suit various locomotive types. Packs such as these, from Mainly Trains, cover a number of different locos according to region and, although some are a little over-scale, they do offer an economical solution to missing or inferior footsteps on r-t-r models.

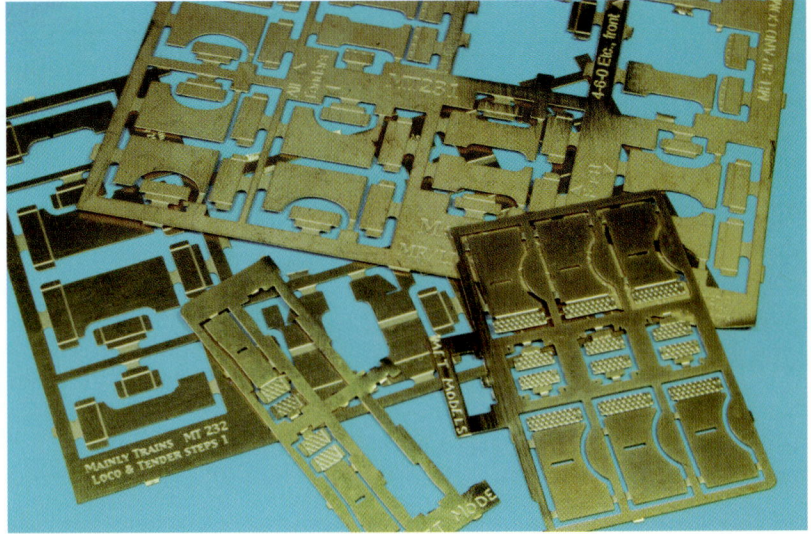

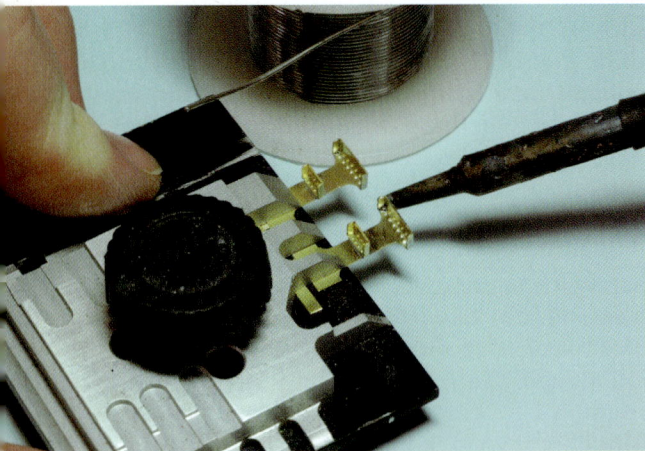

Clamping the etch in something like a Hold 'n' Fold tool leaves both hands free to hold the soldering iron and the footsteps (in a pair of tweezers) while the joint is made. Use a dab of flux on each part before applying a little solder. The parts that require folding-up can be made rigid by adding a smidgen of solder to the corners, again using flux to help things along.

Just like the real things, a diagonal strengthening bracket can be improvised from strip brass and soldered to the inside of the steps, reinforcing the upper mounting bracket. Remove any excess solder with a fine file and clean away any flux residues now, before gluing the parts to the engine.

The Mainly Trains parallel footsteps pack (ref. MT232) was utilized to allow these steps to be added to the rear of a Bachmann Fairburn 2-6-4T, although the distinctive cut-outs had to be made with a drill and fine jeweller's file.

At the other end of the Fairburn, the front footsteps were scratch-built simply from 1mm brass strip (also from Mainly Trains) with small pieces of etched chequer plate cut and folded to right angles to form the steps. The trickiest part was holding it together while soldering, a spring clamp being used to grip the ensemble lightly. The strip was folded at the top edges to form mounting brackets to sit onto the underside of the running plate.

ADDING PERIOD-SPECIFIC DETAIL AND A NEW SET OF WHEELS

Although a ready-to-run model may score highly in looks, detail and performance, there may still be a few variations lacking in the versions being offered of a particular locomotive. As major manufacturers have to maximize their investments in new models, those offered will be aimed at appealing to as large a customer base as possible, so an engine type is bound to be produced in the condition in which it ran for the longest period. Only limited edition runs of a loco in an experimental livery or with a short-lived detail variation are commercially sensible undertakings. That leaves some models open to a few minor detail errors and the Ivatt '4MT' in post-War LMS black livery is one such item.

As only two of these engines were built before nationalization, the LMS livery offers a narrow timeframe and, as the first twenty or so Ivatts were originally fitted with a few different details

to the other production batches, there are subsequently a few errors on the model. Firstly, the rectangular inspection cover sitting on the boiler's top feed valve shouldn't be there as this was a later modification, though it had been retrofitted to all by the late 1950s. Secondly, the guard irons hanging in front of the leading axle ought to be mounted to the locomotive's frames, not the pony truck – a highly distinctive difference when noted on prototype photographs. Thirdly, the handrail and footstep arrangement on the sides of the tender are also indicative of later, modified machines and so are unsuited either to the LMS livery or to very early BR condition.

I wanted my model to carry the interim livery of the embryonic British Railways, with a fully lettered tender and an 'M'-prefixed running number as applied to all former LMS machines before the 4xxxx series of numbering was adopted. But how do you go about removing the lovely factory-printed characters without damaging the paintwork? The following chapter reveals all.

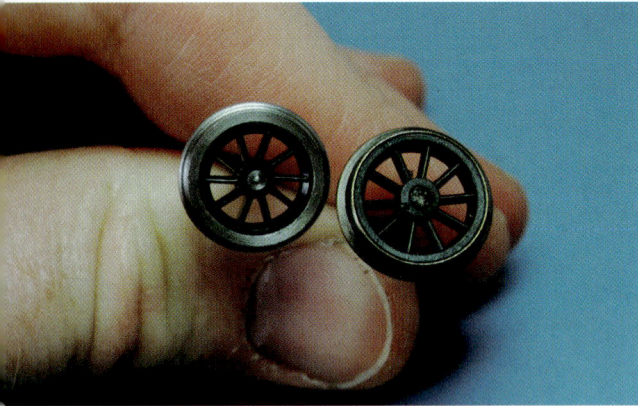

The first enhancement concerns the leading pony truck and wheels. A replacement set can be obtained from the Alan Gibson range, either direct or via Mainly Trains, and the difference in appearance is clearly illustrated in this view (the Gibson wheel is on the left). For an Ivatt '4MT', a 3ft diameter, nine-spoke wheel set is required.

The Bachmann Ivatt '4MT' is one of my favourite r-t-r releases of recent years, with a wealth of fine detail fitted as standard. However, there are still a few worthwhile tweaks to undertake, not least in altering some of the fittings in order to better represent a particular prototype in early 1950s condition.

Gibson wheels come unassembled with a choice of axles in each pack. Choose the shortest one and gently press one wheel onto the axle, stopping when the centre boss sits flush with the front of the wheel. Usually, the friction fit is more than satisfactory, but, if the wheels can be turned a little too easily on the axle, secure it with a tiny amount of a penetrating, cyano-type glue such as Roket Hot. This glue is very thin and can easily make a mess if not applied with care. Use a micro-tip applicator or an old paintbrush.

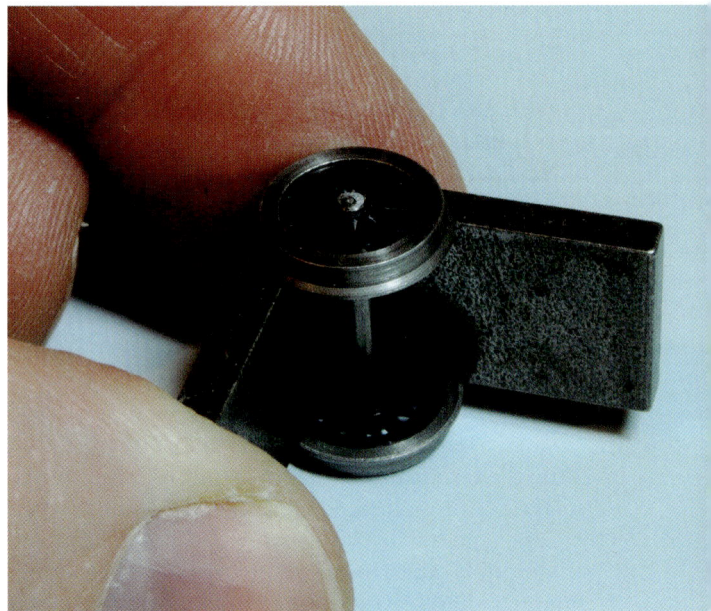

To ensure that the new wheels are fitted true to the axle and set the correct distance apart, a back-to-back gauge, as offered in the Gibson range, can be used. Check carefully at this stage as any discrepancies will ruin the engine's running performance.

As the leading truck is such a highly visible part of the model and, being an early 1950s-era subject, there will be no AWS plate to disguise the front of the truck, the NEM coupling pocket detracts from the engine's otherwise authentic front-end looks, although it can be cut away easily enough. I also removed the moulded spring detail and the guard irons. Brassmasters produce a comprehensive etched kit to build a replacement pony truck with full bearing and spring detail, but I felt unwilling to devote so much time to this task. Instead, I used some of the kit's parts to detail the Bachmann truck and, as each Brassmasters kit provides so much detail, two models can be treated. The top plate was removed from the fret and cut in half before folding as per the instructions, then fixed to the top of the truck.

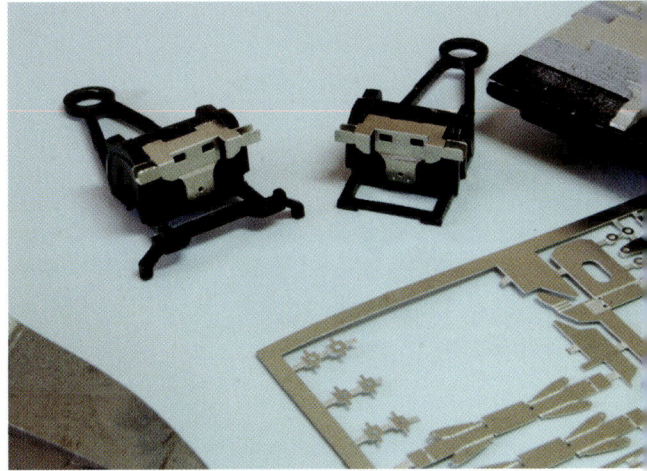

The central spring mount was also folded to shape before gluing in place and the length of wire-wound steel guitar string, included with the Brassmasters kit, was cut to the appropriate size and fixed in place.

A bit of trial and error was needed to get the steel strings to fit neatly; this is a very convincing way of portraying coil springs. Two lengths of plastic rod (1.5mm and 0.75mm diameter) were cut to form the central spring damper.

ABOVE: The new wheel set will clip back into the pony truck. Test-fit the completed unit to ensure that the new parts do not interfere with the underside of the frames. If so, file away the new top plate, taking care not to dislodge the spring detail, then recheck until all is well. The new wheel rims will benefit from a coat of black paint, although they should be cleaned of any oil first, as the bare metal surfaces are usually given a coating of light oil to prevent corrosion during storage and shipment. Wipe with a cotton bud dipped in white spirit and allow it to dry before applying a primer and paint. Be sure to keep the wheel treads clean.

ABOVE: Ivatt's original '4MT' design stipulated that the front guard irons should be fixed to the frames of the locomotive itself and it was some years before the whole class was modified to carry the guards on the pony truck frame instead. As the Bachmann model only offers the later fittings, I made a pair of frame overlays from 0.0010in thick plastic card, cut to incorporate a slightly lower curve over the new wheel set, thus reducing the unsightly gap. The final shape was refined by trial-fitting and checking that the wheels could move without hindrance, then bending the guards to the standard swan-neck shape before fixing in place.

BELOW: Another period detail to correct was the unwanted rectangular inspection panel moulded onto the top feed cover. These were only fitted to the first batches of '4MTs' late into the 1950s. A knife and file reformed the profile of the cover, finishing off with fine abrasive papers.

BELOW: Ivatt '4MT' tenders were also modified over time as the original pattern of the top footstep was deemed unsafe. However, my prototype would not have been altered, so a bit of Milliput filler was used to plug the upper step and the handrails and knobs were also removed and the holes filled in.

A combination of a drill, knife and files was used to form the foot aperture, working from period photographs to ascertain the location and size.

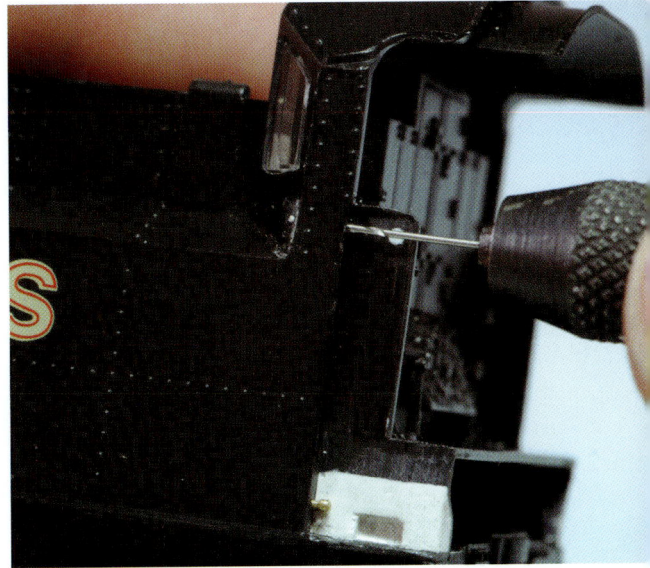

The handrails were resited, fixed to the side of the tender apron. As the prototype's mounting knobs looked rather small, I used 'N' gauge handrail knobs (from Markits), glued into newly drilled holes.

Handrail wire was added along with other general details such as new buffers, smokebox door handle, brake and steam pipes and the supplied plastic components that consist of front footsteps and cylinder drainpipes. As I intended to change the identity of this model, the printed digits were removed, ready for a new set of transfers.

CHAPTER 7

Identity Swap

Rare is the time that a model is released in ready-to-run form carrying the individual number and name that you may desire – and not least when we're talking about an ex-LMS '8F' or a 'Black Five', of which there were many hundreds of individual machines. Even taking into account the burgeoning limited-edition market, there are only so many models that Hornby or Bachmann will add to their catalogues every year, so you may be waiting a long time before a seemingly anonymous locomotive becomes the subject of a mass-produced miniature replica.

Even if you're not interested in sticking lots of little fiddly bits of wire or brass onto your new model, changing the running number is one of those tasks that can be done with the minimum of tools and fuss, provided you know what you're doing. I've spent the last decade or so changing the numbers, names, BR logos and shed codes on countless OO gauge locomotives and, through trial and error plus a little experimentation, a seemingly foolproof group of techniques has been developed. I can't claim to have come up with all of these methods myself, as some have been poached from magazine articles or through the recommendations of other modellers.

The most important factor in the identity-swapping process is the preservation of the model's paintwork. Start interfering with this and touching-in or patch-painting becomes necessary, which not only creates extra work but also demands great care to get right, especially if a pristine finish is to be retained. Another essential point of consideration is the suitability of the model at hand for the chosen new number: that is, does it carry the correct details?

Don't forget to check for prototype images or information as to where the engine was allocated at a certain time and whether it carried the early- or late-period BR logo as this might dictate which model to purchase as a 'donor'. I was recently asked to change the identity of a Hornby Stanier 2-6-4T to represent a mid-1960s engine, so, naturally, obtained a model with the later BR crest (introduced in the late 1950s). However, after having sourced a reference image, dated from 1964, I was surprised that the machine in question still carried the earlier 'lion-on-wheel' symbol. So, don't be as presumptuous as me!

There are a number of ways to alter the factory-printed numbers and insignia on r-t-r models, each requiring only a few tools and no specialist equipment. This first method is probably the easiest and utilizes T-cut automotive paint restorer, which is widely available from DIY, hardware or motor accessory stores. Cotton buds and cocktail sticks are the main tools necessary.

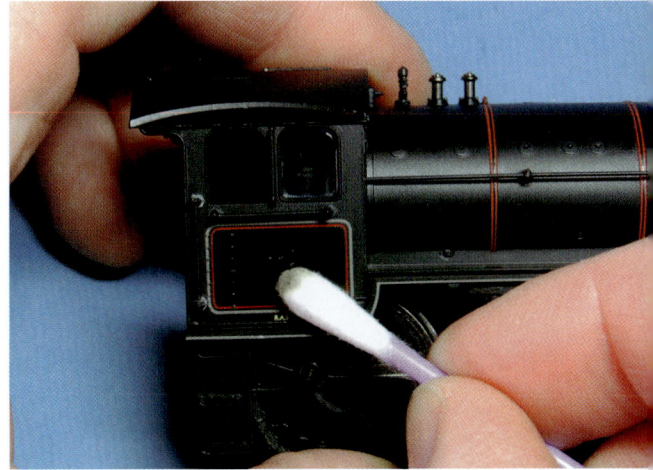

After decanting a little of the T-cut into the lid, dip a slightly blunted cocktail stick into the liquid and begin rubbing the printed detail. Apply fairly gentle pressure, using the stick's side edge to do the rubbing, rather than the point itself, so as to avoid damaging the paintwork. Keep the liquid away from any lining or other details that are to remain. After a few minutes, the characters will begin to disappear. Clean the stick regularly, applying fresh T-cut as you work.

This process can't be rushed without risking damage to the paint and surrounding detail, so be patient and keep rubbing. Depending on the model, it should only take five minutes to remove an entire cab side number set. Remove any remaining T-cut and buff the surface with a clean cotton bud until it is streak-free. A nice, shiny surface should be left and this can be further burnished by rubbing with an old, clean toothbrush.

An alternative and quicker method requires more experience as it runs the risk of damaging the model's paintwork. A very sharp scalpel can be used gently to scrape away the majority of the printed detail, taking care to avoid any raised rivet detail.

Using either T-cut or white spirit, the remnants of the printed characters can be rubbed away. White spirit is just as effective as T-cut, but it can cause problems if it comes into contact with clear glazing material.

Another point where T-cut has the edge over white spirit is that the former leaves the paintwork with a suitably high sheen that makes adding new decals easier. An alternative is to use a soft, nylon-brushed buffing head in a mini-drill (set to the lowest speed setting) to burnish the surface ever so gently.

By using T-cut automotive finish restorer (a blend of petroleum distillates), the printed characters can be softened and removed. As long as this is done gently and without flooding the model in the solution, the base livery colour should not be damaged in any way. However, care must be taken if working around raised details such as riveted areas on cab or tender sides. As the raised areas are prone to excessive abrasion from the cocktail stick, the paint is more likely to be softened here and when working on 'coloured' liveries (as opposed to plain or lined black), this can result in the bare plastic beginning to show through. In cases such as this, I'd recommend confining the cocktail stick to the flat areas, working around the base of the rivets and following with a cotton bud soaked in T-cut to deal with any remaining traces. In all cases, simply taking your time and working gently provides the foolproof defence against such risks.

One of the convenient by-products of using T-cut is that, as it is designed for restoring the shine and lustre of a car's bodywork, so it will with the paintwork on your model. As all decals benefit greatly from being applied onto a high-gloss surface, sufficient buffing of the T-cut with clean, dry cotton buds will produce an almost mirror-like finish. Ensure that no traces of the solution remain in any nooks and crannies as it will leave a powdery deposit as the solvents evaporate. If more 'shine' is needed, a gloss varnish should be applied, preferably sprayed with an airbrush or aerosol to gain a flat, even finish. If only the cab sides are to be treated, the rest of the model can be masked-off before spraying, along with any glazing. Steam locomotives are conveniently shaped to provide many natural surface breaks with which to disguise new paintwork or varnish, such as boiler bands, cabs, smokeboxes and so on. I prefer enamel varnish for this purpose, rather than most acrylics, as it gives a much harder finish. On the other hand, Johnson's Klear floor polish is an acrylic formula, but, being designed for use on floors, is very hard-wearing. It is also thin enough to be airbrushed straight from the bottle and can be hand-applied to a high-quality finish using a good sable-haired brush.

DECALS

Not only is there plenty of choice in railway decals, there are also various brands and formats out there. You can even make your own these days, as long as you're fairly proficient on a computer and own a half-decent colour printer. I'm only recently coming to appreciate the benefits of making my own decals, not least in terms of economy but also in creating adornments that are otherwise unavailable, such as numerals and hand-painted names suitable for freelance and industrial locomotives.

Many of us are familiar with water-slide decals from building Airfix kits and the railway equivalents follow the same principles. As long as the surface is prepared properly, these transfers are perfectly reliable and easy to use, particularly as they allow for repositioning, something that can be vital when making up a five-figure cabside number. Good-quality water-slide decals contain only the minimum of clear carrier film around each character and, with a high-gloss background followed by sealing coats of clear varnish, this should be rendered completely invisible. 'Silvering' of this film occurs when the surface has not been prepared correctly and will spoil a model, so, as with all things, put the work into the preparation stage and reap the rewards later.

To avoid such considerations, dry rub-down decals offer the convenience of no carrier films and avoid the need for a high-gloss surface preparation; simply a clean, dry, grease-free area is all that's required. However, this is weighed against the lack of any possibility of repositioning a character once it has been applied. Only dissolving it with white spirit and starting again will cure a mistake.

Combining the benefits of both rub-down and water-slide decals are the Pressfix range produced by the Historical Model Railway Society (HMRS). Available to suit a variety of eras and regions, there are also separate packs with various lining patterns. Application consists of cutting the chosen character from the dual-layer backing sheet and using its self-adhesive qualities to position it. Until firm pressure is applied, the decal can be repositioned until you're satisfied with the location and, once a little water is added, the translucent backing paper will eventually float away, leaving the decal in place. No further movement is possible, however, so positioning must be accurate in the first instance.

In common with rub-down transfers, the Pressfix range does not require much in the way of surface preparation, provided that the area is clean. A variation on this theme – the Methfix method – is also offered by HMRS and is tailored more towards the perfectionist, requiring methylated spirit to dissolve the backing paper. This is a much slower (and smellier) process, although the resulting finish is superior.

Various decal manufacturers offer extensive ranges to cater for many eras, regions and prototypes. Fox, Modelmaster and HMRS are some of the better known brands and a choice of water-slide, dry rub-down, Pressfix and Methfix application methods are on offer.

A clean work area is essential when applying new decals as dust or fibres can be trapped beneath the numbers or logos and leave an uneven finish. A sharp pair of scissors is handy to cut out individual decals, while cocktail sticks and fine tweezers help with positioning.

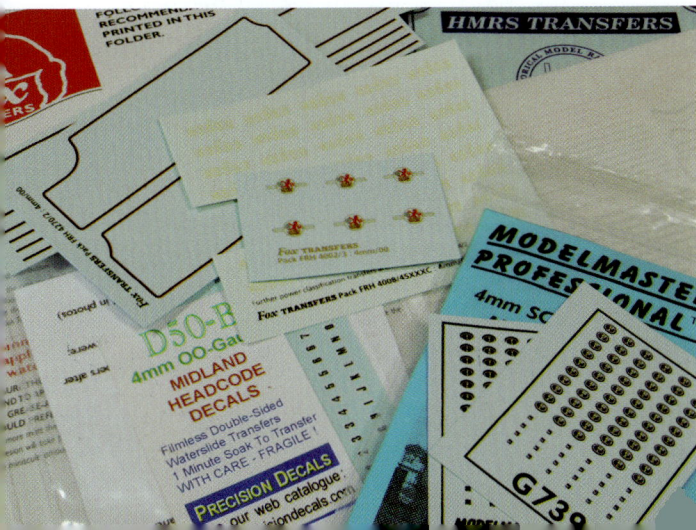

ABOVE: The perils of trying to change a single digit: so many renumbering tasks may only include the desire to change but one or two of the factory-applied numbers. However, attempting to match new decals to printed characters is virtually impossible. The No.6 here stands out a mile, despite being of the correct specification for this BR Class 5.

BELOW: Add the outer characters, checking that they are straight, square and equidistant from each other before setting aside to dry out completely.

ABOVE: It's far better to remove the entire number set and start again with a consistent array of decals. A set of individual water-slide transfers (from the Fox range) has been added here.

BELOW: Although ready made-up number sets are available from Fox Transfers, buying packs of individual numbers proves more economical if a number of projects are envisaged. In order to align them correctly, start assembling the number from the centre outwards, having marked the base height and centre line with a tailor's chalk pencil. Remember that the centre of the cab may not tally with the centre of the number set, as the width of individual numbers can differ. Therefore, the length of the whole set must be derived and then halved to get the centre point, for example with 68111, the middle '1' will not necessarily sit in the middle of the cab as the two other '1's take up less space than the round '6' and '8'. Cut the numbers from the backing paper and arrange them on the bench as they will sit on the engine, then measure the overall length. Divide this to find the centre line. A strip of masking tape across the base line will help to align the characters and keep them level.

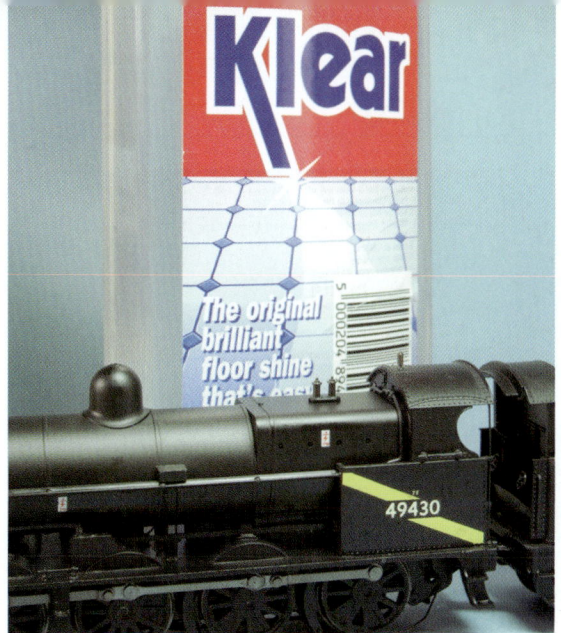

The areas of glossy black visible on this 'Super D' show where T-cut has been applied to not only remove the former numbers but also to provide a base for the new decals, including the overhead warning flashes along the boiler. A yellow warning stripe is being added to the cab side, but wait – it's pointing the wrong way!

The beauty of water-slide decals is that they can be repositioned or removed easily before they dry completely. Even then, they can be carefully scraped away without leaving any traces, providing they have yet to be sealed with varnish. With the yellow stripe corrected and all other new decals added, Johnson's Klear floor polish forms an ideal, quick-drying and durable varnish coat that can easily be applied by hand or with an airbrush. Although it dries to a glossy finish, this can be toned down with subsequent coats of a satin or matt varnish if desired. Don't forget to mask any cab windows.

If a weathering coat is to be applied, I seldom add an all-over clear coat after adding decals. Instead I usually just apply a coat or two of Klear over the new details with a soft, sable-haired brush. Any discrepancies between the surface sheen will soon be lost under a spray of light grime.

Virtually all BR-era engines also carried their running numbers on smokebox-mounted plates and changing these on an r-t-r model is easy. As long as the model's moulded plate is of the correct size, new digits can be added on top of the originals, following a coat of Johnson's Klear or other gloss varnish. Again, made-up number sets are available as well as individual digits, although the latter may need the originals covering with a little gloss black paint beforehand. Seal the new numbers with a clear coat as usual.

If only all engines had been fitted with Great Western-style cast number plates! Changing the identity of a GWR engine is usually just a matter of adding new etched brass plates over the printed originals, along with changing the smokebox number plate. Transfers are also available for this task, but lack the obvious relief of the etched parts. Not every number is available in etched brass, however, so choosing your prototype may require checking what is available first.

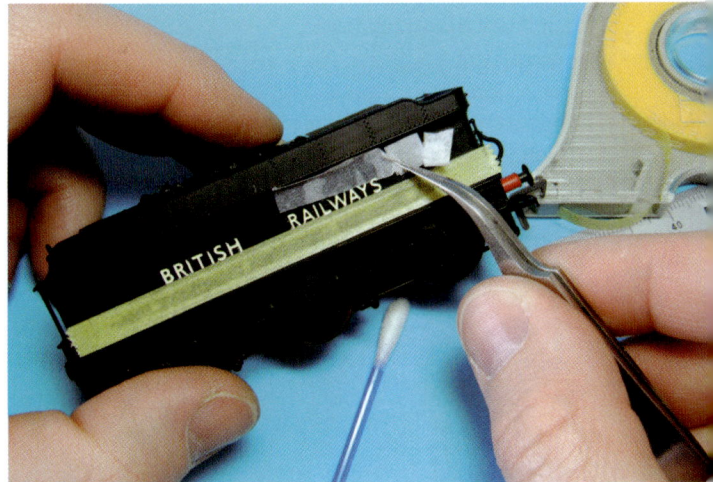

Removing tender crests follows exactly the same procedure as that for the running numbers. However, as these devices are built up from several different colour layers, a little more elbow work with the T-cut and cocktail stick will be needed. Take care around any raised rivet detail as it can be easy to remove too much paint here.

Correctly aligning the new crests on the tender is essential if the model is not to be spoiled. Mark out the location carefully and add a length of low-tack masking tape to act as a guide if necessary. This is particularly handy if backdating a model to carry the original BR tender lettering.

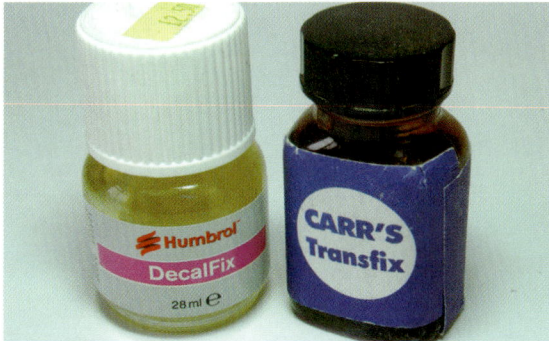

If adding water-slide decals onto uneven surfaces, such as a riveted tender or cab side, it can sometimes be difficult for the decal film to sit properly. Applying a softening solution such as Carr's Transfix or Humbrol's DecalFix can help. Add the solution with a small brush, after removing the excess water from the decal. Leave aside for a while and then gently press the transfer down with a clean, slightly damp cotton bud. The film should now be sufficiently elastic to cope with any unevenness.

CHANGING NAMES

With a change of number may also come a change of name and, by and large, this may consist of a straightforward like-for-like swap of nameplates, or the superimposing of new etched plates over the factory-printed originals (as described in Chapter 3). However, a new name may be shorter, or, in other circumstances, the names may be removed altogether and this can also lead to various problems. Illustrated here is the de-naming of a Bachmann 'B1', to reproduce an unchristened machine and, as the moulded plates were fitted to the smokebox sides by means of plastic tabs glued into a pair of holes, removing them was not easy. In fact, the plates would only break off with some severe persuasion, leaving a few scars. The model's owner insisted on an absolutely pristine finish, so some careful repair work was called for. Luckily, working on the side of a black smokebox meant that only this area would need repainting and, being a separate component on the real thing, meant that any blending and colour matching was unnecessary. Smokeboxes were often a slightly different shade from the rest of a black locomotive, heat-resistant paint being employed in contrast to the heavy gloss of the adjoining boiler barrel.

Swapping the identity of model locomotives not only allows for a larger fleet to be assembled, but also provides scope for creating some unique machines. The techniques outlined here may need a little practising to perfect, but this can always be done on an old model and, as the methods are universal, this doesn't have to be a locomotive. You could even renumber an entire fleet of wagons or carriages if you so desire, perhaps recreating a whole train for that ultra-authentic touch.

A change of number can also mean adding or changing nameplates and the technique for this was mentioned in Chapter 3. Curiously, as I was changing the identity of my BR Class 5 to 73113 *Lyonnesse*, I realized that the new etched nameplates I'd ordered from Modelmaster contained the wrong smokebox number plate!

De-naming may also arise from renumbering and this was the case with this Bachmann 'B1'. The moulded plastic nameplates were a real swine to remove from the smokebox sides, being fixed with a seemingly enormous amount of glue; so much so, that I ended up cutting them away with a fine scalpel blade. This left an area that needed a bit of repair work.

After filling any holes or gashes caused by the removal of the plates, the area was smoothed as much as possible with fine abrasive paper.

The finish of this model had to be pristine, so it left no option but to repaint the entire smokebox. The surrounding areas were masked, applying Humbrol Maskol fluid to any awkward areas or tape joints to stop paint seeping through. A couple of coats of stain black enamel (Railmatch No.205) were then applied by airbrush. After adding all new decals, the whole model was sprayed with satin varnish to give an even overall finish.

Adding small decals such as Overhead Warning flashes can help date a steam engine to the late 1960s period, although application was not universal. I added these water-slide decals after weathering this '8F', as the photographs of the real thing showed that only very small areas had been cleaned away to allow the new warnings to be stuck on. A small dab of black paint, followed by Johnson's Klear, made for a suitable grounding for the decals, followed by a little more Klear to seal them. A light dusting of 'dirt' blended the new signs into the overall picture.

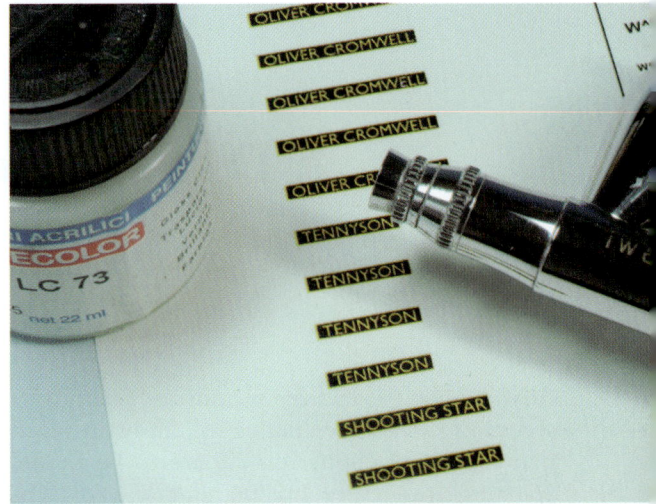

Creating your own decals is now easy, as long as you have a computer and a decent colour printer. I needed some stencilled nameplates for a BR 'Britannia' to replicate *Oliver Cromwell* as it ran towards the end of its life. These were drawn up in Microsoft Word and numerous test prints were made on ordinary paper before inserting a sheet of water-slide decal paper.

Sheets of water-slide decal paper are available from Crafty Computer Paper in either a clear or white-backed form. For these nameplates, I printed them on the white-backed paper to ensure that the light yellow lettering was clear. After printing, a number of coats of acrylic varnish must be applied using an airbrush or aerosol.

The new 'nameplates' were carefully cut before applying in the same manner as regular water-slide decals. Make sure that the new names will cover the factory-printed originals, otherwise use the T-cut method (*see* p.76) to remove these before adding the transfers.

CHAPTER 8

A DIY Guide to Plumbing

Anyone who has had the pleasure of cleaning or servicing a steam locomotive will know just how many miles of copper piping are to be found, reaching into every nook and cranny of the

The array of copper pipework and cast brass valves adorning the side of BR Class 4 76079 is clear in this view. There are few ways to achieve such realistic metallic shades other than by using real materials, such as copper wire.

machine. Bulling-up a loco for museum display can be a particularly onerous task, involving not only an endless supply of elbow grease but also industrial-sized jars of Brasso.

High-specification r-t-r models are constantly evolving and the addition of much of the most prominent pipework as separate components is becoming a standard specification, albeit in plastic. Not all prototypes boasted so much exposed workings, however, as engineers at one time would have baulked at having such things on open display. Austere times, with the desire for easier and cheaper maintenance schedules, saw such sentiments overshadowed by the push towards utility.

On the opposite side of 76079 can be seen the myriad runs of small-bore copper pipe, delivering lubricating oil to various moving parts. Note how they are seldom exactly straight and many curves look a little haphazardly formed, probably being bent over a fitter's knee!

Technological advancements in steam power also led to more ancillary systems being fitted (such as train heating, vacuum and air brakes, steam-powered electricity generators, automated warning systems and mechanical self-lubricating machines), each requiring extra bits and pieces to be accommodated. Developments in injection and ejection equipment also led to more complex and larger components requiring further space in which to be fitted, while also demanding full accessibility for maintenance. Most BR-era designs bore much of these factors in mind from the outset, resulting in various locomotives carrying considerable amounts of exposed piping and components, while older engines had any extra equipment retrofitted, squeezing it in wherever possible.

Chapter 5 outlined the availability of various grades of copper wire, but there are other material options such as brass, lead and nickel silver wire, all of which are available in reels of varying gauges for relatively little cost. Copper is the most useful as it recreates the real thing far better than can be achieved with paint, although coated nickel silver wire is ideal for representing cable conduit, especially the black-coated reels. Even if a colour match is not possible, the plastic coating acts like an efficient primer coat, allowing swift painting with the appropriate shade. All of the above wire is obtainable from jewellery-making craft or modelling suppliers, the Hobbycraft chain being a particularly good source.

Fine metal tubing and rod can also be found in various materials and grades, such as Cammett's packs (see Appendix) of hard or soft stainless steel tubing. These packs are actually aimed at producing telescopic gun barrels for military models, but they are equally useful for producing runs of larger pipework on a locomotive. Stainless steel is, however, a tough material and requires cutting with a junior hacksaw or specific metal-cutting discs in a mini-drill (as supplied by Cammett). Packs of traditional fuse wire can also be highly useful as this material is pliable enough to be bent to shape and can be readily cut with a stout blade or end-cutters.

Another advantage of using metal wire or tube (the uncoated variety) is that it can be soldered to other metal components, allowing durable assemblies to be made up before fitting to the locomotive. An initial example concerns the fabrication of some homemade cylinder drainpipes as both an enhancement of the moulded plastic (and often generic) types offered with various models, but also as an economy over buying cast replacements. By clamping three strands of 0.3mm (30SWG) copper wire in a spring vice, a tiny blob of solder will hold them together, allowing the drains to be bent to the desired shape with a pair of round-nose pliers before trimming to length.

Other applications for runs of wire piping include upgrading engine lubricators, whether of the basic gravity-fed or mechanically driven variety, as they each boast runs of copper pipework that distribute oil to the necessary moving parts. Various engine types included distinctive mechanical lubricators mounted on the side of the running plate and powered by a small linkage from the valve gear. Exact working arrangements differed according to class and designer, but they usually followed the practice of a crank lever turning a pump that moved the lubricant through a network of pipes, increasing the flow as the engine's speed increased. A hand-operated handle was also included to permit oiling when stationary.

Non-mechanical systems relied on gravity to move the oil through the system, a number of brass oil pots being located at strategic points, and these required topping up at regular intervals by the driver. The pipes that emanated from these pots contained fibre wicks, which used capillary action to draw the oil through at a regulated quantity, delivering a steady supply to working surfaces such as wheel bearings, slide rods and piston valves. The oil pots could be either box- or globe-shaped, the latter being common on pre-Grouping designs.

Moulded representations of lubricating, steam and sanding pipes can all be replaced with wire or fine metal rod with minimum fuss, having cut away the excess plastic and making good the surface with fine abrasives. Judge for yourself whether the model's livery will be affected by this action and if any blemishes can be disguised with a little paint. Areas such as smokeboxes, running plates and underframes can usually accept some form of modification without the need for much repainting, but cutting away moulded pipes from the firebox of a Hornby '9F' or an older 'Britannia' will make a mess of the livery unless done with extreme care. In any case, if repainting is likely, do this before adding the new copper wire to preserve the material's authentic appearance.

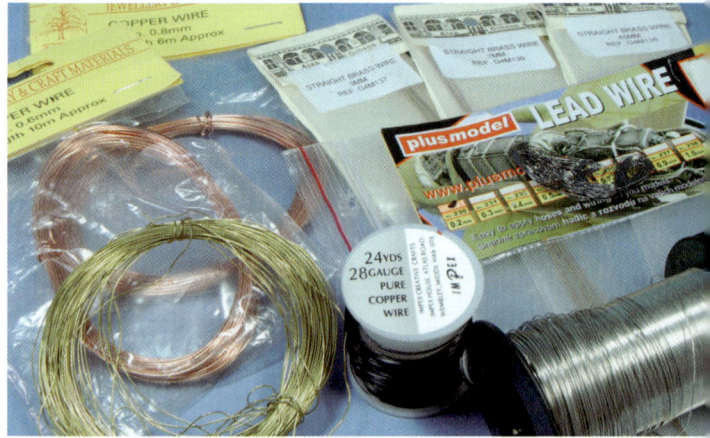

ABOVE: Copper, brass, lead and nickel-silver wire are obtainable from modelling suppliers or craft stores such as Hobbycraft. Various gauges and reel lengths are available and some, such as the beading wire seen here, are offered in a plastic-coated variety, with several colours to choose from. Each has its own use and these reels can prove very economical.

Three separate lengths of 0.3mm (30SWG) copper wire can be soldered together and formed into realistic cylinder drains. Hold the assembly in a spring vice and add just a drop of solder to the joint, being careful not to drown the individual wires. Drill some suitable mounting holes, trim the wire to size and fix in place.

As this view shows (of an LMS three-cylinder 2-6-4T), cylinder drains should also boast a row of brass valves from which the copper pipes emanate. A further option is to retain any moulded items that may be supplied with the loco, cutting away the plastic pipes and drilling out mounting holes for copper wire. The 'valves' can then be painted with metallic enamel.

Mechanical lubricators became standard fittings to many locomotive types from the 1930s onwards and were also retrofitted to some earlier machines. Patterns and fitting locations varied, although they each achieved the same goal of distributing oil to the many moving parts such as bearings, piston valves, slide bars and so on. This unit sits in front of the front driving wheel of a Southern Railway 'Q1' 0-6-0, being driven by the cranked rod in the lower foreground. The hand-wheel provides a manual override for use whilst the engine is stationary.

A different arrangement of lubricator is seen fitted to the running plate of LMS 'Jubilee' 4-6-0 *Leander*. The drive is the rod that disappears vertically from the centre of the unit, being connected to the valve gear and the T-shaped handle allows for manual operation. The arrangement beside the lubricator is interesting as it includes what looks like a form of return valve.

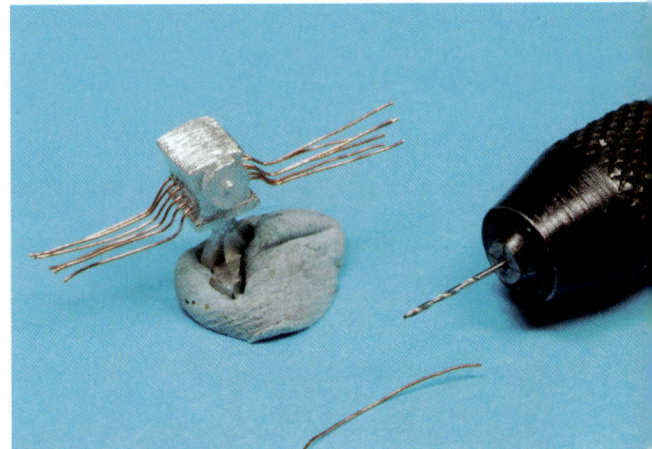

RIGHT: This beautiful lost-wax brass casting of an LMS Wakefield lubricator (from the Alan Gibson range) has been enhanced by adding lengths of 0.3mm copper wire, fitted into shallow holes drilled into either side and a small disc of plastic added to the top, representing a filling/inspection lid. Solid brass is much more difficult to drill into than white-metal castings, although the enhanced sharp detail is a benefit. A model's plastic lubricator can also be enhanced in this way.

LEFT: With a new lubricator in place, the copper piping can be stowed behind the running plate. This small feature adds an eye-catching improvement.

Having cut away the moulded representation of the lubricating pipes running from the tanks of this LMS 'Jinty', the underside of the box was drilled to accept lengths of 0.3mm copper wire. The model had to be dismantled to allow the drill to reach this area, but the results are worth the effort. Check your prototype to see how many pipes ran from each oiling point.

Older steam locomotive types featured globe-shaped lubricators, such as has been fitted to this freelance 0-6-0T, formed from round handrail knobs with short lengths of copper wire added.

Other possible upgrades involving piping and metal wire include adding or enhancing sanding pipes, such as the distinctive run from the large sandboxes on a Bachmann 'B1'. The crude plastic representation was cut away, retaining the mounting bracket on the lower edge of the frames. This and the underside of the sandbox were drilled to accept some 0.9mm copper wire. Ensure that the new pipes are shaped to allow the coupling rods free movement.

Further plumbing relevant to the LNER 'B1' includes provision of a Stones electric generator, as fitted to a good many of these mixed traffic engines. The generator, a white-metal casting from Alexander Models, can be seen on the side of the smokebox with various runs of cable conduit running from it to the electric lamps on the front and rear of the loco. The 'B1' in the background has not been fitted with this equipment and is included by way of comparison. Note also the copper piping behind the steam pipe that has replaced the moulded detail. Cylinder drains have also been fabricated from copper wire, as have smaller sanding pipes, such as the one visible behind the leading brake shoe; itself another extra detail missing from the original model.

It's not always necessary to replace a moulded component just for the sake of it. Indeed, upgrading by cutting away the plastic piping and drilling out for copper wire can be effective, as with this injector assembly for a 'Duchess'.

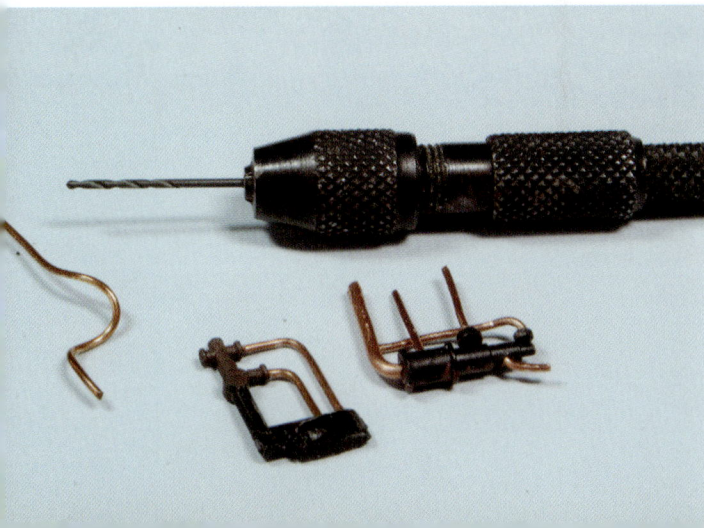

As many locomotive detailing components are offered in cast-metal form, being able to fix any new lengths of wire securely to them is important and can be made easier by drilling out the mounting points to a depth of a few millimetres. This will provide the wire with a firm location and cyano- or epoxy-type adhesives will hold the parts well enough, although items such as under-slung injector/ejector assemblies are prone to the odd knock whilst handling, so making a soldered joint will provide a much sturdier bond. Lost-wax brass castings can be soldered in the usual fashion (as described in Chapter 6), provided that the joint surface is prepared properly by using a file or glass-fibre scratch brush to remove any casting residues. Use a good flux to allow the solder to penetrate the joint fully and to negate the need for excessive heating with the iron.

White-metal castings, on the other hand, are much more sensitive to heat and will be damaged unless a temperature-controlled iron is used. White-metal is an alloy containing tin and lead, although pewter is becoming a popular alternative, as it is a less hazardous ingredient. Specific grades of solder and flux can be obtained for use with white-metal, brands such as Carr's offering suitable products.

Investing in an adjustable soldering iron will make working with white-metal easier, as well as providing a very versatile tool. An operating temperature of around 80°C is usual for small white-metal parts, although very delicate components may need less heat, provided of course that the solder can still melt! Carr's low-temperature solder is specified to flow at 70°C, but a drawback of this low temperature is that the solder will not penetrate joints as efficiently, posing the problem of combining white-metal with brass or copper, as the latter require more heat to form a reliable joint. A cure for this is to 'tin' brass, nickel silver or copper components first with 145°C solder before forming a joint with white-metal parts, using 70°C solder.

Low-temperature soldering is basically similar to working with brass or nickel silver and it pays to practise the technique before working on the actual components. It may not always be easy to find some scraps to practise with, but a browse around the stands at a model railway exhibition may offer the chance to pick up some spare components for little cost. What is important is the control of the iron's temperature and purpose-built tools can be had with digital bit temperature displays, allowing for accurate settings, which can be crucial when working with very delicate objects. Alternatively, a more economical option is to use a power regulator in place of the soldering iron's mains plug, such as the Antex product featured here. This may not offer the same sort of accuracy in adjustment, but, with a little familiarity, it can be a reliable device.

If a model is deemed to have enough plumbing detail already, or if the idea of adding much extra wire turns you cold, using paint to enhance what is already there is also an option – metallic enamel paints can offer decent results. A further idea is to add some texture to the paint with a little talcum powder, which, when applied carefully with a fine brush, can mimic the look of insulation lagging.

Piping is an essential feature of any steam locomotive and, therefore, enhancing this aspect is another important facet of superdetailing r-t-r models. Although these tasks can sometimes seem fiddly, the results are more than worth the effort.

A genuine Davies and Metcalfe exhaust steam injector valve, hanging beneath preserved '8F' 48151. A moulded representation of this component sits beneath the cab of the Hornby model, but a similar arrangement is missing from the same firm's 'Black Five'.

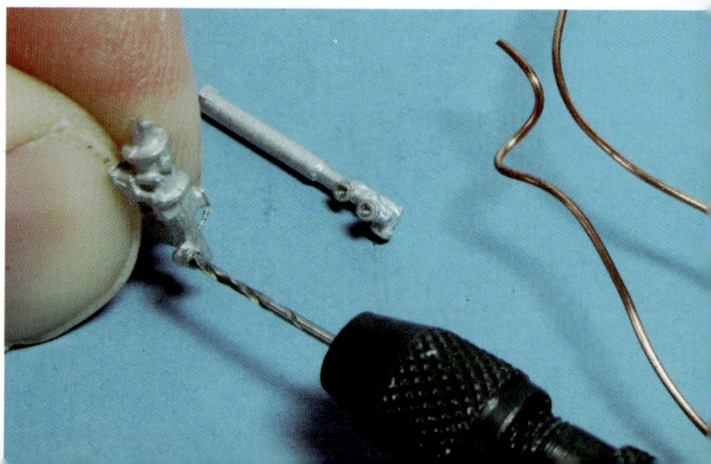

A complete detailing kit is offered by Brassmasters for the Hornby 'Black Five' and is described in more detail in Chapter 9. However, here are the cast white-metal injector assemblies being drilled out to accept lengths of copper wire. The holes need only be 2–3mm deep, just enough to provide a firm location.

ABOVE: In order to solder white-metal parts safely, a temperature-controlled iron is a necessity. These can be expensive, however, so an economy measure is to fit a power regulator to a regular iron, in place of the mains plug, such as this unit from Antex. With practice, the level of power required for different applications can be discerned and I've added some markings onto the dial accordingly! Choosing the correct flux and solder is also important and Carr's offer solutions to these needs.

ABOVE: If joining white-metal to other metals, such as brass or copper, it's important to 'tin' the latter with regular solder first, as this provides a compatible bridge between the two materials. Low-temperature solders often contain antimony, which can react adversely with brass unless the 'tinning' is undertaken first. Adding flux to the joint before the iron is applied will allow the joint to be made quickly, thus avoiding the risk of overheating the metal.

RIGHT: With the various assemblies made up away from the model, the completed parts can then have the wire trimmed to size before fitting. Marking out and drilling locating holes for the wire provides a durable joint.

LEFT: The various grades of copper wire look particularly effective once fitted. Note the black-coated nickel wire running along the edge of the running plate; using this plastic-coated wire saves the awkward task of touching in with paint; only the small brackets (tiny strips of electrician's tape) need painting.

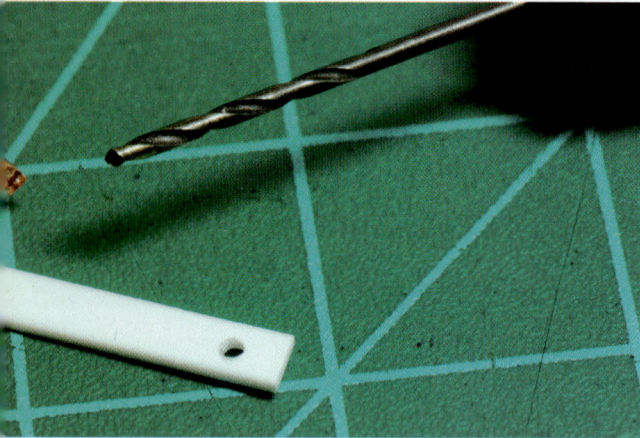

ABOVE: Longer runs of pipes often include flanged joints and these can be recreated using strips of plastic. Here, a hole has been drilled through a strip of 0.080in × 0.020in to suit the diameter of the wire.

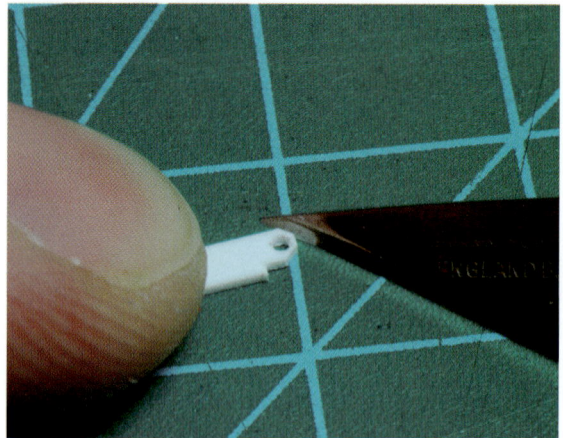

ABOVE: Using a sharp blade, trim around the hole to a square or octagonal shape, according to prototype, leaving just enough material to retain the part's integrity.

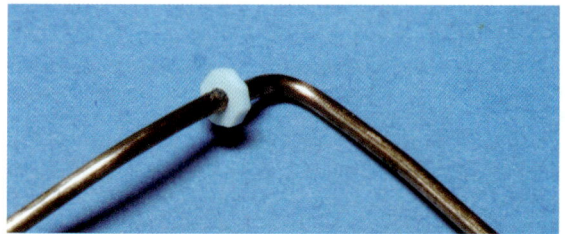

RIGHT: The flange can then be threaded onto the wire and fixed with superglue in the appropriate place.

RIGHT: All of the plumbing on this Bachmann (ex-Mainline) 'Jubilee' has been added from wire and fine metal tubing, while the injector valve is a lost-wax brass casting. Incorporating the square flange on the main input pipe is an important feature.

The benefit of using tube instead of solid wire or rod, in some instances, is self-evident in this view of a water tank vent pipe. Cammett produces various packs of stainless steel tube aimed at miniature gun barrel production, but it's a perfect material for applications such as this.

Bachmann's 2006 release of '9F' 92220 *Evening Star* was a must on my shopping list, having been responsible for maintaining it in pristine condition when I worked at the National Railway Museum. I thought it was a shame that the model came with all the pipework rendered in black plastic, so some metallic enamel paints were used to pick these out and correct the brass-coloured pipes leading to the clack valves, which should be copper.

An alternative treatment for the various injector/ejector array on a '9F' is to add some texture to a dirty mix of white and brown enamels (by adding talcum powder) and carefully painting onto the plastic pipes. Hopefully, this should give a good impression of the insulating lagging applied to some examples. After suitable weathering, this workaday '9F' looks very authentic.

CHAPTER 9

Superdetailing: Part 2

Returning to the theme of superdetailing, as outlined in Chapter 6, an alternative to the prospect of sourcing a cornucopia of separate castings and sheets of etched components from various makers is to take advantage of some of the bespoke detailing kits offered by the likes of Comet, Brassmasters and Mainly Trains. Not all of these kits offer a complete package, but they do include a broad range of bits, accompanied by a set of detailed instructions, prototype notes and, sometimes, options for variations or further detailing with additional recommended products. Brassmasters, in particular, provides excellent instructions with its detailing packs and additional guidance, including step-by-step photographs, can be downloaded from the firm's website. Various modelling magazines, such as *Model Rail*, regularly cover such kits in the form of in-depth evaluations and may expand on any supplied instructions with detailed images and further explanations.

In addition to a detailing pack, it may be necessary to source items such as sprung buffers, couplings and possibly a set of finer-profile trailing wheels. These are often left to the individual to decide upon, as we all have our own particular specifications for such things. Economy wise, purchasing a kit may offer a degree of cost saving over collecting individual parts, but it pays to be discerning and to have in mind the areas of a model where improvements are desired. Certain kits are tailored towards modellers of a finescale bent, optimizing the components for use when regauging the loco to EM or P4 and, thus, a good

number of parts may be superfluous to us mere OO types.

Besides, if you have already embarked on more than a few detailing exercises, it should now be possible to discern which facets of a model may benefit from replacement parts in terms of upgrading or detail variations. The research part of the hobby again comes into play here and it helps to have read up a little and to have chosen a particular prototype, about which enough information has been obtained regarding fittings to suit a chosen period. Later in this chapter we shall look into replacement chimneys and it pays to know whether, for example, an individual 'Jinty' had received a Stanier-pattern stack, or if the original Fowler fitting was still *in situ* at the time. Some of the better detailing kits allow for a choice of such components, which can lead to a range of invaluable spares being amassed for future projects.

A MASTERFUL 'BLACK FIVE'

Hornby's 'Black Five' portrays one of the most numerous steam locomotive types built in the pre-BR era, a total of 842 being built between 1934 and 1951 and, not surprisingly, there were many minor (and some major) variations within this large class. Hornby may offer a choice of boiler and tender options in its catalogue, but a mass-produced product cannot hope to cover all of the alternatives and this is where superdetailing comes in. Brassmasters offers a well thought-out detailing kit for this model that provides a number of optional components to suit specific

Choosing a detailing pack tailored to a specific locomotive type is a convenient way of amassing the necessary components for an upgrade project. The Hornby 'Black Five' is probably a good place to start as an excellent kit is available from Brassmasters that not only includes a range of cast and etched parts, but also incorporates some detailed instructions and prototype notes.

production batches. Adding the full complement of parts is quite a straightforward project, requiring minimal knifework and just a little retouching of the paintwork.

The kit can be complemented by adding a new set of sprung buffers, although the originals aren't bad, so this is an arbitrary choice. What does make a huge difference in appearance is the substitution of a new set of wheels for the front bogie, in tandem with the act of trimming the solid steel casting to reduce the amount to which it protrudes from under the bufferbeam. The leading axle (or axles if a bogie is fitted) of any locomotive is important in terms of visual impact, but also in terms of performance as it acts to guide the locomotive through curved track and point-work. As a sop to the latter, most r-t-r makers err on the side of caution and provide wheels with heavy flanges and wide tyres to conform to 'universal' track standards. However, provided that your track is in good order, a finer set of wheels is not an unrealistic goal.

A set of 3ft 3½in, ten-spoke bevelled-rim wheels and axles, such as those in the Alan Gibson catalogue, look much more appropriate when fitted to the bogie. The method of fitting the wheels is as was described in Chapter 6 and, as long as they are gauged correctly, lubricated and turning freely, they should be as reliable as the originals.

The Brassmasters 'Black Five' components include white-metal and lost-wax castings and a sheet of etched nickel-silver parts. However, buffers must be sourced separately (if replacements are desired), along with a new set of wheels for the leading bogie.

As per the real thing, a choice of flush or riveted bufferbeams is available (the Hornby model coming with the flush variety) to suit particular prototypes. Cylinder covers, lifting eye reinforcement plates, AWS guards and buffer footsteps are also provided.

Tender details are also provided in the Brassmasters kit, including a strip of rivets to fit inside the lip of the tank and lifting eyes.

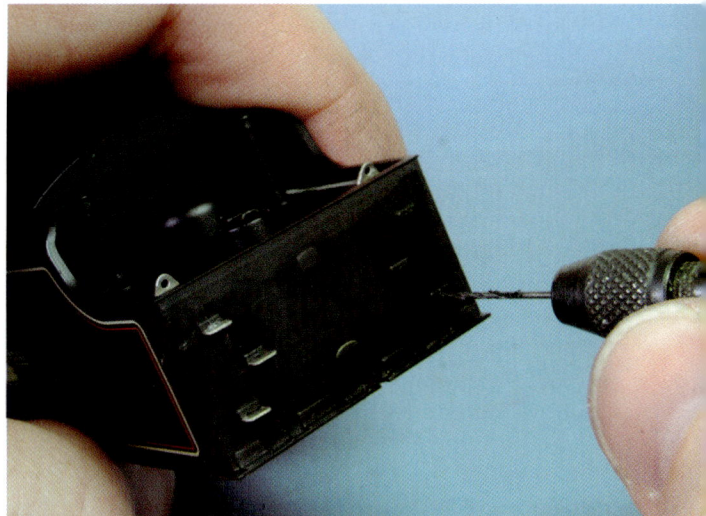

As I intended to replace the buffers in favour of a set of turned-brass and steel units from Slater's, the moulded buffer shanks had to be cut back flush with the face of the bufferbeam, but this was not easy to do without removing the moulded bolt heads at each corner. Therefore, these small details were reinstated using tiny slices of 0.010in × 0.010in plastic strip, fixed in place with Johnson's Klear floor polish. By using a fine brush loaded with the polish, the parts were picked up and positioned carefully and left overnight to set. A further coat of Klear helped to seal them in place.

An error in the tooling for the Hornby Stanier tender is the inclusion of raised rivet detail when it should be flush, just like the sides. Having rubbed this extraneous detail away with abrasive paper, new etched footsteps can be added, drilling small pilot holes first.

To improve the look of the tender chassis, gradually slice away the moulded axle boxes and springs with a sharp scalpel.

Leave the chassis frames flush and smooth, using a scratch brush to reach into any awkward corners and polishing the surface with fine abrasive paper.

Glue the new white-metal castings in place, ensuring they're aligned properly. The axle box retaining strips are hard to salvage when removing the rest of the moulded detail, so I didn't bother and made up a new set from 1mm wide (0.010in thick) strip brass and separate rivets punched from metal foil with a Nutter tool (see Chapter 10 for more details).

An etched overlay adds some missing detail to the bunker bulkhead, capped with a realistic beading strip. A set of lifeguards, buffer steps and steam pipe completes the tender modifications.

Both Hornby's 'Black Five' and '8F' carry a cast-metal leading bogie or pony truck that protrudes too far forward to permit the use of scale couplings or fitting of an AWS coupling guard plate. Cutting back with a junior hacksaw cures the problem, retaining the lifeguards if possible, although the mount for the tension-lock coupling will be lost. Mark out the cut line and remove the waste, clamping firmly in a vice while cutting.

Tidy the cut with a file, leaving a straight, square edge and ensure that all metal filings are removed, especially from around the axle bearing surfaces.

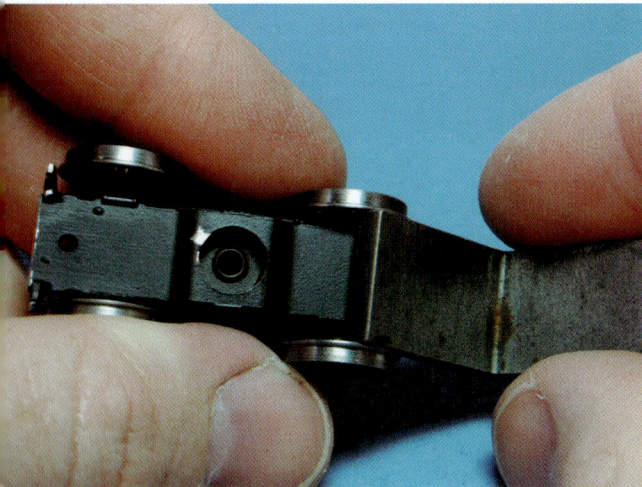

The Gibson replacement wheels offer a much finer appearance with reliable performance, provided that they are fitted properly (see Chapter 6). Using a back-to-back gauge, check that the wheels are true and correctly spaced (14.5mm back-to-back). A tiny drop of light model oil onto the axles will encourage free running.

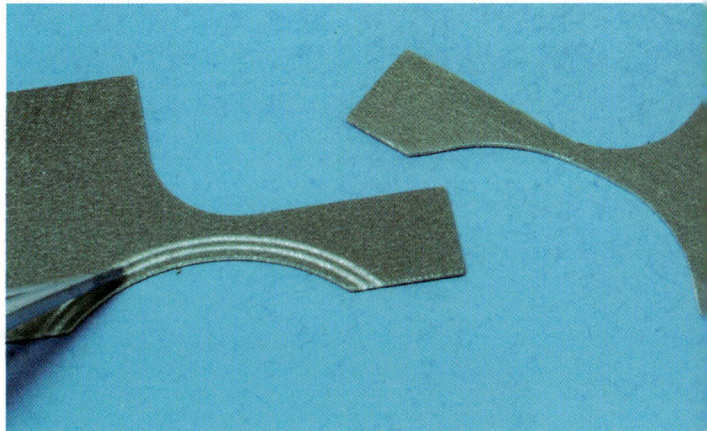

The Brassmasters kit provides etched frame overlays that sit above the front bogie to reduce the amount of daylight visible under the running plate. A series of half-etched lines is included around each wheel arch as a guide to how much to file away to clear various wheels. When using the Gibson set but allowing for plenty of swing around medium radius curves, I worked to the larger radius line.

After folding to shape, the frame overlays simply glue in place and also form missing motion brackets, sitting just behind the piston rod slide bars. Fettle away any excess metal if necessary to ensure a good fit before applying the glue.

With all the other detailing components fitted, the 'Black Five' is ready to have the livery touched up.

With just a hint of weathering to blend in the patches of new paint, the extra components look at home on the finished model. The trimmed bogie chassis and finer wheels add a high degree of finesse to the front end.

The replacement tender axle boxes provide extra relief to the chassis and a footplate crew finish the job nicely.

The Hornby '8F' carries not only an over-scale front wheel set but also a rather clumsy solid steel pony truck that, just like the 'Black Five', benefits greatly from trimming. The mass of the truck is designed to help the front wheels keep to the rails when negotiating short radius curves and turnouts; a particularly fearsome prospect for an eight-coupled locomotive, but trimming a few millimetres from the end will create no adverse effects. The difference between the original (right) and Gibson wheels is clear in this view.

COMET'S 'DUCHESS' UPGRADE

Comet Models, in addition to its locomotive kits, also produces a small range of detailing packs aimed primarily at BR 'Standard' classes as well as the odd LMS prototype. The LMS 'Duchess' is catered for with three separate kits to suit both the curved and 'utility' front versions as well as the final two examples built with Ivatt's modified trailing truck and altered cab. The variations in the front end appearance result from the class originally being envisaged as a fleet of streamlined locomotives, although they were not all built as such. Those that originally wore the sleek styling eventually succumbed to de-streamlining during the 1940s, resulting in a stepped, or 'utility', aspect to the front of the running plate. On the other hand, engines constructed in the traditional manner had the front end styled correctly, with a downward curve from running plate to bufferbeam.

I can't say that the LMS version of streamlining was as successful as the LNER's beautiful 'A4's. It had been my original intention to include a streamlined 'Duchess' in this book, not least for reasons of topicality as, by the time this tome reaches the shelves, the NRM's *Duchess of*

Hamilton should be nearing completion in its retrofitted streamlined casing. However, these engines were not long in the BR era in this condition and, besides, I'm not sure I want to celebrate the defacing of one of the nation's most beautiful artefacts.

An interesting quote from railway author Roger Lloyd, dating from 1951, is worth repeating here:

it is an axiom of all good art that one must never design a thing to look like something other than what it is. Thus a railway engine should always have wheels, a boiler, a cab, a chimney; that is to say, whether it is a very large engine or a very small engine, it should still look like an engine, and trying to camouflage it to look like something else is vulgarity. That many people love to have it so, does not make its vulgarity any less distressing. This, I think, is the real condemnation of the craze for taking a perfectly honest engine, fastening a metal casing all over it, and calling it streamlined, so that it looks like anything in heaven or earth except what it actually is.

(From *The Fascination of Railways* by Roger Lloyd, Allen & Unwin, 1951.)

Gosh, he wasn't keen on them either, was he? In mitigation, he did say that the 'A4's were the 'least displeasing' of the streamliners and I can only imagine what he thought of the GWR's ham-fisted attempts at air-smoothing the 'Castle' class. Anyway, I digress.

Each of the Comet detailing kits for the non-streamlined 'Duchesses' contain new cast inside cylinder covers, AWS fittings, cylinder vacuum relief valves, sandbox covers and fillers, safety valve cover, speedometer cable, cab doors, cab seats, fallplate and floor boards, frame extensions, turned-brass whistle, smokebox door handle, handrail knobs and wire. This comprehensive list can be added to by also obtaining etched brass Stanier-pattern footsteps and a replacement kit for the trailing truck, in which case a new loco-tender power connector will be required. Cylinder drainpipes are also needed and the tender can be treated to a new set of axle boxes, water scoop and a casting to represent the steam-operated coal pusher (see Chapter 12). Quite a shopping list, especially when you throw in a replacement set of bogie wheels, etched name-plates, transfers and paint. However, all of these ingredients add up to a significantly improved Hornby model.

Much of the improvement lies in the etched brass smoke deflectors that are much more delicate than the moulded plastic originals, although they are a little tricky to assemble by soldering. Glue might be an easier option, but, as these components are in quite an exposed position, adhesives will not offer the same level of durability as solder. The upper straps are perhaps the most difficult bits to get right as they are intended to wrap around the handrails once the deflector has been fixed onto the running plate. It took me several attempts to get these looking right, but, fortunately, the 0.005in thick brass is flexible enough to forgive a few aborted attempts to achieve a tidy appearance.

This is not the only model that can benefit from replacement smoke deflectors and suitable parts can be had for the BR '9F' and 'Britannia', amongst others. Incidentally, in preservation, '9F' *Evening Star* has carried lengths of timber wedged in the gap between the top of the deflectors and the smokebox, resting on top of the handrails. I'm not sure why, as this would interrupt the updraught that is required to disperse the smoke from the chimney; perhaps it was to allow safer access to polish the chimney's copper cap!

Another bespoke detailing kit that offers a range of options to suit various prototypes is that offered by Comet Models for the Hornby LMS 'Duchess' Pacifics. Catering for both the 'utility' and 'curved' front variants, suitable smoke deflectors are available to suit each type. Conveniently, much of these kits' individual parts are also available separately, allowing the modeller to mix and match the desired components. This model has been stripped ready for the job, the new handrails and knobs being the first bits to have been added.

The distinctive inside cylinder cover is offered as a superior white-metal casting, requiring the original moulding to be drilled and cut away. Open the cavity out gradually, checking against the new part to gain a good, close fit, then fix with epoxy.

Although Hornby now offers its 'Duchess' with a fixed trailing truck (with flangeless wheel set), models produced prior to 2008 possessed a large expanse of fresh air beneath the firebox and the truck and the Comet kit supplies a pair of etched frame extensions to disguise this. The original pony truck can be retained, although it needs to be heavily modified, or a separately available kit can be utilized, the latter option being pursued here. Due to the nature of the frame extensions, the lateral movement of the truck is inhibited, so this modification is not recommended for those with tight curves on their layouts.

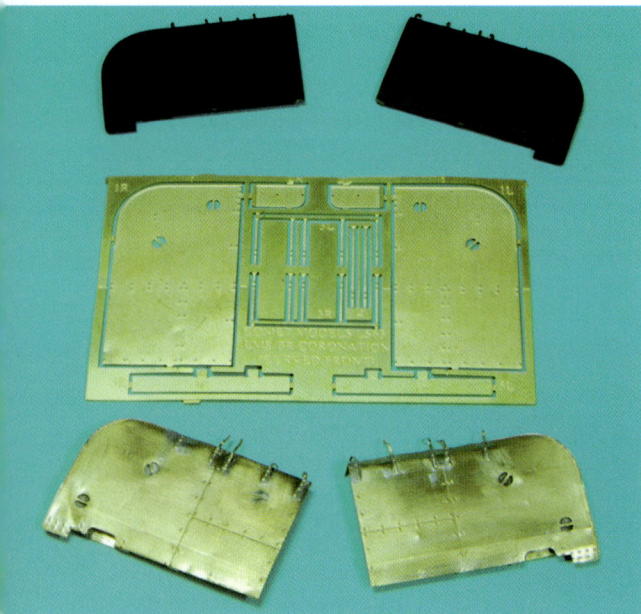

A choice of smoke deflectors is available to suit the different patterns of front end to be found on the 'Duchesses' and each set requires some careful assembly; the strap brackets being especially delicate. The improvement over the moulded plastic deflectors is substantial.

A small bulldog clip is perfect for clamping the fine strap brackets and hand-hold cups in place whilst soldering. 'Tinning' each part first helps the job along and, combined with the use of a suitable flux, minimizes the need for prolonged contact with the hot iron.

Fit the completed deflectors with epoxy glue, folding the straps over the handrails and securing the brackets to the side of the smokebox. Work in stages as this can be a bit fiddly, mixing enough epoxy to cope with each individual.

The finished 'Duchess', ready for service. Despite plenty of new components being added, the need for a full repaint was avoided, touching in with primer and enamel top coats, along with a little weathering, blending everything together.

CHIMNEY MATTERS

An engine's chimney is another of those small components that can make or break a model's looks. By and large, most r-t-r models get this feature right, but there are still a few instances, including some very recent releases, where the designers haven't quite captured the character of the original, or where an incorrect pattern is included, not well suited to a particular prototype. Many engines did undergo chimney changes throughout their lives, so it may be a question of the right chimney shape, but portrayed in the wrong period.

Correcting an unsatisfactory component can sometimes be achieved by means of filler and files, but it is often more agreeable to chop the chimney off and start again with a new cast-metal or turned-brass chimney. Some of these replacements, however, may still need a little prepara-tion or enhancement to get them up to scratch, as casting 'pips' often remain while others may have little or no rendering of the real thing's hollow nature. Having to drill out a metal casting is a real pain and it can leave one wondering whether it was worth replacing the original, but with care and the right approach, it can be done to good effect.

Detailing kits often include a replacement chimney if the subject model has been widely acknowledged to have an inferior representa-tion, Brassmasters' project pack for the Hornby 'Royal Scot' and 'Patriot' being a prime example. Alternatively, a choice of new castings may be on offer to suit a conversion project, or to cater for batch differences not covered in the r-t-r range. Again, Brassmasters offers a comprehensive detailing kit for the Bachmann LMS 'Jinty' and a choice of Fowler- or Stanier-pattern chimney is included to suit different prototypes and periods, the model's original chimney looking like neither one nor the other.

Cutting away the incumbent chimney is a quick task, but being sure to file and abrade the surface flush with the smokebox's profile is important as this will provide the seat for the replacement. Check for a good fit before applying any adhesive as, particularly with white-metal castings, the lower flange may have become distorted in transit or may need excess material removing from the underside. Epoxy glue is preferable for this job as it provides not only a strong bond but also allows for constant adjustments before setting (using a five-minute formula will provide plenty of time). Check that the stack stands truly vertically, looking at the model in every plane, with a set square as a visual reference point. If it sets cock-eyed, the model will look awful. A thick, slow-setting superglue can also be employed, but the epoxy bond often provides a less brittle joint than that of a cyanoacrylate formula.

There's little doubt that obtaining a dedicated detailing kit saves a lot of ferreting through various parts lists from a range of component makers. They can also offer up ideas for projects you may not have thought of and give an idea of where an r-t-r model is let down (if the kit offers a replacement for something, the original is probably deemed inferior by someone); this may be subjective, but then so is most of the railway modelling hobby. However, be prepared to source some extra bits and pieces, having decided how far you want to go in terms of cutting up the original product.

Remember to bear in mind the consequences of your actions and whether any major component exchanges will result in the need for some wholesale repainting, or if a little retouching will suffice. It goes without saying that the more detailing undertaken on a single locomotive, the more finishing work will be necessary, although, even with the comprehensive 'Black Five' and 'Duchess' projects featured in this chapter, the original livery schemes were retained. Careful priming and painting of the new parts, plus some gentle weathering, blends everything together.

In contrast, the following chapter goes much further, taking a model back to its bare bones and building it back up with various off-the-shelf and scratch-built components. In instances like this, there is no choice but to effect a complete repaint.

Changing an engine's chimney is not always due to a poor rendering by a model's designer, but rather that certain locomotives received different patterns throughout their lives. Use either a saw or a good pair of end-cutters to snip off the offending item, leaving a little waste to be filed back flush. Don't be tempted into cutting the chimney flush in one action, as the profile of the smokebox must be followed exactly, otherwise the new component will not seat properly. File away the remaining plastic and finish with abrasive paper until the surface is smooth and free of tool marks.

Choose a suitable replacement and remove any casting flash with files and abrasives before fitting. The top opening may also benefit from opening out slightly with a hand reamer if necessary. Check for a good fit, then fix in place with five-minute epoxy glue, utilizing a set square as a visual reference to ensure the stack stands vertically. Look from the front and sides and make any adjustments before the glue sets; any error here will ruin the look of the model.

LEFT: A criticism of the Hornby rebuilt 'Royal Scots' and 'Patriots' concerned the profile of the double chimney. My own model has received a white-metal casting from Brassmasters and looks much the better for it.

BELOW: A replacement is not always necessary, as this Bachmann GWR '57xx' demonstrates. The overall shape of the chimney looked fine to me, but what let it down was the noticeable gap between the twin components. Fill the crevice with a little model putty and, once this has been carefully rubbed down and painted, there should be no discernible trace of the joint.

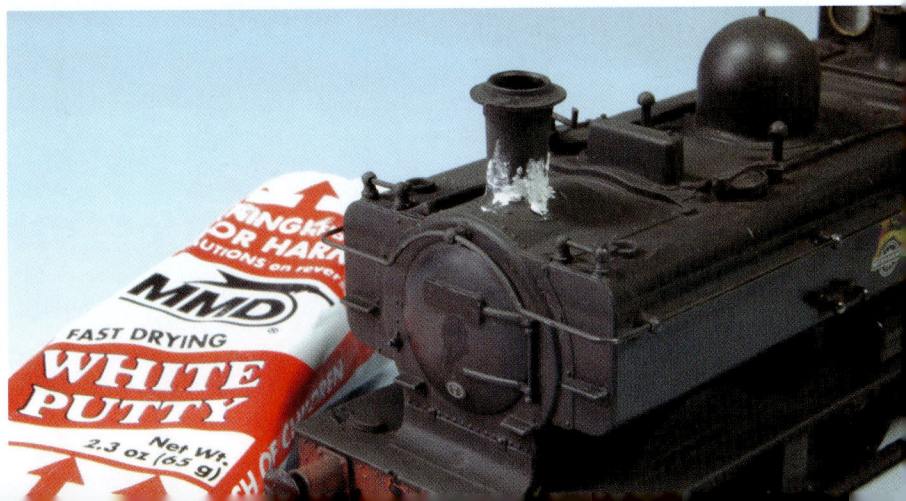

Detailing Cab Interiors

The cab of a locomotive forms the nerve centre of the machine, but too often this area is neglected by manufacturers and modellers, especially where older products are concerned. The interiors of certain tank locomotives, such as the various LMS and BR 2-6-4Ts and 2-6-2Ts, are not readily accessible, just as is the case with the Bachmann '57xx' and 'Jinty', despite plenty of interior detail being applied at the factory. Even just adding a driver and fireman can be a job and a half, demanding the model to be almost completely dismantled.

Open-cab tender engines are now being supplied with a breathtaking degree of detail as standard, as has been demonstrated in Chapter 2, but how difficult is it to bring other models up to a similar specification? The answer to that depends on the model at hand and how easy it is to get into it. Even using metallic enamel paints to pick out valves, controls and pipework can make a positive impact. In addition to adding a pair of figures, other details such as hose pipes, tools, bucket and a spare oil lamp are all simple things to include, but which go a long way to creating a believable working environment.

Steam cabs can be very cluttered spaces and it was rare that a pre-1950s engineer would design the interior with the comfort of the crew paramount in his thinking. After all, it took more than one hundred years before cabs were fully enclosed, protecting driver and fireman from the elements, and even then this was not a universally accepted practice.

The amount of control equipment to be found in the cab depends upon the type of locomotive and its intended use, although all engines share a small number of basic controls and cab fittings: a regulator handle; boiler pressure and water level gauges; reverser; steam brake; hand brake; water-injection controls; sanding operation; and whistle. Passenger classes required extra gear to govern carriage heating and so on, as well as later warning systems such as AWS. In addition, screw reversing apparatus was favoured for passenger work, as this allowed for fine-tuning of the valve gear through the full speed range, increasing fuel economy and steam efficiency, whereas freight and shunting engines often carried a lever reverser that offered forward, mid and reverse with only a few settings in-between as well as the advantage of rapid changes in direction.

One of the most important features to add to the inside of a locomotive cab is a layer of dirt, especially across the floor. Any engine in day-to-day use would gain an ingrained layer of coal dust, soot and grease, despite one of the fireman's main responsibilities being to maintain a clean and safe environment on the footplate. He was unlikely to be on his knees with soap and a brush however, so applying a dusting of soot-coloured weathering powder across the floor, around the boiler backhead and cab sides won't go amiss and this aspect is discussed further in Chapter 14.

The interior of a locomotive's cab will benefit from some extra detailing attention, although some models already come supplied with a beautiful array of fittings and a high level of decoration; Hornby's 'King Arthur' and 'T9' spring to mind. Looking at the real thing, there is certainly plenty going on inside every cab and other models can be brought up to the same specification with a little extra work. This is the cab of Great Central No.506 Butler Henderson. Photo by Nick Brodrick

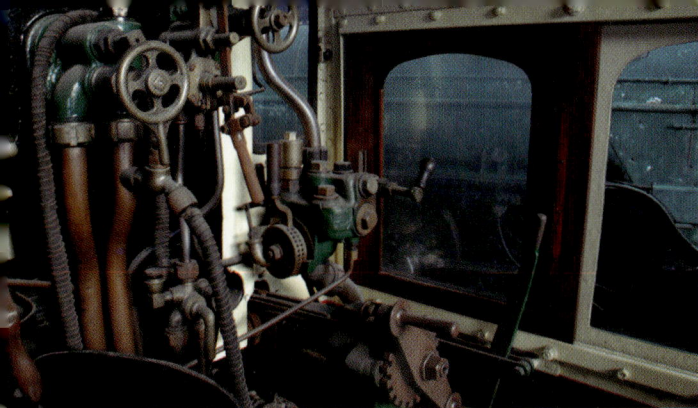

It pains me to see Butler Henderson in its present condition, as the National Collection locomotive has (in 2009) been banished from the Great Hall of the NRM for Barrow Hill roundhouse. I spent many hours keeping the cab and exterior of this engine immaculate, but nowadays the copper and brass are tarnished and the formerly polished steel red with rust. Why? Anyway, look at the sliding side window panel, encased in what looks like teak, and the screw reverser control. Note also that, the GCR having been a right-hand drive railway, the fireman's controls governing the boiler water are sited on the left-hand side. A folding door shields the driver from the blast from the firebox whilst it is open and a hosepipe and tap can be seen, provided to keep the cab interior clean of coal dust.
Photo by Nick Brodrick

A contrast to Butler Henderson is the interior of a Southern 'Q1' 0-6-0. These freight engines were certainly austere in their external looks and the cabs were no different. The regulator has been designed to be operable from both sides of the cab – helpful when shunting in a goods yard – and there are few auxiliary systems to maintain. The brass box is a lubricator pot and the twin, rectangular glass gauges monitor the level of water in the boiler, the zebra-striped background aiding visibility.

ABOVE: Wooden floorboards are an easy detail to replicate using strips of wood veneer. Choose a close-grained wood and fix in place with double-sided tape, scoring into individual planks after fitting. Applying dark wood stain will help to weather the appearance. Cutting away the moulded cab doors of this 'Jinty' leaves the cab interior more visible, making the extra work worthwhile.

LEFT: Looking equally as basic is the cab of Midland Railway '1F' 0-6-0T 41708. Dating from 1880, this venerable machine retains the everyday appearance of a working steam locomotive and, like the 'Q1', the regulator has twin handles to permit easier shunting manoeuvres. Note also the open front spectacle and the wooden floorboards can also just be discerned.
Photo by Nick Brodrick

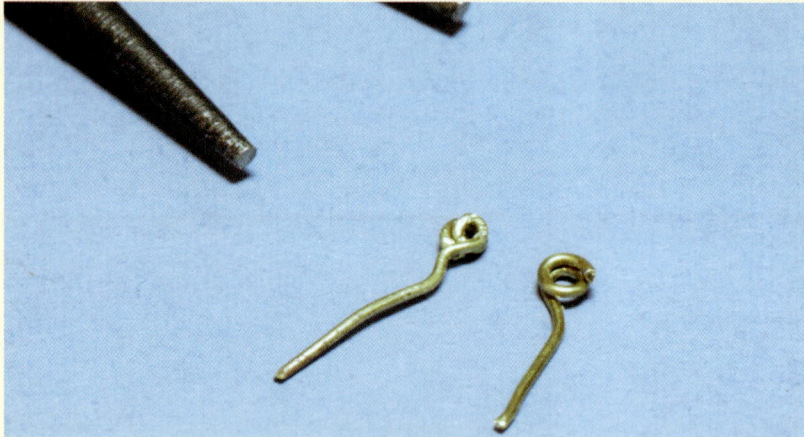

Some models with an older pedigree may not have much in the way of internal cab fittings, so scratch-building may be necessary and some of the following techniques have been lifted from an article by Eric Taylor in the 1987 Annual edition of Model Railway Constructor. Taking lengths of copper or brass wire, form it into tight coils using round-nose pliers.

After flooding the coiled wire with solder, file the faces flat and the edges square and you have the beginnings of a steam pressure gauge!

A combination of gauges, piping and some etched hand-wheels and a regulator (from a Mainly Trains detailing etch, ref. MT227) make up the controls of this 'Terrier'. A cast brass oil pot on the side of the reversing lever, with attendant piping, is an Alan Gibson product and veneer has been added to the floor. The horizontal length of wire above the regulator forms the whistle handle.

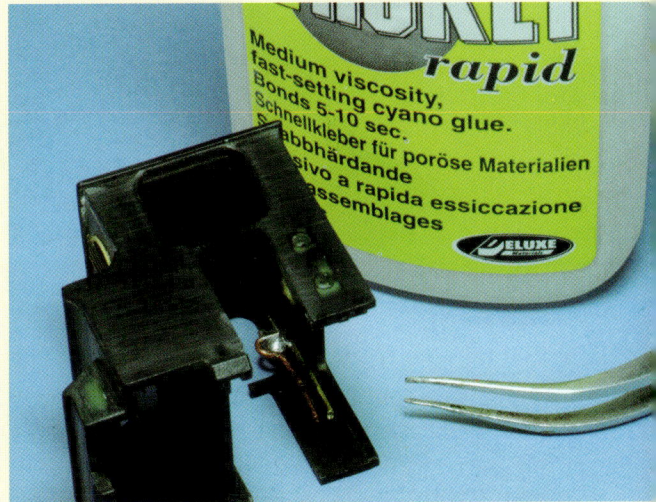

Slightly more complex valves can be formed using the same mix of wire and solder, although, in this case, the brass has been folded into an S-shape to allow a wide section of solder to adhere. The length of fine wire will be trimmed to form an operating handle.

The completed ejector valve assembly can be fixed to the inside wall of the cab before the locomotive is reassembled. Painting the various dials, complete with needle and gradations, adds some extra finesse, while the interior walls will benefit from a lick of paint; the top half is often cream and the lower reaches black.

The finished 'Terrier' looks all the better for a full complement of interior details, giving the miniature footplate crew something to work with! A full description of this project is given in the following chapter.

CHAPTER 10

Detailing Case Study: LBSC 'Terrier' 0-6-0T

This episode is intended to demonstrate not only a comprehensive detailing project, but also the way that a period of thorough research can help to create a more accurate representation of an individual locomotive. By choosing to develop the diminutive Hornby 'Terrier', a model that owes its origins to a former Dapol product, such is the age of the model that it requires a large amount of the original fittings to be cut away and replaced with improved components.

Moreover, if a truly high-grade model is desired, the chassis could also be upgraded using a new etched brass kit from Comet that comes complete with new wheels, motor and gearbox, thus leaving only the basic plastic mouldings of boiler, cab, tanks and running plate from

the Hornby model. As was outlined in the Introduction, I have shied away from going to these lengths in this particular volume as such an approach is more redolent of kit-building. Instead, I have aimed to get the very best out of what Hornby has provided and, hopefully, the level of realism elsewhere on the model helps to detract from any other shortcomings.

Still in current production at the time of writing (and also featuring in *Thomas the Tank Engine*), the 'Terrier' is beginning to show its age in terms of over-scale wheel profiles and coupling rods, as well as the heavily moulded details such as piping, brakes, handrails and safety valves. However, the model is relatively cheap and the level of decoration, particularly those offered in

Looking like a pocket-sized locomotive, the Stroudley 'Terrier' has been popular amongst steam-era modellers since its initial release under the Dapol brand in 1989. Now produced by Hornby, a slightly better mechanism has been fitted and the standard of decoration is high, but the crude details and large tension-lock couplings leave it looking a little toy-like.

lined London, Brighton & South Coast Railway (LBSCR) livery, is impressive. With care, the original livery could be salvaged in the main part, despite adding plenty of new parts, in a similar way to the LMS 'Duchess' featured in Chapter 9, although recreating certain examples with modified bunkers and sandboxes may prove more challenging.

There are, as pointed out in contemporary reviews and magazine features back in 1989, a number of inherent detail inaccuracies present on this model, centred around the halfway-house of period condition and particularly concerning the sandbox arrangement. No specific detailing kit has been marketed for this popular prototype, although plenty of individual components can be readily obtained from various sources. An opportunity for scratch-building also arises and making use of certain general resource packs, such as those in the Mainly Trains range of etched brake gear and footsteps, will help the project along.

A prototype should be chosen with care, as no two Terriers seem to have been the same, particularly by the time they reached BR ownership. Putting in the effort to research an individual's history will help, not least as it pays to know what details are required before drawing up a shopping list of components and materials. The following information was gleaned from a couple of hours' worth of searching across the Internet, entering 'Terrier 32670' into a search engine and also obtaining a few relevant books and magazine articles from a second-hand transport book shop.

'TERRIER' 32670: A HISTORY

Having the honour of being the oldest survivor of William Stroudley's class of 'Terrier' 0-6-0Ts, 32670 was built at Brighton Works by the London, Brighton & South Coast Railway in December 1872, one of the original batch of five machines built in that year. From new, the number 70 was carried, along with the name *Poplar*, reflecting that the purpose of these engines was to work the East London lines.

At the turn of the century, No.70 was sold as surplus to the Kent & East Sussex Railway (K&ESR), where it remained until the line closed in 1954, having since passed into BR ownership upon nationalization in 1948. Although known as No.3 *Bodiam* under K&ESR ownership, the engine was renumbered to 32670 – and denamed – by BR.

After the K&ESR closure, 32670 moved to the Havant–Hayling Island branch, being given a general overhaul in 1960, despite now being nearly ninety years old. Just three years later, this branch line was also closed under the Beeching Report and the engine was withdrawn by BR. Preservation immediately beckoned and a swift move to the reopened K&ESR followed, where it worked into the mid-1980s before a major overhaul was required, this being completed relatively recently and, at the time of writing, *Bodiam* is still in working order.

This 'Terrier' possesses some unique characteristics, such as the tall coal bunker that is a result of a rebuild by the K&ESR. The LBSCR engineer, Marsh, had begun a rebuilding programme for the 'Terriers' and this was rolled out to all surviving examples. New, longer boilers were fitted and classification changed from Class A1 to A1X, this particular engine having the honour of being the last to be rebuilt in this fashion, receiving the modifications as late as 1943; this explains why it retains the original sandboxes above the running plate despite all other rebuilds having these components relocated.

Although Westinghouse pumps were provided on the LBSCR for use with air-braked suburban stock, this equipment was removed from 32670 by the K&ESR, being replaced by vacuum brake gear, including a distinctive, cylindrical tank below the rear bunker. Since its latest overhaul, the engine once again sports the Westinghouse pump on the cab side.

CHOOSING A PERIOD TO MODEL

Pinning down a specific era in which to model 32670 took quite a bit of consideration, as livery and detail fittings seemed to vary during the 1950s and 1960s. Finding suitable photographs to work from also proved difficult, despite this being a well-documented machine, particularly in the latter few years of the ex-K&ESR before closure by BR. As is often the case, nearly all of the images that I could trace showed the engine in the traditional three-quarter portrait composition, but these failed to reveal certain features, such as the exact nature of the vacuum pump arrangement. After much head-scratching, I eventually opted to portray 32670 as it appeared in the late 1940s, sporting a plain black livery that had been applied immediately following nationalization, with a new BR number in place on the bunker sides.

Other confusing messages that I gleaned from studying period photographs surrounded the fitting of extra headcode disc brackets in the Southern Region pattern, sprouting from each side of the smokebox. Initially, I added these to my model, using the Mainly Trains lamp bracket

etch, but then thought better of it and removed them. I'm hazarding a guess that they were only fitted after the engine left the K&ESR line in the mid-1950s.

SETTING TO WORK

The Hornby model includes a complement of sandboxes cast into the chassis frame in addition to those incorporated into the front splashers. These two features contradict each other as the 'Terriers', as originally built, had all sandboxes mounted above the running plate. However, upon rebuilding to 'A1X' specification, these were moved to sit on the sides of the chassis frames. This means that the front splashers must be reshaped if a true A1X is desired; not an easy thing to do and requiring much filling and carving to gain a suitable profile. Luckily for me, 32670 retains this pattern of splashers to this day, so removing the sanding gear from the chassis proved much more straightforward.

Sanding pipes are moulded into the plastic section of the chassis, so can be cut away with a knife. However, the steel bit is different and it's essential to avoid getting any metal filings or waste into the various moving parts and, especially, into the electric motor, as this will lead to a plague of short circuits as well as excess wear to the bearings. In this case, a lot of material has to be removed, so it seemed safer to dismantle the whole chassis, including motor, wheels and power pick-ups. Cut away the waste with a hacksaw, following with files until the surface is flush. Complete the job with emery paper and fine abrasives to leave a smooth finish and clean away all traces of swarf. Degrease the metal with white spirit before touching in with matt black paint prior to reassembly, reoiling the wheels and gears as necessary.

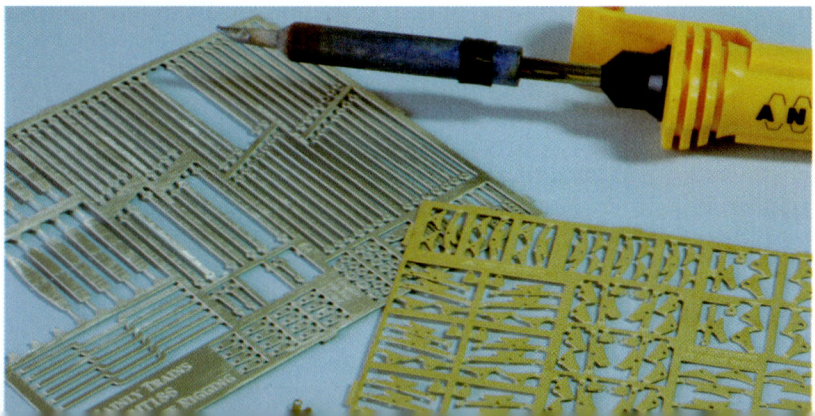

Mainly Trains offers some excellent resource packs as aids to scratch-building and detailing work; the sets of locomotive brake rods (MT186) and shoes (for SR types MT182) are perfect for replacing the moulded gear on the 'Terrier' model.

Assemble a full set for the locomotive before finally cutting them from the fret, noting how the parts are 'handed' to suit the opposite sides of the chassis.

The brake shoes are designed to be laminated from three separate layers and it helps to leave the middle part of the sandwich attached to the fret whilst soldering the overlays, using a length of brass wire through the centre hole to aid alignment. A small bulldog clip makes a handy clamp.

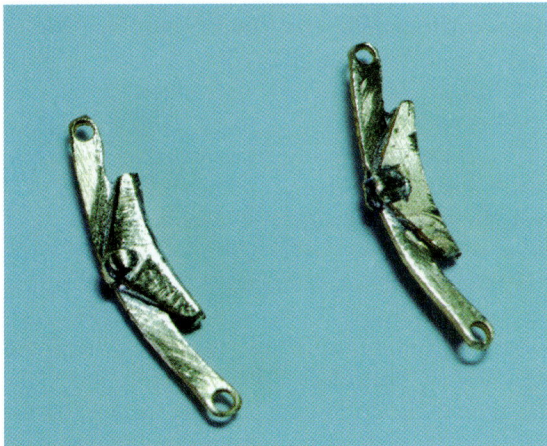

Use a file and a glass-fibre scratch brush to clean up each component, as well as removing excess solder and any traces of flux. The twin mounting holes may need opening out slightly to accept the 0.7mm mounting wire.

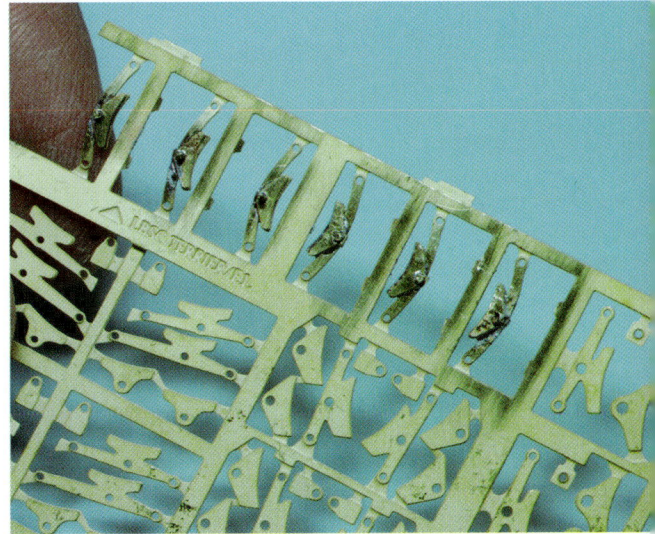

Having marked out the locations for the mounting points, drill shallow holes into the steel chassis (approx. 3mm deep), taking care to leave enough clearance for the wheels and observing the amount of side-play in each axle. It's important that the shoes do not come into contact with the wheels, as this may cause short circuits. Don't forget to allow for the free movement of the coupling rods, too.

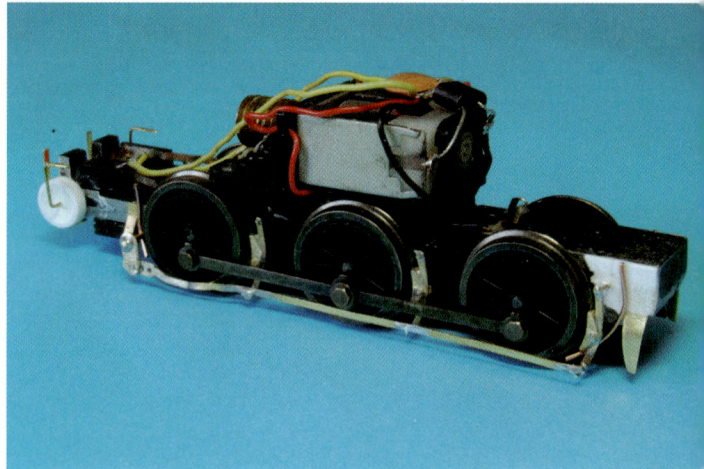

Soldering as much of the brake assembly as possible produces a stronger set-up, although the mounts into the chassis are better suited to being glued with epoxy. The outside actuating rods visible here were improvised from 1mm brass strip, soldered to an adjustable bracket from the Mainly Trains brake rod pack, from which the cams were also sourced. The motor can now be reassembled into the chassis.

Wire sanding pipes, strip brass lifeguards and 0.010in plastic card frame extension overlays complete the chassis. Working screw link couplings are to be employed, so no provision has been made for fitting NEM-compatible units. However, if tension locks were to be used, a low-profile coupling bar could be fashioned from stiff brass (0.7mm 22SWG) and fixed to the chassis at the appropriate height.

One of the first boiler fittings to feel the steel of my hacksaw was the plastic chimney, which, although not bad in terms of profile and execution, was deemed inferior to a cast unit produced by 247 Developments. This pleasant white-metal component, purchased from the 247 stand at the Warley model show, unfortunately suffered a bit of damage on the way home from the National Exhibition Centre, squashed along with its owner into Cattle Class on the West Coast Main Line. The lower flange is delicately rendered in the soft metal and a degree of rebuilding was needed after fitting to the smokebox, using Milliput and a round file to blend with the rest of the stack.

Incidentally, a mounting lug is incorporated into the casting, something that is not common to all replacement chimneys, and requires either to be cut away before fitting or a locating hole to be drilled into the smokebox. I plumped for the latter as I thought this would give the chimney a bit of extra security. However, a cast steel weight

lurks inside the boiler and smokebox and this will interfere with the drill. To circumvent this problem, prise away the smokebox door and remove the small screw underneath the boiler that retains the weight. After drilling a pilot hole (of 3mm diameter), use a hand reamer to open the aperture out to the desired size before refitting the weight and replacing the smokebox door. Trim the chimney's lug to a length that will allow it to fit above the weight, then fix it in place.

Refining the safety valves was another priority task, although I was a bit frustrated after forgetting to buy some replacements at the same time as the chimney. I'd planned to work on the model the following day, so, being a stubborn sort of chap, I thought about trying to do something with the original mouldings before ordering a new set (Alan Gibson produces a nice brass casting that is suitable). By turning the plastic valve's shaft in an electric mini-drill, set on a low speed and mounted in a vice, a file was held gently against it, working as if it were mounted in a lathe. By moving the file along the shaft's length, the diameter was narrowed and the profile refined. The bracket linking the shaft to the dome was replaced with 1mm-wide, 0.010in-thick strip brass, mounted to the shaft with a dowel of 0.3mm stiff brass wire. The completed valves are by no means perfect, but they're certainly better than the originals. I may yet upgrade them to the Gibson set, however.

The moulded smokebox door hinges are not only a bit on the crude side, but also too short. The door is best shorn of all raised detail to leave a blank canvas and new straps can be formed from plastic strip (0.020in × 0.010in), wrapping the ends around a length of 0.7mm wire to form the hinge (soften the plastic with liquid poly cement). A new smokebox door handle and front handrail, plus a new chimney, complete the engine's 'face'.

A distinctive feature of the 'Terriers' is the location of the buffers, fitted slightly above the running plate. This makes adding working sprung buffers somewhat tricky and, in order to fit my favourite Slater's units, the mounting holes were drilled only just deep enough to accommodate the new shanks. It's not possible to mount the buffer heads in the usual way, so, for a quick compromise, I cut the head rods short and dispensed with the sprung action. Instead, the heads are fixed in place with epoxy, although this wasn't done until after the model had been primed and painted.

Through my own fault, I forgot to order replacement safety valves and, as I've mentioned elsewhere, I hate having to postpone a project in progress while waiting on the postman, so I tried to refine the original moulded valves, turning the shafts against a file, whilst spinning slowly in a mini-drill.

The slender profile of the modified valves, plus the new strip brass brackets, offer a big improvement.

For many 'Terriers' the addition of a Westinghouse air-brake pump is essential and, although my chosen prototype had lost its air-brake equipment by the time it reached BR ownership, I've demonstrated the fittings here. The brass casting is by Alan Gibson and a length of copper pipe links it with the ejection port in the smokebox, from where the pump drew its steam supply. The new wire cab handrails can also be seen in this view, replacing strips of moulded plastic and threaded through holes drilled into the top of the brackets. The handrails along the boiler were much easier to fit! Note that new footsteps have been constructed (Mainly Trains ref. MT232) and the water tank hatches have been moved to a more accurate position closer to the cab.

Moulded clack valves were cut away from the sides of the boiler and replaced with brass castings (Gibson), which also incorporate short lengths of piping that can be bent to follow the engine's contours. On the real thing, these water-feed pipes actually perform a U-bend, running back to the cab along the top of the tanks. Depending on the individual 'Terrier', the fitter who last replaced them and, probably, on the length of pipe available at the time, the actual position of the U-bend could vary from just below the clack valves, to being discreetly hidden behind the running plate.

The key facet of 32670 to capture is the modified bunker and this was built up from the original moulding using various layers of plastic card and strip. It doesn't matter about keeping this hollow, like the real thing, as a full load of coal will disguise the flat top surface and the addition of a scratch-built brass coal rail allows the fuel to be stacked to the maximum level.

These replacement clack valves, cast in brass by Alan Gibson, are superb, as they include all the relevant bolt head detail as well as incorporating the feed pipes. New oil boxes have been fixed to the front panel of the tanks (Gibson again) and short lengths of 0.3mm copper wire run from the underside. Note also the improvised 'globe'-type lubricators on the front of the splashers, using short handrail knobs and wire. Etched sandbox lids originate from a Mainly Trains loco detailing pack (ref. MT256).

This interesting tool, known as 'the Nutter', allows individual rivets, bolt heads and nuts to be stamped from thin metal foil using a selection of tips in a metal punch. The foil is clamped in the tool over a rubber pad and, after stamping out a quantity of rivets or bolts, the tiny details can be fixed onto a flat surface using Johnson's Klear floor polish, leaving an invisible bond. As the 'Terrier' in question wore distinct raised rivets on the side tanks and bunker rear, this was a detail that I wanted to include and the Nutter facilitates this.

Adding the small rivets is not as fiddly as it may seem. Mark out the locations and apply a thin coat of Klear over the surface. Before this dries, use a fine brush, loaded with the clear polish, to pick up the individual details and drop them in place, manipulating gently until accurately positioned. Another coat or two of Klear, applied a little later by hand or airbrush, will seal everything in place.

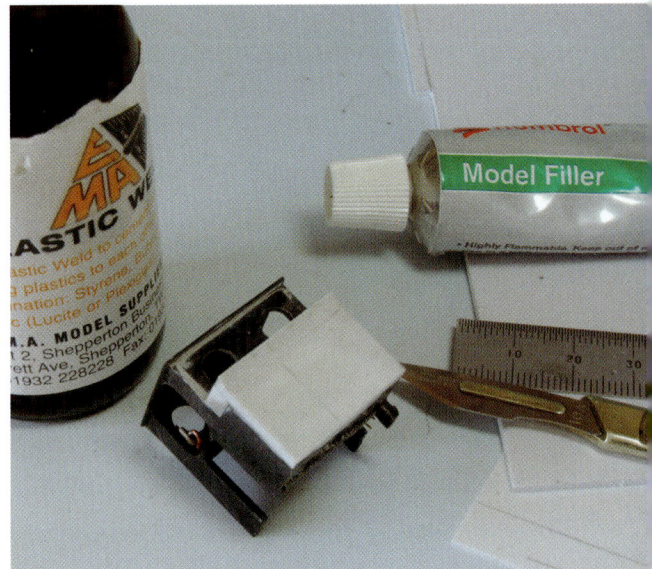

In order to make the changes to the bunker, the rear tool box must first be cut away using a razor saw, leaving a little waste to be worked flush with a flat file.

Plastic card and strip are perfect for making alterations such as this as they can be laminated and, once the glue has set, carved or filed to shape. Employ model putty to fill any gaps.

Forming the elegant curve of the bunker top took numerous attempts to get right, checking against photographs until satisfied that it looked correct. A scratch-built coal rail was folded up and soldered from 1mm strip brass, then numerous Nutter-derived bolt and rivet heads added in appropriate places.

As a steel weight has been displaced during the bunker modifications, I set an amount of lead shot inside the new bunker with PVA-type glue and left it to set completely overnight. This extra ballast will aid the model's adhesion to the rails.

The moulded relief that alludes to spectacle plates was cut away and replaced with etched brass overlays from a Mainly Trains detailing fret (ref. MT226). Barred versions are provided in that pack, but none of them exactly matched those on 32670, so I made my own by fixing individual lengths of 0.3mm brass wire over the round plates.

My chosen prototype carried a distinctive cylindrical vacuum tank under the bunker and this was recreated using a short length (15mm) of Evergreen ¼in (7.25mm) plastic tube, cut in a mitre box to keep the ends square.

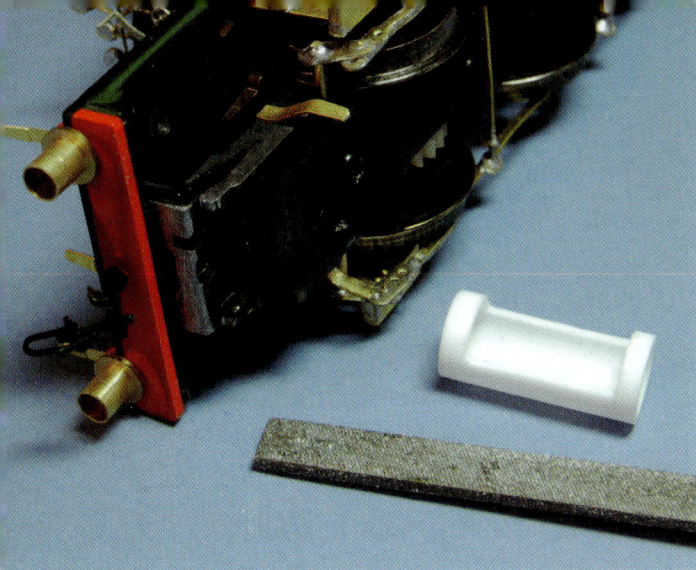

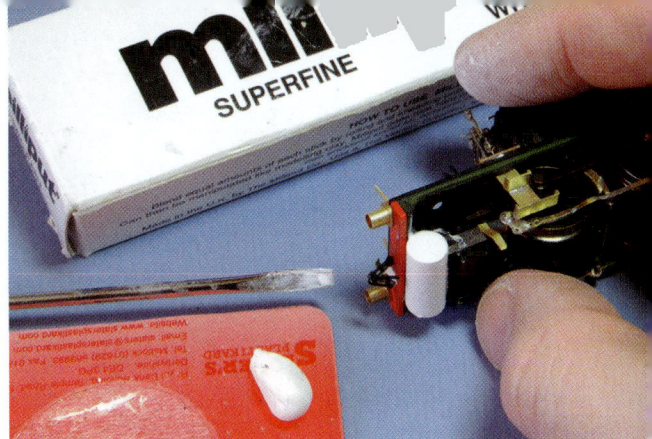

Fill the open ends of the cylinder with Milliput, or similar, and before it sets hard, smooth it over with a wet finger before pressing a slight concave profile into the putty with a suitably shaped scrap of wooden dowelling. Once the filler has set, the ends can be tidied up with abrasive paper.

In order to clear the chassis block, a notch had to be cut in the cylinder. Employ trial and error to get this right before fixing it in place. Secure it to the chassis only, however, to retain access to the motor.

Strap hangers for the cylinder are easy to form from 1mm strip brass, using round-nose pliers.

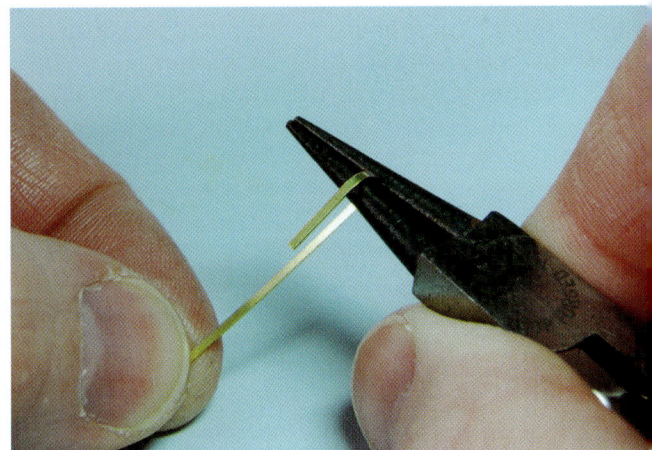

Fix the hangers in place, glued to the bufferbeam only. When the body is to be removed, the cylinder, being fixed to the chassis block, simply slides out of the brass hoops, as they only continue under the cylinder just enough to fool the eye into thinking they completely surround it.

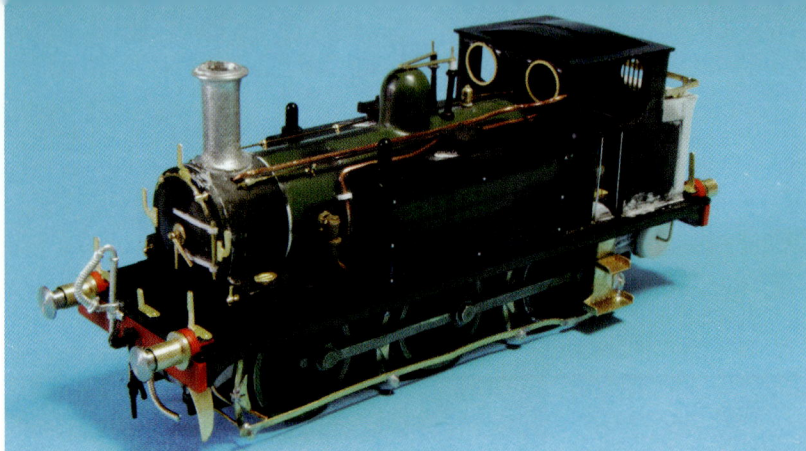

With all the new parts fitted, the engine is ready for the paint shop. Some parts will be removed before painting, such as the exposed copper piping and buffer heads, so as to preserve their bare metal appearance. The body, cab and chassis will all be treated separately.

CONCLUSION

How successful has this project been? The wheels may still betray the model's origins, but the comprehensive overhaul of the bodyshell and chassis block makes an enormous difference. Total expenditure on aftermarket products amounts to about £40 and, in terms of time, it took me about fifteen hours to complete, plus the time invested in researching the subject. The model performs admirably over universal OO track, as it was designed to do, and the convenience of avoiding the need for building and running-in a new drive system, plus the attendant cost of chassis, wheels, motor and gears (at least an extra £50), leaves me satisfied with the results.

Many modellers are put off by the thought of constructing miniature mechanisms. While such tasks are a natural progression from accurately assembling etched metal components, the mental leap can seem daunting, but this is the ideal sort of project through which to practise a wide range of skills and techniques that will enable you to go further in future.

When compared with the image of the 'Terrier' as it came out of the box, the amount of work visited upon the model can be appreciated. The new brake gear and chassis fittings add refinement to the underframe and take attention away from the wide wheel profiles.

Fixing the bare copper pipes after painting keeps their realistic appearance and the various flanged joints in the pipes (see Chapter 8) look effective, the plastic being touched in with metallic paint. The fully fitted-out cab (see Chapter 9), uniquely shaped bunker and individual rivet details all play important roles in the upgrade of this delightful little model.

CHAPTER 11

Superdetailing: Part 3

In this final instalment of superdetailing projects, the aim is to spruce up a number of underframe features, carry out some minor conversion work and see what can be achieved when using some of the cheaper, 'junior' products available. This latter task is one that will put our practical skills to the test.

CYLINDER ISSUES

Let's begin by looking at a few possible tweaks to a locomotive's cylinders, the front aspects of which are sometimes modified to allow for the model's reliable use over sharply curved track. A couple of pertinent examples are a pair of Great Western engines in the Hornby catalogue: the '28xx' 2-8-0 and the 'Grange' 4-6-0. Both of these locomotives carry the typical Swindon design of low-slung cylinders, set with the piston rods working horizontally and in line with the centre of each driving wheel.

The size and position of the cylinders not only meant that the real GWR engines were restricted as to which routes they could safely traverse without striking platform edges, but also, in miniaturizing the design, Hornby has been forced to mould the inside edge of the cylinders with pronounced cut-outs to permit the leading pony truck or bogie to swing from left to right around curved rails. Both the 'Grange' and '28xx' are specified by Hornby to be suitable for a minimum radius of 438mm (or Second Radius under Hornby's track system), but if, however, your layout is fairly straight and equipped with medium-radius points, there should be no

reason why these compromising details cannot be corrected, or, at the least, refined.

Etched covers are available for different cylinder types, particularly in the Comet Models range, within which packs of white-metal cylinders are complemented by a set of etched nickel silver components, plus some cast relief valves where appropriate. These cylinder kits are intended for use when constructing a new brass chassis and valve gear, but are available separately for a relatively modest cost. Simply taking the cover components, filing the edges smooth and fixing over the flattened plastic mouldings is all there is to do in some cases. Moreover, each pack can often yield enough parts to treat two engines and the 'Grange' treated here has gained a pair of etched covers left over from a kit designed for a different engine altogether and, apart from needing some areas filling, the diameter was virtually perfect. The original moulded relief valve was sliced off with a sharp blade before the covers were glued back in place, along with central rod covers cut from plastic rod.

A cheaper alternative is to make your own covers using thin plastic card (0.010in) and a compass cutting tool, available from art shops. Just discern the diameter required, set the cutting tool accordingly and apply light pressure over several revolutions until the plastic has been cut through. File the model's cylinder cover face with a flat file to provide a perfectly flat and clean surface and glue the new cover in place. If some degree of extra lateral movement is needed for the front wheels, the new parts can be shaped to suit, customizing the amount of material cut out for the purpose. Swapping the leading wheels for a finer profile, such as has been mentioned previously, will mean that less material will need to be removed, particularly where the '28xx' is concerned, as this model's standard wheel set boasts huge tyres in comparison to a pair of Gibson wheels.

Hornby's GWR 'Grange' features cut-outs in the front of the cylinders, essential to permit the front bogie to cope with tightly curved track. However, this can detract from the model's appearance and, if the need for this lateral movement of the bogie is not essential – for layouts with gentle curves – the cylinders can have full covers applied. These etched nickel-silver discs were left spare from a Comet pack of LMS cylinders, but, with a little filler and fettling, they proved just the job.

After preparing the surface, the new discs can be added. The moulded relief valve was salvaged by slicing it off as cleanly as possible with a sharp blade, before refixing it to the new cover. The central rod cover is just a length of plastic rod.

Instead of buying a Comet cylinder kit just for the covers, you could always make your own from scratch. The Hornby '28xx' is another type with the cut-out cylinder fronts and, by using a compass cutting tool, some 0.005in plastic card can be cut to the appropriate diameter and fixed in place. Don't forget that the new covers can always retain some degree of cut-out if necessary, but the extent can be tailored to suit your own needs.

SPEEDOMETERS

Despite railways having long been governed by speed limits, locomotives only began to receive speedometer equipment towards the final few decades of steam power. Special dynamometer cars had to be hauled in order to measure such things accurately, drivers usually ascertaining their steed's progress by the use of a pocket watch, observation of the line-side quarter-mile posts and mathematics.

As British Railways moved towards a 'modernized' network, issues of safety and punctuality meant that it became advantageous to set about fitting passenger and mixed traffic engines with some form of speed indicating device. Such fittings became common, although by no means universal, from the mid-1950s onwards and usually consisted of a disc-shaped device, suspended from the running plate and powered by a short crank derived from the coupling rod of one of the rear driving wheels. This disc contained a dynamo that, as the wheels turned, created an electric current and this registered the engine's speed via a calibrated gauge inside the cab. The visible linkage between wheel and running plate followed a common pattern across most of the fleet, only the ex-GWR and early BR Western Region engines having a different design.

In model terms, some r-t-r locomotives come ready fitted with speedometer units where appropriate but, if renumbering a particular machine or forward-dating a model in terms of livery and details, adding a suitable 'speedo' may be necessary. Besides, those units fitted to Hornby models consist of fine lengths of flexible plastic wire that may be very durable, but do not entirely capture the character of the real thing. Cast white-metal and brass components are available for the standard BR pattern and these each require an extra crank to be added to the wheel's centre. Such cranks can be obtained from Craftsman Models or, alternatively, fabricated from scraps of 0.010in-thick brass or nickel silver. Depending on the model, it may be possible to glue the 'big end' of the new crank to the top of a crankpin bolt as seen on the 'Duchess' (*see* Chapter 9), but make sure that the 'little end' sits directly over the wheel's centre.

Fix the casting to the underside of the running frame, creating a small bracket or wire dowel, if necessary, to achieve a strong joint. The speedometer unit should then hover just above the 'little end' of the crank, in line with the centre of the wheel, with just enough clearance to allow for any side-play in the axle. Note that other than on ex-GWR or BR WR engines, the 'speedo' was mounted on the left-hand side (as looking forward from the cab). The Western was a right-hand-drive railway, so speedometers on its fleet were fitted on the right.

Speedometers were a relatively late addition to British steam locomotives and were not universally fitted. If they were installed, however, they usually followed the same pattern of fixing to the rear coupled wheel on the driver's side. This cast white-metal speedometer drive is from the Comet range and requires an extra crank to be fixed to the wheel's crank pin, centred over the axle. The 'speedo' is then fixed to the underside of the running plate and hovers just above the crank, allowing it to rotate freely.

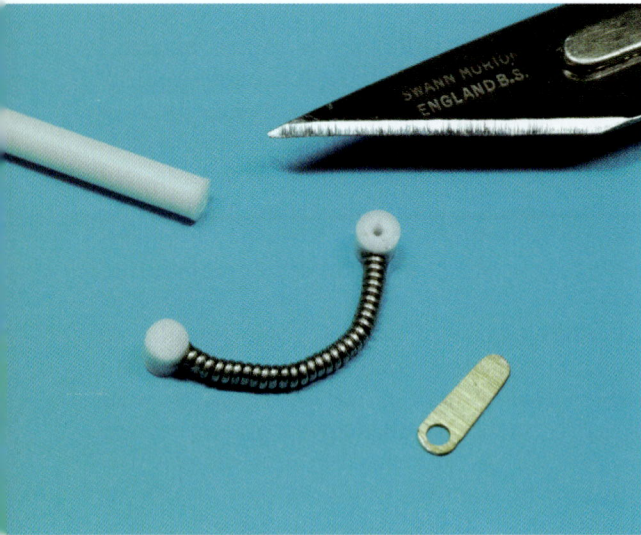

As usual, scratch-building a suitable component will prove cheaper and, using a length of wound steel guitar string and two sections of plastic rod, a convincing representation of the ubiquitous BR speedometer can be created.

Wherever appropriate, r-t-r models often come with speedometer drives in place, albeit in varying degrees of authenticity. Hornby's rendition on the BR 'Britannia', for instance, employs a length of fine plastic wire and, although proving quite durable, does not really capture the essence of the real thing.

Drilling one of the bosses of the speedometer to take a short brass wire dowel will provide a better fixing for the unit to the running plate, with a corresponding hole being drilled into the latter as well.

APPLYING THE BRAKES

Plastic brake rod arrangements are common to all r-t-r products, as metal components are deemed too risky in terms of the likelihood of short circuits. However, with careful installation and handling of the model in use, there should be no problems in fitting fine-section etched metal parts in place of the heavy plastic. Not all of the brake gear may need upgrading, the comprehensive work visited upon the 'Terrier' in Chapter 10 being quite a rare necessity (thankfully!).

Returning to the Brassmasters detailing kit for the Bachmann 'Jinty', as mentioned in Chapter 9, the pack also provides a set of longitudinal brake rods that can be fixed to the original plastic brake shoes and hangers. By drilling through the lower bosses, brass wire can be fed through and, whilst forming mounting points for the actuating rods, also go towards adding some authentic cross shafts. An operating arm and linkage are also provided to sit under the cab – the whole assembly moves the steel block chassis into another dimension of realism. Etched frame extension overlays complete the chassis upgrade, with integral guard irons that can be bent to shape before fitting. These parts also look great and incorporate various runs of half-etched rivets that are gently punched into relief from the underside with a sharp point.

A different option concerns the use of one of the general detailing resource packs in the Mainly Trains range, namely the pack of etched nickel silver brake rigging (ref. MT186). A raft of straight brake rods are provided in multiples of each length, a choice of 6ft to 9ft being supplied in 3in increments. Other useful parts include parallel and tapered cross shafts, cranks and adjusters. By choosing the appropriate lengths of rod and fixing mounting dowels of brass wire into the plastic shoe hanger bosses, the new parts are simple to fit, only the end with the adjuster needing a spot of trimming and soldering (or gluing). Adding a set of these parts to a Bachmann '57xx' certainly enriches the underframe of this model.

Upgrading plastic brake rods is a useful way of adding extra realism to the underframe area, particularly where smaller engines are concerned. The comprehensive detailing kit for the Bachmann 'Jinty' 0-6-0T contains replacement etched nickel-silver actuating rods that require wire dowels to be inserted into the lower bosses of the brake shoe hangers, after the plastic rods have been gently pared away. These must be drilled (to 0.4mm) with care to prevent the delicate plastic parts from being damaged.

Once set in place and checked to allow clearance for the wheels and coupling rods, the new brake rigging is a huge improvement over the heavy plastic moulding.

The wire mounting dowels also act as authentic cross shafts, linking brake hangers on both sides of the chassis and the completed set-up, once the glue has set, is quite strong. Also provided in the Brassmasters kit are suitable parts to make up the crank levers linking the rods with the engine's brake valve. The kit's instructions are thoughtfully produced and well illustrated.

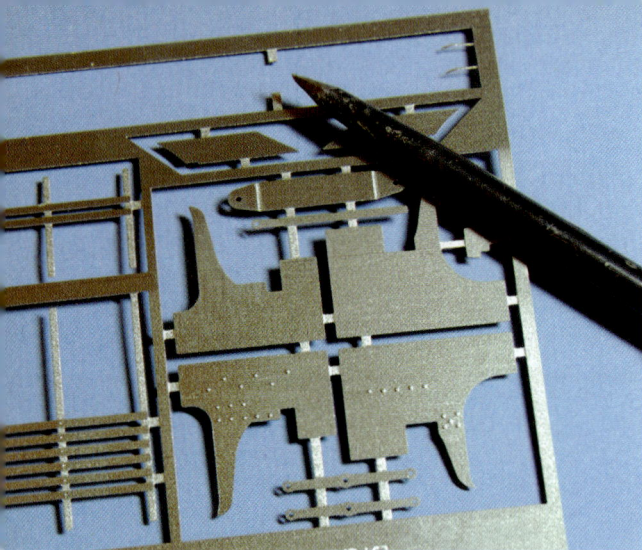

To complete the chassis detailing, the kit offers a set of frame extension overlays, incorporating half-etched rivets that should be punched through from behind before fitting. The guard irons also need folding to shape.

Enhancing brake components doesn't always require the resources of a specific detailing kit, as the work on this Bachmann GWR '57xx' illustrates. Using a pack of etched brake rigging from Mainly Trains, suitable lengths can be fitted between each brake hanger using a similar wire dowel method. At the cab end, fit one of the various adjuster components, studying the prototype to discern the appropriate arrangement.

Once primed and painted, with a little weathering added to blend the new parts with the rest of the locomotive, the results speak for themselves.

BOGIE UPGRADE

We've talked about upgrading the leading, non-driving wheels of a steam locomotive to refine the characteristics of the front end, but what about the bogie itself? Etched brass bogie units, sold as separate items from locomotive kits, are straightforward to assemble as long as you're okay with a soldering iron. Certain models will benefit greatly from a new bogie, not least the Hornby LMS 'Princess' or 'Duchess' classes. A look at the comparison photograph of the two 'Princesses' shows the difference that this modification can make, although adding some extra ballast to the front of the bogie will help to keep the leading wheels on the track.

As with many such modifications, a new bogie will undoubtedly mean the loss of the coupling mounts as supplied for tension-lock couplings. However, when dealing with a loco such as a 'Princess', having any coupling at the smokebox end is pointless, as these machines virtually never worked tender first. If a coupling is desired, the benefits of replacing the bogie have to be weighed against the difficulty of improvising a replacement mount. Never discount the possibilities of modifying a kit or using aspects of it to enhance the existing component: one of the main benefits of the new bogie is the superior aspect offered when looking at the engine side-on, the Hornby casting being too shallow with a large gap between it and the lower edge of the frames. Therefore, a possible solution to retaining the original bogie is to file the sides of the casting square before fixing the etched side overlays from the Comet kit, suitably modified to fit.

A real locomotive's leading bogie is much more than just a solid block of steel, as portrayed on some r-t-r models. This short wheelbase, double-framed unit was under repair at Carnforth in 2008 and shows well the slender frames, horizontal bearing plates and, just visible, is the upturned leaf spring between the outer and inner frames.

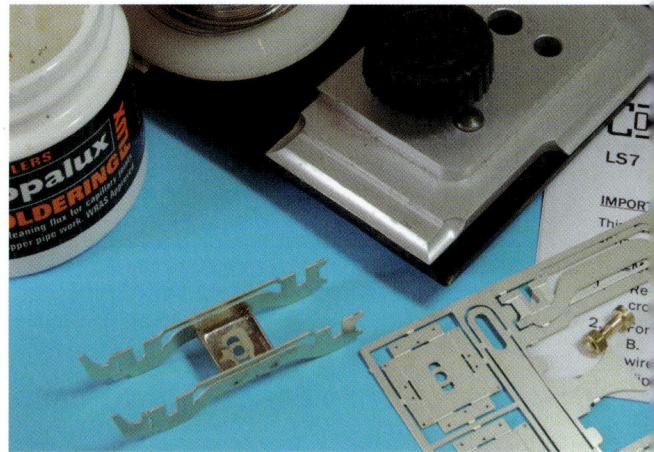

The Comet bogie kit (ref. LS7) is suitable for LMS Pacifics with a wheelbase of 7ft 6in, which includes both the 'Princess' and 'Duchess' types, and can be built to OO gauge or either of the finescale alternatives of P4 or EM. Begin assembly by folding up the main stretcher, checking that the sides and cross members sit at right angles. A little solder inside the fold lines will keep it rigid.

The Hornby LMS 'Princess' takes only a few minor tweaks to produce a truly impressive model, but it is let down by the functional front bogie casting (rear). The loco in the foreground, however, has received a Comet etched bogie kit and, despite retaining the original wheels, the difference in appearance is marked.

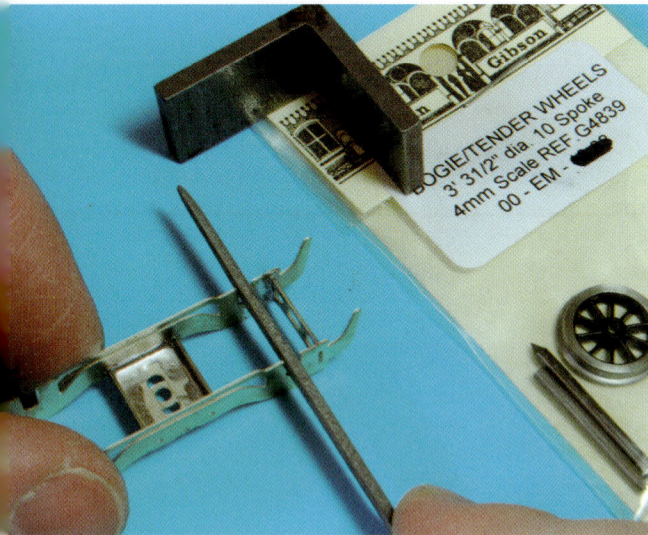

Fit the OO gauge stretchers to the front and rear, noting which way up the parts should face and, with the sides now feeling sturdy, fettle the hornways to allow an easy – but not sloppy – fit for the axles.

With short lengths of wire fitted as a guide, add the side overlays, checking for correct alignment before clamping and soldering.

The axles are retained in the bogie by adding lengths of wire through the holes provided and the front guard irons should be formed to an appropriate shape to align with the tops of the rails. The swing link provided with the kit is ideal for fitting the unit to the Hornby 'Princess' or 'Duchess' models, a washer being soldered at the appropriate location to form the mounting point, having folded the link to suit.

Also from Comet is this bogie kit for LMS 4-6-0s, such as the ex-Mainline 'Jubilee' seen here. The bogie has been mounted in the same way as the original, utilizing a nut and bolt with a spring added to aid road-holding. Adding a finer bogie to any model results in a loss of ballast over the front axles, which can cause problems on tightly curved (or poorly laid) track, so be warned. However, fixing some small pieces of lead inside the frames of the bogie, wherever possible, will improve performance.

Portraying a minor variant within a locomotive class is a way of achieving a unique model that probably won't feature in an r-t-r range, or at least for the foreseeable future. The Bachmann 'B1' on the left has had numerous alterations to the smokebox door to represent a later-build example. Note the different strap hinges, footstep and relocated number plate. The electric lamps and generator, with attendant cable conduit are also new additions, along with a scratch-built AWS plunger, just visible behind the coupling. Viewing next to a 'B1' straight from the box provides a stark comparison.

A MINOR CONVERSION

How often does an r-t-r manufacturer offer every conceivable variant of each locomotive type that it produces? Especially when that would mean subtle, but expensive, changes to tooling and the creation of various extra components? Take the LNER 'B1' for example: such a large fleet of locomotives, constructed at various works, naturally contained some detail differences between batches. One very visual disparity could be found on the front of the smokebox door of some later-build machines, where the hinges and smokebox number plate followed a different arrangement to earlier batches. Additionally, the profile of the door was also slightly more convex and the overall diameter also differed.

Bachmann's 'B1' offers only the original pattern of smokebox door, so if a chosen prototype falls within the bracket of those later machines, the only option is to perform a little

surgery. Such a job can be classed as a conversion project, albeit rather minor, that is, we're not talking about taking one class of locomotive and butchering it to produce another, vaguely similar type that isn't available r-t-r. Indeed, such extreme conversion projects are deserving of a book of their own.

However, producing class variations that haven't been – and are unlikely to be – catered for by Bachmann or Hornby, such as the 'B1' already mentioned, requires nothing more than the skills and techniques already described. Illustrated here is a straightforward conversion of an LMS 'Jinty' 0-6-0T that consists of removing from the Bachmann model the various accoutrements that hint at vacuum-creating mechanisms: the ejector on the side of the boiler and the bufferbeam-mounted pipes.

In choosing a suitable 'Jinty' to recreate, I found a rather nice image of 47629 in use as a yard shunter near Derby station in the early

1960s, clearly showing the lack of any vacuum brake gear. This loco also sported one of the six-bar coal rails atop the bunker, as opposed to the twin-bar rail with which the Bachmann model is supplied. Happily, the Brassmasters detailing kit that had been obtained to spruce up this model's finer points also includes a choice of etched coal rails to suit both two- and six-bar varieties.

Another aspect of the real 47629 that varied from the Bachmann product is the provision of flat-section coupling rods. Although the Brassmasters detailing kit includes a choice of replacement coupling rods, these are designed for use with replacement wheel sets, should it be desired to change the gauge or simply to upgrade the wheels to a more finescale specification. For my purposes, I deemed it sufficient to modify the existing rods by flooding the fluted section with solder and this has proved more than satisfactory.

Another variation from the standard Bachmann specification that my chosen prototype contained was the larger, six-bar coal rail around the bunker. The Brassmasters detailing kit for the 'Jinty' includes just such a component, which requires folding to shape before fitting in place.

The LMS 'Jinty' 0-6-0T was a type built in large numbers (422) over seven years and spread over various works, including outside contractors. Varying traffic requirements led to the need for a range of specifications and this illustrates why not all 'Jinties' were the same. However pleasing the Bachmann model may be, it only caters for certain versions of the prototype and, for those wanting a little variety, a minor conversion project is the answer. I wanted a steam brake-only example, so removed all traces of vacuum-brake equipment, most notably the ejector on the side of the boiler, making good any holes that were left.

With a little persuasion, the original moulding can be pulled out of the bunker and the new part slotted into the existing mounting holes. Check that it sits square and level before the glue sets.

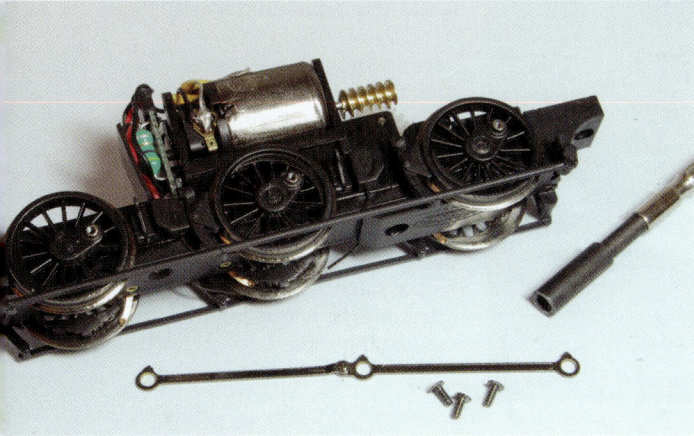

A slightly more testing aspect of the portrayal of my chosen 'Jinty' was the fact that 47629 carried flush-sided coupling rods as opposed to the fluted variety on the Bachmann model. A fairly simple solution was devised, requiring the rods to be removed, using a small box spanner to unscrew the crank pins.

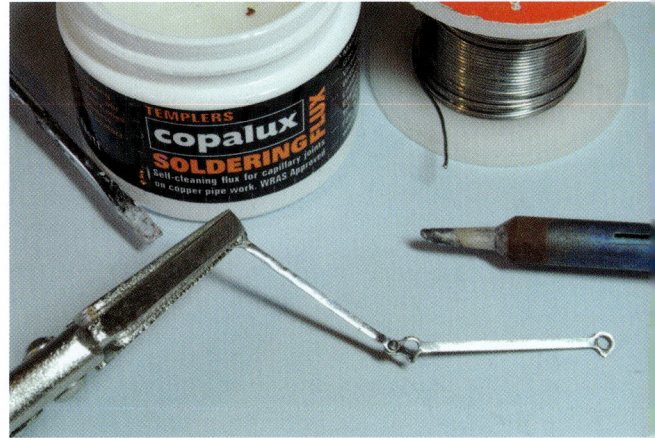

After burnishing thoroughly with a glass-fibre scratch brush to remove any dirt, grease and oil, plus the chemical blackening agent applied in the factory, the rods were wiped with a little white spirit and left to dry. The recessed sections of the fluted rods were then flooded with solder, using a little flux paste to help it flow across the area. Held securely in a spring clamp, an 18 watt iron sufficed for the job and the solder was kept well away from the crankpin holes and the articulated joint.

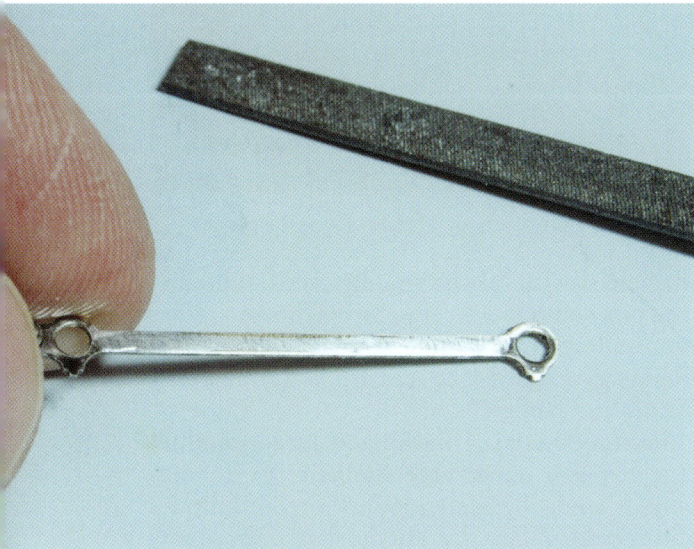

Once the solder had cooled, the faces of the rods were filed flat and polished with abrasive paper until smooth and free of scratches and tool marks. By adding enough solder in the first place, there should be no reason to have to fill any gaps. Clean the rods of any flux residues and the crankpin holes of any filings, then refit the rods.

With all the appropriate parts from the Brassmasters kit fitted and a new length of handrail added to the boiler in place of the vacuum ejector, the new additions can be given a light brush of primer before the top coats are applied.

A suitably weathered finish not only blends in the new components and the modified connecting rods, but also portrays the real 47629 as it appeared in the photograph by which I was inspired. After applying the coats of 'dirt' from an airbrush, a tiny drop of light model oil was applied to the crankpins to relubricate the connecting rods.

A relatively minor conversion job has produced some welcome variety to my fleet of 'Jinties'.

BUDGET RANGE POTENTIAL

Both Hornby and Bachmann have added so-called budget ranges to their product lines, aiming to tap into the beginner/train set market. In the case of Hornby's Railroad range, certain products that may have been around for a few decades, such as the 'Jinty' and original, pre-high-specification 'A3', have been repackaged, shorn of any delicate fittings and retailed at lower prices. The Junior branch of Bachmann, however, uses a selection of small 0-6-0 steam and diesel shunters, all sharing a common chassis and, as licence holders of the global 'Thomas' brand in the United States, some of these models bear a startling similarity to certain famous characters, without the smiling faces, naturally. It makes commercial sense for Bachmann to get extra mileage out of these toolings and, for the European market, the engines carry fictional liveries and names.

Featured here is a Bachmann Junior product that carries a remarkable similarity to Thomas himself and, by drawing on the techniques of superdetailing, this model has been transformed into a believable, albeit fictional, industrial shunting locomotive. The power unit may not be top of the range, but it is a five-pole, skew-wound unit and gives a relatively smooth performance. With adequate ballast added to the bodyshell, the diminutive motor still packs a decent punch.

LEFT: Another prospect for the Bachmann 'Jinty' is conversion to the Midland Railway '2441' class, on which the 'Jinty' was based. A shorter smokebox, taller side tanks, smaller bunker and the remains of condensing equipment (the vent pipes emerging from the tanks) are some of the more visible modifications.

RIGHT: The recent growth of the 'budget' lines of r-t-r makers provides the modeller with some interesting possibilities. Compare the Hornby Railroad 'Jinty' to the Bachmann model, the former dating back to the days of Tri-ang and, although the exterior needs some enhancement, the fitting of the virtually indestructible X04-type motor (designed for use in reconnaissance cameras on RAF bombers during the Second World War) means that the mechanics of the thing are certainly reliable. Bachmann's Junior line also offers decent motors and wheels with basic bodyshells that can be improved.

LEFT: This Bachmann Junior 0-6-0T looks familiar and, in the USA would probably carry a cheeky face on the smokebox, blue paint and a No.1 on the tanks. With Hornby holding the 'Thomas' licence in Europe, however, Bachmann is utilizing the same toolings to address the market for beginner's train sets and the various diminutive shunters have great potential for the modeller, particularly in terms of industrial and freelance subjects.

RIGHT: After complete dismantling, various facets can be remodelled such as the smokebox front (a Gibson casting designed for a Midland Railway loco) and chimney, dome and safety valves all replaced. For some reason, the front bufferbeam of this particular model is set at the wrong height, so a wedge of Milliput and plastic card will correct this and change the character of the front end to a more 'industrial' aspect.

I chose to cut away the large bunker top, but this revealed that the cab rear plate was too short, so a patch of black plastic card fills the void and a shelf has been added for the coal to sit on. The Junior range all feature solid windows that must be drilled out and filed to shape, or, in the case of the front and rear spectacles, reamed to the final size. The cab doors were modified in height, as well as having the top edges tapered with a file to give the impression of thinner material. To accommodate a roof ventilator, a hole was drilled and filed to a square shape before the etched overlay (Mainly Trains pack MT256) was added and a spare coal rail from a Brassmasters 'Jinty' detailing kit was modified to fit. Note the roof guttering, improvised from thin strips of electrical insulation tape.

Other typical fittings include handrails, tank filler hatches and vent pipes, boiler wash-out plugs, a vertical whistle (Stanier pattern no less!), lifting lugs and fire iron brackets, most of which were either scratch-built or found in the scrap box. Strips of insulation tape have been used again, this time to form boiler bands.

RIGHT: The rebuilt front end has also gained an inspection cover for the inside cylinders, complete with chequer plate foot-boarding. Turned-brass buffers with etched backing plates (A1 Models), coupling hook, lamp brackets (Mainly Trains) and individually applied rivet heads, courtesy of a Nutter tool, finish things off, giving the engine a more purposeful aspect.

LEFT: The arrangement of the internal components had to be redressed as the cab had been home to the array of resistors that served the motor. A bit of trimming and relocation freed up the cab for a representation of the firebox backhead, salvaged from a Dapol plastic kit for a GWR Prairie tank, with the addition of etched controls from another Mainly Trains detailing pack (MT227).

LEFT: In addition to brass footsteps and cast injectors, the chassis received frame extensions of plastic card to fill the wide voids at either end, incorporating shaped guard irons and rivet detail. A set of etched brake gear (Mainly Trains packs MT175 and MT186) was also fitted, in a similar fashion to that added to the 'Terrier' in Chapter 10, along with sandboxes and pipes.

RIGHT: With a fictitious livery, number and name, this little engine is perfect for an industrial setting such as a dockyard, colliery or factory shunter. Taking the time to consider the location of new parts will be rewarded with a believable model. For instance, a full complement of steps and handrails lead up to the tank filling points and the set-up of brake shoes, hangers and actuating rods looks right.

There is certainly plenty of potential to be exploited in these budget ranges and not only for industrial-themed subjects. The Railroad '9F' may lack the high standard of detail shown on the Bachmann product, but the loco-mounted drive unit is impressive and the Railroad pricing means that it can be obtained for around £40 less. Even adding in a Comet '9F' detailing pack (which is comprehensive) and other various new components, the total cost of an upgrade can still come in at less than the retail price of the Bachmann '9F'. Incidentally, the Bachmann Junior conversion cost about £55 all in, including £25 for the locomotive. I, for one, consider this terrific value, not least as it also provided an interesting and enjoyable project.

As well as providing economical and rewarding projects, converting models such as this offers a viable alternative to kit building. Freelance prototypes allow your imagination to stretch beyond the confines of ultra-authenticity, particularly where livery and names are concerned.

CHAPTER 12

The Tender Trap

Modifications unique to tender locomotives or, to be precise, to the tenders themselves are discussed here and it may be pertinent to begin this chapter by looking at how the tender is attached to the locomotive. Older, tender-driven locomotives are gradually being phased-out in favour of motors fitted within the locomotive, but there has been a recent shift to including space for a DCC decoder in the tender as a way of circumventing space issues inside a narrow boiler. While DCC chip fitting doesn't concern us in this book, the fact that the bypass circuitry is important means that both DCC- and conventional DC-operated engines are now carrying a number of delicate wires between loco and tender.

Various tender-drive models, such as the Hornby LMS '2P' 4-4-0 or '4F' 0-6-0, possess fixed drawbars and a pair of power cables linking the engine's current-collecting driving wheels to the motor. Others, such as the GWR '28xx', are fitted with a hook and pin coupling that also incorporates copper contacts, carrying the power between the two vehicles. This has become Hornby's standard arrangement, although modern-specification products transmit the power in reverse, that is, with the tender wheels being used as auxiliary collectors for the loco-mounted motor. This set-up can have the benefit of virtually all-wheel power collection and provides for smooth and reliable running.

Bachmann has yet to offer tender power collection, although it has played a trump card with the versatile loco-tender coupling fitted on the LNWR 'Super D' 0-8-0. This can be adjusted in length to suit your own personal layout require-

One of the most impressive examples of design innovation over the last few years has been the adjustable loco-tender coupling on the Bachmann 'Super D', allowing the gap between the cab and tender to be tailored to suit the curvature of your layout. The screw and washer, to the right of the tender's leading axle, governs the length of the drawbar and the various wires transmit the power to the DCC or DC bypass circuit in the tender.

ments. Indeed, if you have only very minor curves, the gap between the two units can be set ultra-close. Previously, any potential for choice of coupling gap lay in the drawbar having separate perforations, providing only two options, the shorter of these still resembling a gaping chasm, although permitting reliable use on most layouts.

WATCHING THE GAP

Altering a fixed drawbar can often just be a case of drilling a new mounting hole, having derived the desired gap. However, this could throw up the problem of there being enough material to drill into, or, if only a minor change is needed, the existing hole needs filling in before redrilling. In both cases, it's easier to fabricate an entirely new drawbar from some brass strip, as demonstrated here on a Bachmann Ivatt '4MT'.

Tender couplings with power connections can cause a few headaches if any modifications are made. For example, the 'Duchess' given the Comet detailing treatment in Chapter 9 also called for a new trailing truck kit to be built, which meant the loss of the original tender coupling, along with the extra power collection. This is not always a bad thing, especially if your layout is fitted with 'electrofrog' points, but the added reliability of tender collection is not to be sniffed at. Therefore, with an improvised coupling made up from scrap brass, the power connection is retained by fitting a miniature two-pin plug and socket (also from the Comet range), this being surreptitiously placed out of sight when the engine is in use.

Of course, the Hornby coupling itself can be modified with care and forethought, without upsetting the intended contact arrangement. Illustrated is a Bulleid 'Light Pacific' with the drawbar shortened by drilling a new hole and filing away the excess to form a suitable profile to sit into the chassis. The gap has been substantially reduced, although this does limit the model's 'route availability', being confined to medium- and long-radius turnouts and gentle curves only.

LEFT: Hornby's common tender drawbar arrangement for loco-drive models incorporates a set of fine copper spring contacts to convey electric current from the tender wheel pick-ups to the motor. Shown here is a standard fitting and a shortened version, allowing close-coupling without the loss of the extra power collection.

BELOW: A miniature two-pin connector set can be obtained from Comet to maintain the loco-tender power flow, but this requires a little modification to the wiring. Cut the cables leading to the existing coupling contact points and solder some new lengths of fine wire, protecting the joints with heat-shrink tube or insulation tape. Pass them through a hole drilled into the top of the chassis.

BELOW: After building a new trailing truck for the Hornby 'Duchess', to complement the etched brass frame extensions of the Comet detailing kit (see Chapter 9), the facility for fitting the original drawbar was lost. However, a new coupling was fashioned from scrap brass.

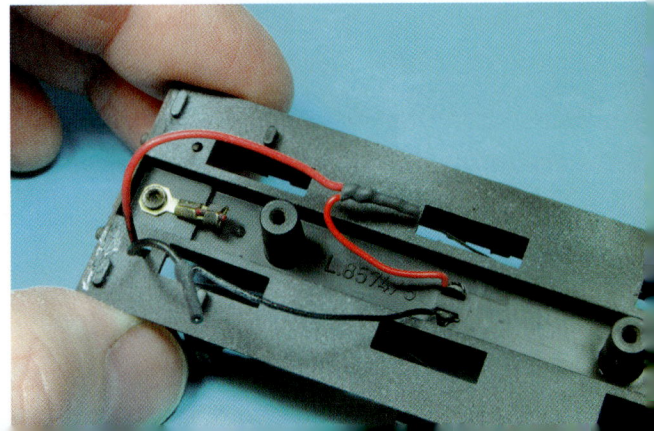

The wires can then be soldered to the two-pin plug, again insulating with heat-shrink tubing. Add a little black paint to the red cable where it becomes visible. The socket can be fixed to the motor's power leads in a similar way, noting the polarity of each wire to match with the tender's. Connect and test.

In some cases, the supplied drawbar cannot be shortened without weakening the material or because there is insufficient room to drill a new hole. Either way, fabricating a replacement is not difficult using strip brass. For the Bachmann Ivatt '4MT', a strip of 0.025in brass, 6mm wide, was marked out and drilled for holes of the same diameter as the original, but 3mm closer together.

An overall profile similar to the original drawbar was achieved with files and the brass cleaned and polished before fitting.

Having decided that the tender and loco could be brought 3mm closer together, that was the difference between positions of the locating holes in the new drawbar from the original. Incidentally, cutting the moulded cab doors in half vertically, then refixing them at an inward angle, creates more freedom for the tender to move around curves unhindered.

The finished result can be discerned in this view. The '4MT' in the background has the factory-supplied drawbar set on the shorter notch, while the new coupling on the nearer machine leaves a much smaller gap.

DETAIL REFINEMENTS

In terms of refining tender-specific details, a few suggestions include opening up water filling hatches or coal bunker doors and adding a missing fire iron tunnel. Steam-operated coal pushers were not widely employed in Britain, the LMS 'Duchess' being one class that received these labour-saving devices. Although a white-metal casting is available from Comet Models, this provides only the large cylinder and piston, leaving the rest of the fittings to be scratch-built. The degree of faithfulness to the real thing is dependent upon how full the bunker will be, as the coal will hide much of the equipment. However, it is an important detail to include.

In certain cases, the r-t-r tender chassis may be deemed inferior, in particular when a high level of detail has been added above the level of the running plate. Shortcomings, in terms of a lack of moulded relief in axle boxes and springs, for example, can often be addressed by cast-metal replacements that are freely available from the likes of Comet, Brassmasters and so on (see Chapter 9). On the other hand, certain products contain perfunctory representations of brake shoes and rigging as well as heavily moulded frames, over-scale wheels and some pretty chunky footsteps.

Comet produces some impressive tender kits (both chassis and bodies), but Mainly Trains also offers a range of attractively priced packages to suit various r-t-r tenders. No modifications are necessary to the existing bodyshell, but the new chassis offers the clean lines and realistic profile of metal frames with sharply cast axle boxes and springs, as well as the full complement of other details such as footsteps, water scoops, brake shoes and rigging. Full instructions are provided and the components are designed with ease of construction paramount. Indeed, as long as the inner chassis and bearings are soldered properly and the unit remains straight and true, there should be no problems with running performance.

Once a tender's moulded coal load has been removed, it may become apparent that a fire iron tunnel has been omitted, such as is the case with the Bachmann BR Class 5 models fitted with BR1F tenders. Plastic strip or card, plus a little filler, will provide the raw materials for a tunnel.

Another modification can be made to any tender that possesses doors into the coal space by drilling out the moulding and paring back to a suitable aperture with a file ...

... before making up some new doors from plastic strip and fixing them in an open position. Some handles from brass wire will add extra realism.

BELOW: Once the new additions have been painted, plus a little weathering, some fire irons fitted and real coal added to the bunker, the Class 5's tender looks much the better for the extra work.

Studying contemporary photographs shows that many engines were seen pottering about in steam days with their water filler hatches left open. So, why not recreate this in miniature? Carefully cut away the hatch lid with a razor or jeweller's piercing saw (as seen here), keeping the moulding intact for reuse.

After dressing the hatch with a flat file, open out the aperture with successive drill bits, rotating them gently by hand until the edges take on a low-profile appearance.

File the base of the hatch flat and drill out two holes for a short wire handle. Fix in place, perhaps resting against another raised feature such as the dome.

After painting and weathering, an impression of water in the tank can be created using Glue 'n' Glaze, or similar liquid glazing products, poured into the aperture and, perhaps, a small puddle.

RIGHT: The 'Duchess' class Pacifics of the LMS were fitted with steam-operated coal pushers inside the bunker, intended to aid the fireman in reaching into his fuel supply. Comet offers a white-metal casting of the main piston unit, but the real thing was much more complex, as seen in this view of *Duchess of Hamilton.* How much of this would be visible – and worth modelling – depends on how much coal you intend adding to the bunker. Note the steam pipe leading along the top left-hand edge towards the operating gear. By the way, the two long rods wrapped in rags are not connected with the pushing equipment, but are connecting rods from the loco's inside valve gear. Photo: Ben Jones

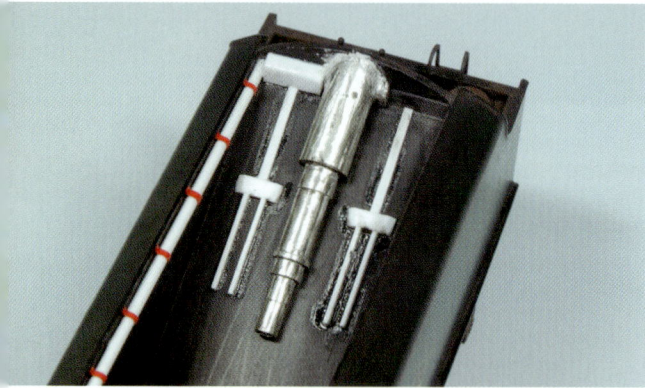

LEFT: Using the Comet casting as a starting point, the rest of the equipment must be scratch-built from plastic strip.

BELOW: With a suitable load of coal to show off the new components, the tender of this 'Duchess' now looks far more authentic.

FURTHER OPTIONS

There is scope for changing the type of tender that accompanies a locomotive and this may be a necessity stemming from changing its identity, or just visiting upon it a minor conversion project. Steam engines often switched tenders during their working lives and did not retain the same pattern every time. Differences may have been subtle or drastic, depending on the period and prototype and, once again, a spot of research will prove useful in determining what, where and when. The Mainly Trains tender chassis kits can also be supplied with plastic bodies, as can some of the Comet kits, providing the chance of your own tender swap.

If your chosen type isn't available by these means, or from Bachmann or Hornby spare parts dealers (*see* Appendix), building an entire kit may be the answer. There is very nearly a kit for every tender type that existed on all but the most obscure locomotive types of the BR era and trawling through the catalogues of Comet or Alexander Models, for instance, should provide a raft of options.

Whatever may be needed to bring a tender up to scratch, it's important that the running characteristics are preserved (or improved), the coupling remains reliable and the level of detail and finish matches up to that on the locomotive.

Improving an r-t-r tender chassis is made easier by building a replacement kit, such as those offered by Mainly Trains, which are designed to be direct replacements and therefore negate any need for modifying the existing bodyshell. This kit, to replace the Bachmann LNER 'Group Standard' tender chassis, is being constructed to upgrade a 'J39' 0-6-0. Follow the comprehensive instructions and ensure that the chassis unit is entirely straight and true; a Hold 'n' Fold tool is just the job for this.

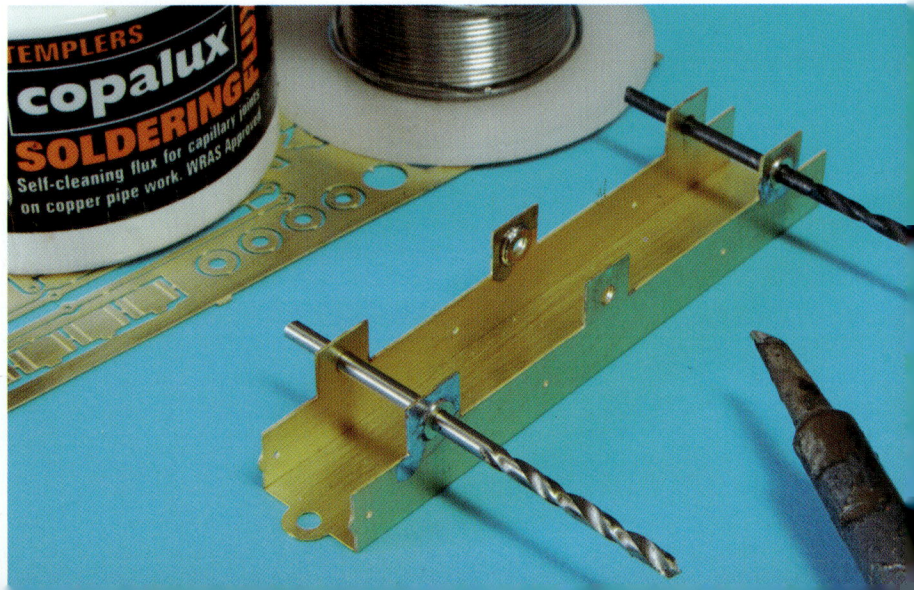

Use a drill bit of the same diameter as the axles to retain the bearing washers whilst soldering them in place and to check true alignment.

Add the wheels and check that they are correctly spaced using a back-to-back gauge. Lengths of 0.7mm wire should be passed through the etched holes to form brake hangers.

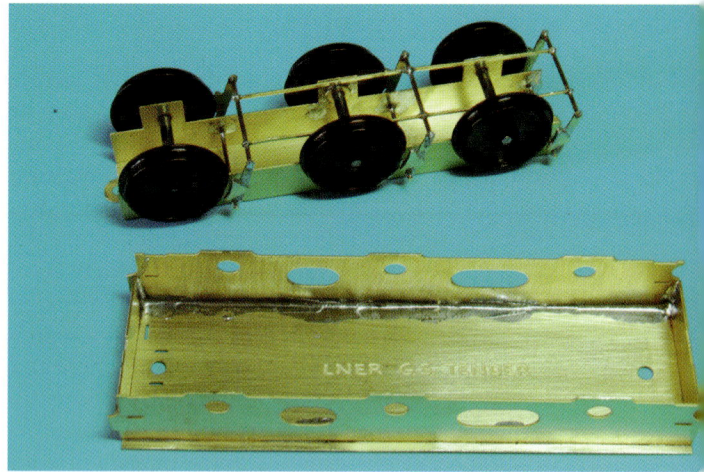

After fitting the brake gear, leaving room for the wheels to operate freely, the outer frames can be assembled.

The mounting points for the plastic body should be fitted and checked for a good fit, along with the loco-tender coupling hook, footsteps and axle boxes and springs (glued). Once complete and tested, remove the wheels again, then prime and paint the chassis before final fitting.

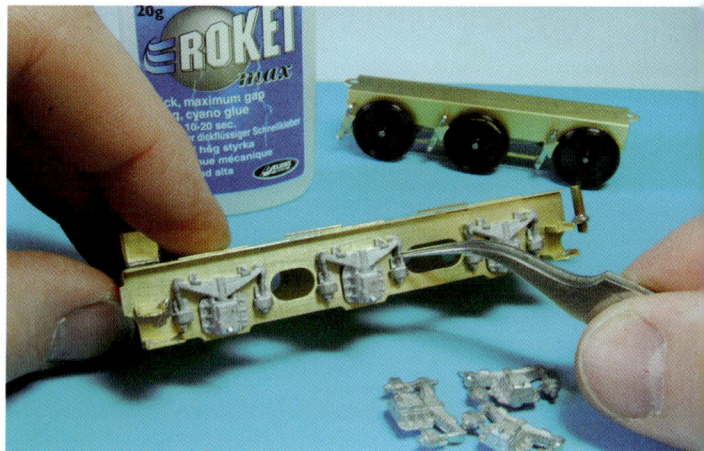

The difference between the original plastic chassis (left) and the replacement brass kit (right) is stark. Not only is there more definition on the cast components, but also the brake shoes are in a more appropriate location and boast a full complement of rigging.

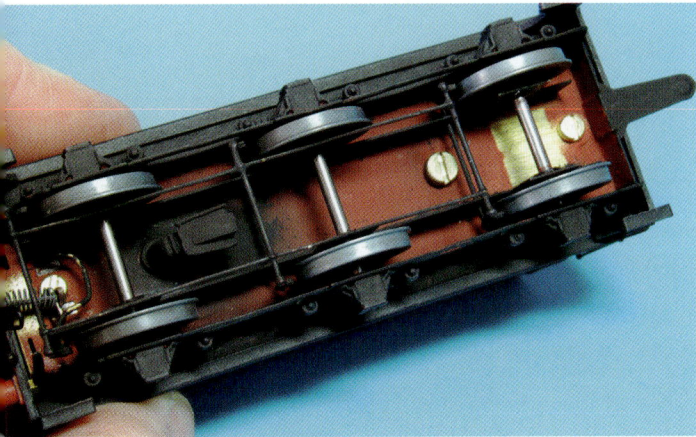

LEFT: This is another Mainly Trains chassis kit, for a Bachmann Stanier 4,000 gallon tender. Note the full brake rigging and shoes in line with the wheels. The rear cross shaft has been shaped to accommodate a working screw coupling drawbar and a water scoop has also been added.

BELOW: It's not only Bachmann models that benefit from a replacement kit. This Hornby GWR 'Castle' tender has been improved substantially by building a superior chassis. At the time of writing, Hornby was planning a timely upgrade to the 'Castle', including a retooled tender. In lieu of that, this model was crying out for an upgrade, not least as the supplied tender wheels looked enormous!

A glimpse at the top of this tender's tank reveals some extra reserves of coal! Note how slim the frames of this tender chassis are, along with the distinctive guard irons and brake rigging, the latter being items that are missing from many r-t-r tenders.

CHAPTER 13

Finishing School

Following each of the detailing and modifying projects outlined in this book, only the most comprehensive of tasks will usually result in the need for a complete repaint. On the other hand, a new livery may be envisaged and the model will no doubt require dismantling to a suitable array of parts to make the job of masking and painting easier. Whatever the level of refinishing required, there are some fundamentals to consider and some rules to observe.

My first recommendation is to practise, practise and practise again. Work on anything from scraps of plastic, old wagons and locomotive bodies; even cast-off kids' toys will suffice to master the techniques of preparation, priming, painting and varnishing. One of the most important skills a model-maker can possess is patience, which can sometimes be put to the test during the finishing process. Waiting for the paint to dry properly before recoating, masking, lining or rubbing down is vital, as is the thorough preparation of all surfaces before commencing work. The facility for swallowing one's pride, admitting a mistake and being prepared to strip the new paint off and start all over again is also necessary, although that bit never comes easily to me!

In my line of work, ultra-tight deadlines don't always allow for such thoroughness in patience and preparation. Being given, say, three weeks to build a complete locomotive kit or to heavily modify a r-t-r model is not conducive to such a methodical approach, especially when facing twenty-four hours in-between coats of primer, multiple paint shades, varnish, lining and weathering. There are times when I find myself silently threatening all manner of violence upon a model as it steadfastly refuses to hurry itself along in the drying process. But, after biting my lip, I always remember that some things just can't be rushed.

PREPARATION

This stage is one of the most important in any undertaking, as an inferior surface will yield an inferior finish. There are no short cuts available to the model painter; no Artex or thick-textured paints to hide cracks and blemishes in OO gauge. Weathering may hide a multitude of sins, but, unless you want your entire fleet to look like an end-of-steam '8F', this should not be treated as a fall-back option. Putting the work in at the early stages will be rewarded with a smoother passage through the later phase of top coats and varnishes.

Before applying any priming coats, the surface of the model should be as clean as possible. If any alterations have been made and abrasives used, not only must the surface finish be smooth, but any traces of dust, filings or scratch brush fibres need to be removed. If possible, wash the model in clean water with a mild detergent such as Cif, which will remove grease and loose contaminants without leaving a residue. Avoid washing-up liquids as these are formulated to leave a shiny film that will impede future coats of paint. Another hazard to the proper adhesion of paint includes traces of flux remaining from soldering and Cif, being an alkali solution, will neutralize any remaining acids. Thorough drying is also important, as trapped moisture will react

Aerosol paints may have their uses but their application to small, intricate surfaces can be a little unpredictable. Dedicated railway colours are offered in aerosol form by RailMatch and Phoenix Precision Paints and these are formulated to the same high quality as the same firms' jars and tinlets. The best results can be achieved by applying several light coats rather than one thick covering; too much paint will drown any small, delicate details. Cans of primer, such as those offered by Halfords, can produce excellent results and form the perfect base for enamel or acrylic top coats.

with both oil- and water-based paints. I usually wrap a model loosely in greaseproof paper and sit it on the top shelf of an airing cupboard (away from fabric fibres) for a few days to be absolutely sure that any moisture has evaporated from all the nooks and crannies. Remember not to leave a plastic model too close to a radiator as distortion may occur.

Priming is another crucial stage and can be used as a proving tool to show up any imperfections in filler or areas where abrasive work has not been as thorough as it should. Sometimes you need a light dusting of white or light grey primer for these areas to become visible, so it's important, therefore, not to drown the model with the initial priming coat. Cans of aerosol primer, as sold in Halfords or DIY stores are okay, but must be used with care as the output of a spray can is much harder to control than, say, a good quality airbrush. Compatibility may be an issue too; these general purpose primers are usually fine when applied over a factory finish, as long as the surface has been rubbed down lightly and cleaned thoroughly, but never spray them over any previously painted surfaces where enamels have been used, as the whole lot will blister into a sticky mess. When in doubt, always test on a scrap piece, just to be sure. Dedicated jars of model primer are available in acrylic and enamel formulas and these are often the safest option and, if sprayed with an airbrush, can produce an excellent basis for the top coats.

PAINT TYPES

Model paints come in three main formulas: acrylics (water based); enamels (solvent based); and cellulose. For the purposes of this book, we shall ignore the latter, as cellulose paints are really only suited to the professional (and perfectionist) painter with many years of experience under his or her belt. They offer ultra-quick drying times, but are not as readily available as enamels or acrylics. Cellulose is a perfect medium for spraying, but, because it dries so quickly, it cannot be brushed and application can be a very fine line between success and failure.

Enamels have been the staple of modellers for generations and, although they may be slow-drying, they invariably produce excellent, durable results without too much expertise being required. Available in a vast number of colours and shades, from various makers such as Revell, Humbrol, Railmatch, Phoenix Precision and Cherry Paints, they can be thinned with either white spirit or fast-evaporation solvents aimed at airbrushing use and available in the same product ranges.

Acrylics, on the other hand, are becoming more popular these days, spreading into Railmatch and Humbrol's rail colour ranges. It's taken me a while to get used to these and, while I still prefer the enamel experience, I'm not averse to using acrylics, especially if I'm working to a deadline, as a number of different colours can be applied and masked over in a day. Correct thinning ratios, thorough mixing, correct air pressure (when spraying) and application technique are essential to gaining quality results. Water is suitable as a thinning agent with most brands, although many will recommend dedicated acrylic thinners, which consist of deionized water with a little alcohol mixed in to aid evaporation. As different brands of acrylics are blended with varying ingredients, I'd recommend using thinners within the same brand as the paints wherever possible. For instance, Tamiya acrylic paints (although not producing rail shades, the general and weathering shades are useful) contain a much higher level of alcohol, so using the right thinner is important to gain maximum results.

Both enamels and acrylics can be brushed or sprayed with equal success, but, again, the vagaries of different brands (and different formulas within the same brand) produces anomalies. I usually spray the main livery colour, then paint the ubiquitous black running plate, smokebox and cab roof by hand. I used to favour Humbrol's No.33 Matt Black for this, but over the past decade the formula has changed and I now find it dries far too quickly. This is not too bad for small areas, but gaining a good brushed finish needs a bit more flexibility. Now, therefore, I tend to use Lifecolor acrylic Matt Black, which produces very satisfactory results when brushed straight from the jar, although I often have to apply two thin layers to gain an even finish. Painting should always be done in a warm environment; cold air is inherently damp and, thus, a cold model will be liable to the formation of condensation. Conversely, warm paint applied in a temperate environment retains a lower viscosity and will therefore flow better during application, whether by brush or spray.

SAFETY NOTES

Health and safety issues seem to permeate our lives in this modern world, but we have to accept that if we are admitting potentially deadly chemicals into our homes, we have to act responsibly. Whatever formula of paint is used, take suitable precautions regarding a supply of fresh air and, if spraying an aerosol or airbrush, always wear a mask with appropriate paint-fume filters, remembering to change them regularly. An extractor booth is also recommended – these are dropping in price these days. If there's one area of modelling where scrimping and cutting costs should not be done, it is here. Don't forget that it's your lungs, nervous system and brain cells at risk here.

Railway modellers are spoilt for choice in terms of authentic rail shades from RailMatch, Phoenix and Humbrol. General colours are also useful and the ranges of LIfecolor, Humbrol, Revell and Tamiya can each offer a wide choice of shades.

Choosing the right thinning agent to suit the various brands and types of paint is important. As paint formulas differ between manufacturers, it's often preferable to utilize the thinner offered by the same brand as the paint in use. For example, although the Tamiya range is classed as an acrylic paint, many general acrylic thinners do not mix well with it, as its alcohol content is much higher than in other water-based paints. White spirit is good for thinning enamels when brushing or spraying, while specific thinners for airbrushing offer rapid evaporation (and faster drying times), but this makes them unsuitable for use when brushing by hand. Cellulose thinner is excellent at cleaning airbrushes, regardless of whether cellulose paint has been used, but other solvent- and water-based airbrush cleaning liquids are available, some in aerosol form.

A high-quality clear coat can make the difference between a successful or an inferior paint job, so choose your varnish carefully. Acrylic formulas offer faster drying times, but they often need more layers to be built up and are not always as hard-wearing as enamels. Humbrol's Clear Cote range combines the convenience of fast-drying acrylics with the resilience of enamels, although quality can be variable. This is particularly the case with the Matt Cote formula, which dries to an ultra-flat finish that is perfect for smokeboxes and interiors, but can lend the livery beneath an odd, greyish sheen. Both RailMatch and Phoenix produce excellent enamel varnishes that may take a few days to cure completely, but do offer superior results. Johnson's Klear, on the other hand, is not a varnish at all, but a clear, acrylic floor polish. When brushed or sprayed it leaves an excellent gloss finish that is more durable than regular acrylics.

AIRBRUSHES

The potential improvement in the quality of finish to your models increases exponentially when using a good-quality airbrush. Brushing by hand takes great skill to get right in such a small scale and uneven and cluttered surfaces, such as to be found on a locomotive, are not conducive to gaining a satisfactory brushed finish. By investing in an airbrush, a small compressor and a moisture trap, the possibilities that arise are astounding.

I must admit that I came to airbrushing relatively late, having been satisfied with my brushwork, refined over years of studying at art school. However, my epiphany came when I borrowed a Badger airbrush and realized – once I'd got the hang of the paint–thinner ratio and the optimum air-pressure range – that I'd been making life so much harder for myself. The increased work rate and superior results made me see the light and, although I do still use a set of high-quality sable brushes for many tasks, the airbrush takes precedence for priming, livery applications, clear coats and most weathering tasks.

There are two basic types of airbrush: external or internal mix. External-mix tools are by far the cheapest and simplest, consisting of a paint nozzle mounted ahead of the air stream and, as the term suggests, sitting on the outside of the tool. In this way, the air and paint are mixed in mid-air, before being thrust towards the model; by moving the paint nozzle closer to the air stream, more paint is emitted. There is no facility for adjusting the airflow, it's either full on or full off, which limits the amount of control you can exert over the paint in terms of quantity and quality of spray.

An advantage of external-mix airbrushes is that they are easier to clean, as the paint is kept outside the tool. Usually retailing for around £20 or under, some of these can be okay as long as you hold modest expectations regarding their performance. Don't think that any airbrush will automatically produce professional results, especially one that costs so little. If you want quality, then you have to be prepared to pay a little more for a precision-made instrument.

Internal-mix airbrushes work in a vaguely similar way as far as the air–paint combination goes, but the mixing occurs inside the tool. Under the 'internal-mix' umbrella come three sub-groups: single action; double action; and semi-double action. With a single-action unit, the paint–air mix adjustment is made by a needle that can be adjusted with a wheel at the rear of the brush. Drawing it further back releases more paint, while pushing it forward reduces the flow. The air pressure is either fully on or fully off, making difficult any adjustment to the paint flow while spraying. Double-action tools, however, allow both the amount of air and paint to be adjusted using a single button or trigger. Semi-double-action airbrushes offer control over the paint flow but not the amount of air.

There are plenty of brands and specifications on the market, for example Iwata, Badger, Premi Air and Paasche. For anyone who might be interested, I use an Iwata Revolution TR2, with a trigger handle, for almost every task, swapping for an Iwata Revolution CR for smaller, detailed work such as weathering.

AIR SUPPLIES

A reliable air supply is an essential element of an airbrush set-up and an electric compressor forms the most convenient solution. Available in varying sizes and specifications, for most hobby work in OO gauge a relatively small, modern desktop unit should suffice. Choosing a compressor with a reservoir tank is preferable, as the air supply is smooth and relatively stable; units that pump air directly to the brush produce a 'pulsing' output that can be difficult to regulate and can make an even finish difficult to achieve.

A pressure-regulator valve is also desirable, though not always essential. My compressor, from Axminster Power Tool Centre in Devon, is probably overpowered for spraying OO gauge models, but it does allow me to spray guitars and small car panels, which is handy. I've jerry-rigged the air valve to allow me some degree of air-pressure control; it is instinctive rather than deadly accurate, but with enough experience, you can usually gain a feel for these things. A new item that has only just come my way is an external MAC valve accessory, in the Iwata range. This allows the airflow to be regulated by means of a small thumbscrew attached to a valve that can simply be fitted between the airbrush and compressor.

Aerosol propellants are, absolutely, the work of the Devil. I've had enough encounters with these things that I find it hard even to look at one without being reminded of the ruinous experiences of times past. Even the large-capacity cans last but a few minutes before freezing up, they emit an unpredictable level of air pressure and are too expensive for what little benefit they offer. Using a spare car tyre is not out of the question, providing you find the right adaptors for your air line, but can you really be bothered taking the spare out of the boot and pumping it up for the sake of a couple of coats of GWR green? A high-quality compressor that will fit on your

Investment in a good-quality airbrush and compressor will immediately repay itself in terms of productivity and soundness of finish. Consider your requirements carefully before choosing a model, and also take into account the reliability and after-sales back-up of the better-known brands such as Iwata, Badger and Paasche. The Airbrush Company of West Sussex (see Appendix) offers a vast range of airbrushes, tools and accessories, as well as expertise across all facets of modelling and hobby work, and can help you to choose the right package. Always use a water trap, wherever you may be working, plus a good-quality compressor with a pressure regulator makes life much easier.

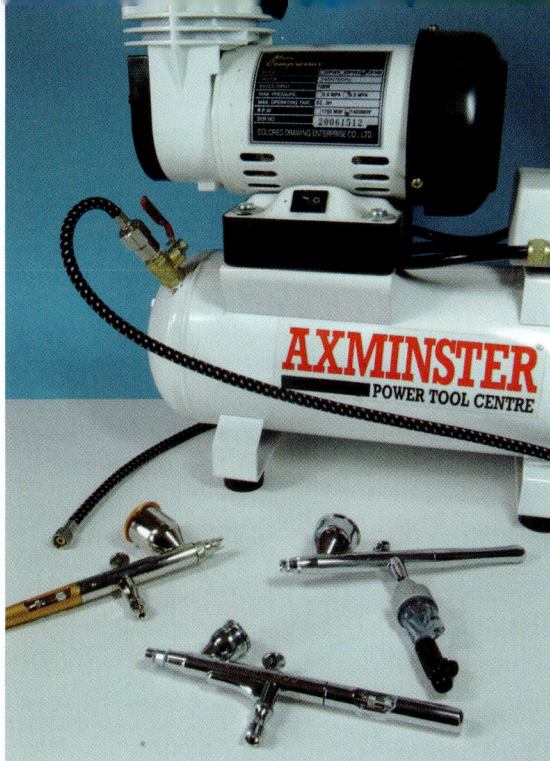

desk, run quietly and smoothly, with a reservoir tank, gauge and pressure regulator, will set you back just a little more than a Bachmann '9F', at retail price. A top-notch airbrush is about the same, although there are a couple of lower-priced Iwata tools about at the moment, for about £80 (2009 prices).

Spraying most model paints requires a fairly low pressure, between 10 and 30psi (pounds per square inch), depending on the type and viscosity of the paint; the thinner the paint, the less pressure is needed. Usually around 15psi is about right for a universal application, but the constancy of the pressure is important and a compressor with a reservoir comes into its own here, especially if fitted with an adjustable regulator. If the pressure is too high, the paint will be hard to control and may be drying before it hits the model, leading to a poor, rough finish. If the pressure is too low, the paint will not atomize properly and, again, an inferior finish results.

Water traps are inexpensive and essential accessories, whatever air supply you may have or what climate you may be spraying in. It's surprising how much water vapour is caught in one of these things, even on a seemingly dry day. If this moisture is not intercepted before it reaches the airbrush, it'll end up in big puddles on your model and necessitate a complete strip-down.

Aerosol cans are fine for primers and acceptable for main livery colours, but, after a few bad experiences, I won't touch them for OO livery work unless I'm desperate. This may have been down to my own errors in application, but I find that they're better suited to large-scale work as the spray pattern is unpredictable. More often than not, too much paint is released for a truly even finish, especially on a surface as complex as a steam locomotive. However, there are certain automotive shades that are dead ringers for railway colours. Ford Burgundy, for example, looks just like LMS crimson to me!

MIXING AND APPLICATION

Mixing the paint correctly is important. There's no hard and fast rule to the paint–thinner ratio, as various brands and formulas react slightly differently. In short, you want the paint to be thin enough to atomize well in the airbrush, but thick enough to adhere to the model properly without running all over the place. My rule of thumb is that, when stirring with a paint spatula, if the paint drops from the tool readily, in self-contained blobs, then it's ready. If, however, the blobs are in the least bit stringy or slow to drop, it's too thick. If it runs off in a torrent, it's too thin. Incidentally, if you've over-thinned the paint, throw it away, as adding more paint won't thicken it again. Add only a drop or two of thinners from a pipette or eye dropper at a time, stir and test for the 'drop', repeating until happy.

When spraying paint, it's desirous to achieve a slightly wet look as it lands on the model. If the paint dries too quickly, the finish will take on the texture of orange peel. Wetness depends on the spraying distance and the air–paint ratio. For livery colours and gloss varnish finishes, spraying should take place in closer proximity than many people realize: around 70–90mm (2.75–3.5in) from the model. Keeping the airbrush moving while spraying is, thus, critical, as is the paint–thinners mix, as too weak a mixture will cause runs. As I said at the beginning, practising is the best way of learning and experience, gained through trial and error, is invaluable.

The order in which the separate livery elements are applied is governed by the need to add top coats over a lighter background. Sometimes, it may be easier to apply certain stages, such as the red of the bufferbeams in the first instance, then mask these areas before adding the overall livery coats. Alternatively, the bufferbeams must be reprimed with a white or grey coat before the red can be added. Masking small areas of a steam locomotive can be awkward, however, as there are very few flat surfaces. Making good use of Humbrol Maskol fluid, Blu-Tack and masking film will help.

Careful and effective masking is as much a part of the finishing process as the application of paint and using good-quality materials will help towards a good-quality result. Rolls of low-tack masking film prove a very economical accessory, especially when working on larger areas, or where intricate shapes need to be formed, such as when masking up the front of an LNER 'A4'. Masking tape comes in various sizes and types, the red roll seen here being a vinyl-backed product from Electrostar that copes well with uneven surfaces as well as being flexible enough to follow gently curving lines. Tamiya tapes come in a handy dispenser and are perfect for general use. Avoid using rolls of decorator's masking tape as even the low-tack rolls can damage a model's surface. Liquid masking fluid, such as Humbrol's Maskol, is invaluable for awkward areas and for sealing the joints of masking tape or film to prevent paint penetration.

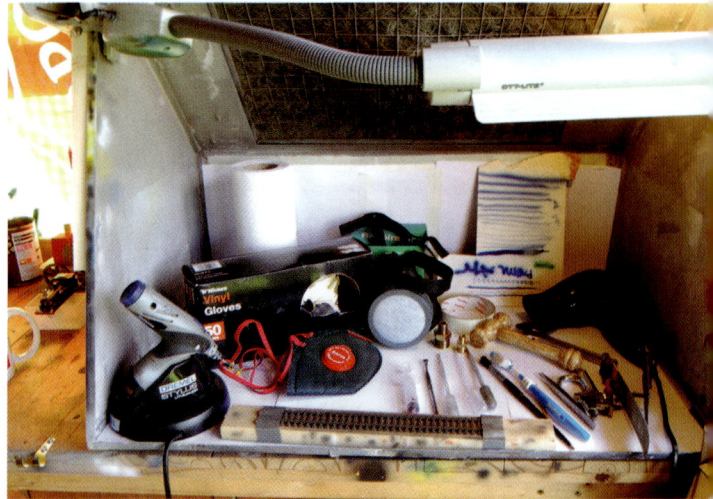

A few specific tools will come in handy during the finishing process, for example a tack-rag and a soft goat-haired brush (for removing dust), a paint stirrer-cum-spatula and spare glass jars for mixing paints. An L-shaped length of stiff wire mounted in a mini-drill makes for a convenient stirrer and a selection of paint handles to hold the model makes life much easier. A fume-extraction booth is essential for safe paint spraying, while working in a dedicated space, such as this corner of a shed, provides plenty of natural light and ventilation, while cleanliness is also important to prevent contamination of wet paint.

ABOVE: Touching in new components is usually achievable without the need for a full, or even partial, repaint. Several light coverings of acrylic primer and top coats, applied by hand, are enough for the modified bufferbeam, leading wheel set and pony truck of this Ivatt '4MT'.

BELOW: Cleaning the model prior to priming is imperative to remove all traces of soldering fluxes, dust and filings, greasy fingerprints and oil. Use a household detergent such as Cif, as this won't leave any shiny residues, then rinse thoroughly with clean water before setting aside somewhere warm to dry out completely, preferably over a day or two, as water trapped inside voids may take a while to evaporate. Try not to handle the model again too much before applying a priming coat, so as to reduce the risk of contamination with grease and oil (from your skin!).

BELOW: A priming coat can sometimes be treated as another stage in the modification process – if considerable alterations have been made, with lots of filling and rubbing down, it's usually only once a coat of flat grey paint has been applied that any remaining scratches, imperfections or tool marks become visible. Be prepared to fill and abrade again until perfect, then repeat the cleaning, drying and priming steps.

If a full repaint is needed, it's often agreeable simply to rub down the model's surface with fine abrasive paper or wire wool (00000grade) to provide a key for the new coats, beginning with primer. Ensure that all factory-printed detail such as lining, names and numbers have been flattened, or else they will show through later. Model paint strippers are available, but they seldom take away all of the factory finish, although the liquid offered by Phoenix will move certain elements if left soaking for long enough. This can be useful in areas that are hard to reach with abrasive, or where the fine detail may be degraded by burnishing. As a means of removing previous attempts at repainting with enamels, model paint strippers are ideal, although they won't work with acrylics. Never use DIY strippers such as Nitromors, as these will devour the plastic as well as the paint.

If only a small area of the model has been modified (or repaired in this case), it may be possible to patch-paint, masking up a suitable area that takes advantage of any natural visual breaks, such as the sides of the cab or individual bands of the boiler.

A light primer coat can be followed by the livery shade. If you possess a good airbrush, once the masking has been removed, the livery shade can then be 'feathered' over the paint 'joint' using a very fine spray. Provided the new paint is a close match to the factory finish, the newly painted area can be blended in convincingly. A coat of varnish over the whole model will unify all treated areas.

As we've seen, many minor modifications to r-t-r steam locomotives involve at least a little work to the smokebox. This can be masked and painted in its entirety to achieve a more convincing finish. Besides, even on the shiniest engine, most smokeboxes were finished in a matt black, so recreating this can be effective.

Even with the best intentions, paint can still find its way underneath an area of masking tape or film. If this happens, using a little T-cut and a cocktail stick will remove any unwanted enamel paint. Acrylics are harder to shift once dry, being impervious to water and thinners. Very light scraping with a sharp scalpel blade usually does the trick, but this takes a little practice.

VARNISHING

Varnishing is an essential preparation step, between a livery application and the addition of decals and lining. As described in Chapter 7, the need for a high-gloss surface before applying water-slide decals is paramount. Acrylic varnishes are available, but I find that these require far more coats to achieve a suitable mirror-like finish than enamel equivalents. Johnson's Klear, on the other hand, may be marketed as a floor polish but it's also a wonderfully effective acrylic gloss varnish and the formula means it's thin enough to be airbrushed straight from the bottle.

As with the initial preparation considerations, dust is the enemy of the clear coat and all precautions should be taken to apply varnish in a clean area and to set the model aside in a dust-free

environment, perhaps under a plastic cover, with enough air to allow the solvents to evaporate. Be aware that enamel varnishes usually take much longer than paint to dry completely.

In terms of a final sealing coat of varnish, the choice of matt, satin or gloss is up to the individual and may depend on whether any subsequent weathering is envisaged. Some matt coats, such as Humbrol Matt Cote, can look a little too flat, with the perception of the livery shades beneath being altered, especially under bright lighting. However, this may not be a problem if a weathering coat is to follow. Speaking of which, an important factor to consider is that some of the weathering techniques that follow in Chapter 14 involve the model's surface being slightly distressed or buffed using T-cut. Either way, a hard-wearing varnish coat is essential to protect any new paintwork (factory finishes are fine), which makes enamel varnishes the favoured medium, left to harden off for at least a few days beforehand.

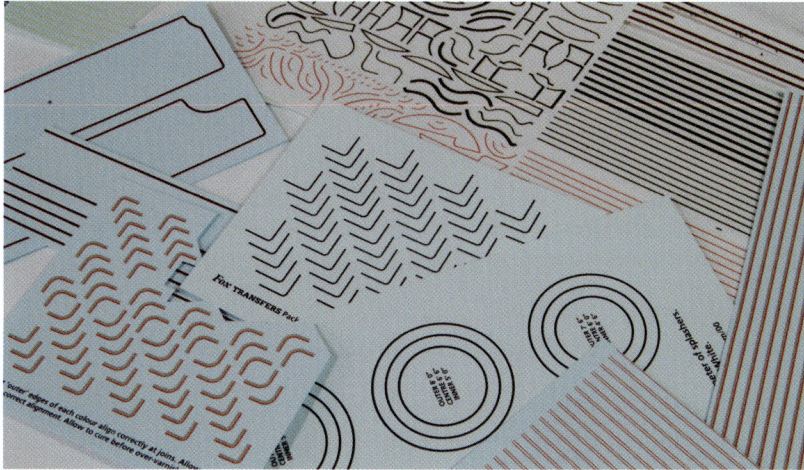

Lining is an integral part of many steam locomotive livery schemes, with only dedicated freight engines receiving plain black. Decals are available in Pressfix, Methfix and water-slide form for a great many lining schemes, from brands such as Fox, Modelmaster and HMRS. These take a lot of the hard work out of the process, although the more complicated schemes involving lining around wheels and underframes can still be very time-consuming.

Careful marking out with a fine chalk pencil before applying any lining will make the job run more smoothly, these marks being washed away later. Add the various corners first, checking with a straight edge that they are aligned properly, then allow time for the water-slide decals to dry out.

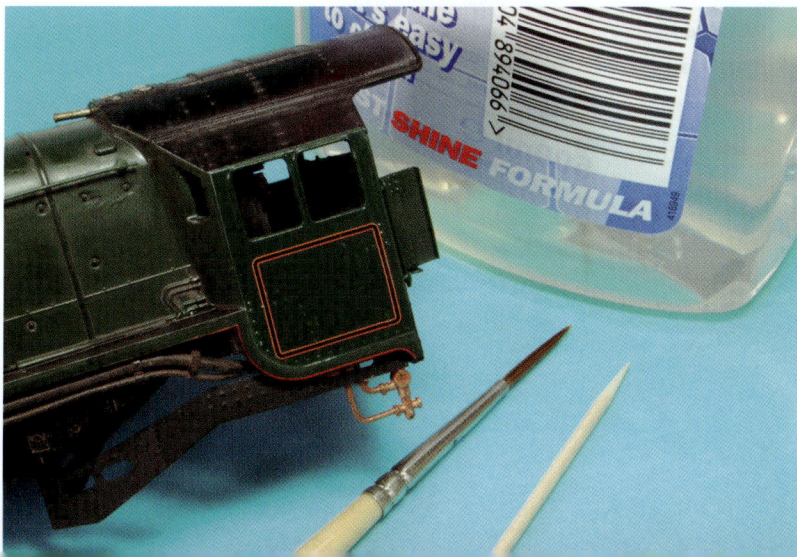

If you're confident that the corners are in exactly the right place, applying a light coat of Johnson's Klear will stop them from moving whilst the straight sections are added. Again, check with a straight edge that all is straight.

This 'Duchess' has received the Wartime black livery of the LMS and the attractive lining was applied using the HMRS pack of Pressfix decals. These were quicker to apply than regular water-slide decals, but, as the variety of shapes and curves did not match all areas correctly, the immovable nature of the Pressfix application method meant that some of the lining joints are not perfect.

More complicated lining can take a few days to apply, such as the LNER Apple Green scheme applied to this model of 60163 *Tornado*. While the water-slide decals were not too difficult to add to the boiler, cab and tender (the pack from Fox offering a comprehensive choice of shapes), the red lines on the chassis proved much harder. In fact, I gave up with the transfers at this point and used a fine brush, as I did for the plain white lining around the edge of the cab.

A sealing coat of varnish not only keeps the various decals safe from damage, but also helps to unite the various shades of paint. A satin coat is usually the most appropriate, as too glossy a shine will give the model a toy-like appearance, while a flat matt finish may change the perception of the underlying colours. The choice of either acrylic or enamel varnish must be considered carefully, because, if any weathering is desired, certain methods of distressing can be incompatible with water-based coats.

CHAPTER 14

Weathering

Before embarking on any degree of weathering, it's important to have in mind what it is that we are attempting to portray. Are we aiming for a full-on, end of steam leviathan that hasn't been cleaned for several years, or an everyday mixed-traffic engine that may not have been polished recently, but is still looking presentable? And then there's the look of a top-link express engine that has been buffed up before leaving the shed, but already gained a small amount of dirt over

To portray 'Britannia' *Oliver Cromwell* in its spruced-up guise as it hauled the final steam service on BR in 1968, it had to be remembered that the engine had been in service for nearly twenty years at that point and, although receiving overhauls, it was never going to look like new, as the (impressive) Hornby model appears straight from the box. A light misting of various 'dirt' shades from an airbrush and some polishing of the green paintwork with T-cut transforms the factory finish, in addition to small patches of grease, oil, soot and brake dust.

the previous hundred or so miles since it began its journey.

Even a buffed-up locomotive will benefit from some degree of weathering. Moreover, the term 'weathering' can sometimes be misleading as it doesn't necessarily mean mucking up a model with layers of grime. It really refers to recreating the look of a railway engine that has been exposed to the elements for either just a few hours or well over a decade. Steam traction is an inherently dirty form of transport and, even in the Victorian and Edwardian period when companies employed armies of engine cleaners, the machines were still prone to soot, ash, oil and grease that would spill out of the chimneys, smokeboxes, bunkers and running gear, as the trains ran through all weathers.

Factory-applied weathering has become a common facet of r-t-r ranges, at least one version of each locomotive type now being offered with a work-stained finish. Although some of these models look acceptable, the one-dimensional appearance of the dirty brown and black paint does not accurately reflect the true nature of dirt accumulation, faded paintwork or oil and limescale stains. Applying a bespoke weathering finish takes time and it is worth considering how and why dirt builds up on specific surfaces more than others before choosing the right technique and material with which to recreate it.

There are many methods and materials that can be applied in the weathering process and plenty of sources of inspiration and instruction. I've gained many useful techniques and learned of interesting products from reading various military modelling magazines and books; this branch of modelling seems to have been very active in distressing and weathering models for decades. Indeed, there are some weird and wonderful ways to add a coating of dirt or portray flaking paint and rusty metal and, as well as proprietary products to help in this task, there are also plenty of DIY solutions; I've even seen Marmite used as a masking medium.

An airbrush, while making the process quicker and offering extra possibilities, is not essential to all weathering techniques. Tamiya pigments, weathering powders, crushed artist's pastels and both acrylic and enamel paints all form part of a wide palette open to the modeller.

One part of any locomotive that would be cleaned regularly is the cab windows and these should be masked before applying any weathering treatments, as clear plastic is difficult to clean without impairing the transparency. Either masking tape or film can be used, but I prefer Maskol fluid, as it is easier to apply and permits irregularly shaped areas to be kept clean, giving the impression that the train crew have just wiped the window, leaving muck in the corners.

A simple upgrade to the texture of a locomotive's finish is to apply a coat of matt black paint to the smokebox. This area was exposed to very high working temperatures and a different grade of paint was often used, invariably offering a flatter sheen than the rest of the engine. Lifecolor acrylic matt black provides an attractive sheen, although it does usually need at least two thin coats; only a single layer has been applied in this view.

Where an airbrush comes into its own is when applying a gentle misting of shades over a model. Here, Railmatch enamel 'Frame Dirt' has been sprayed over the lower areas of the engine and tender, as well as into the coal bunker and across the top of the water tank. Working with the model raised on a small plinth allows better access for the airbrush and permits the model to be rotated without touching it. Treating the front pony truck separately solves the difficult access issue; reaching into nooks and crannies with an airbrush runs the risk of building up an excess of paint in the corners.

To prevent coupling rods and other details acting as stencils on the wheels and frames, it pays to rotate the motion between coats of paint. A 9volt battery is ideal for jogging the motor on a bit when the contacts are pressed against the wheels.

Once the initial misting coats have dried, the enamel paint can be removed from the bodywork, if desired, with either white spirit or T-cut on a cotton bud. Using the latter also allows the paintwork to be buffed up to a pleasing shine (as long as the base colour or varnish beneath is not acrylic). This Hornby 'Grange' came supplied with a factory-weathered finish that I found too flat. Instead, I sprayed a few different shades of underframe dirt to add variety to the chassis and running plate before using T-cut to clean up the body, removing most of the factory-applied weathering too.

After much rubbing and buffing with cotton buds, the surface will begin to take on a convincingly oily sheen, which can then be enhanced with a soft buffing head in a mini-drill. Set the tool to the lowest speed and apply with only minimal pressure, moving the head about constantly to prevent a dangerous build-up of heat. This should remove any excess T-cut and leave a smooth, even finish.

A light dusting of Railmatch 'Roof Dirt' and 'Weathered Black' can be used to layer a general coating of grime.

The cleaning stage can always remain limited to a cab side number or BR emblem, as was the case in real life, particularly into the 1960s as cleaning staff were depleted. Just a little white spirit on a bud will do the trick (if enamel paints have been used), rubbing very gently.

To give the impression of a cleaned area that is once again becoming soiled, simply spray a very fine misting over the area.

I wanted a dirtier finish on this '4MT', so the entire loco was covered in light coats of various shades of 'dirt'. As this Iwata airbrush allows for fine-detail work, the smokebox was given a coat of 'Weathered Black' without the need for masking.

Even the filthiest locomotives possessed a range of shades amongst the layers of grime, often running in vertical streaks, produced by the rain and excess water from filling towers. Again, a good airbrush allows for this to be recreated with subtly different tones.

Brake dust and patches of rust add some relief to the overall grey-brown covering of a working freight engine, such as seen here on a 'Super D'. This effect can be achieved either with an airbrush, weathering powders, or by employing the Tamiya packs of weathering pigments.

To add further realism to an engine's underframe, add a little talcum powder to a mix of enamel or acrylic paints . . .

. . . before applying with a stippling action. The paint and talc will create a wonderful textured effect that speaks of years of soot and ash being trapped in the layers of oil and grease.

This view of a preserved '8F' shows the effects of rain, grease and oil on the paint's surface and the range of textures visible in the overall black livery.

Adding gloss varnish to a mix of paints will impart a greasy finish, as will the use of Humbrol Metal Cote Gunmetal. Building up layers of vertical streaks creates a better impression of accumulating muck and persistent oil leakage.

Tensocrom acrylic weathering agents, from Lifecolor, are also useful for producing realistic effects of oil, grease and limescale staining and are equally suitable for brushing or spraying. These paints are heavily diluted and, when dry, leave just a hint of colour. By building multiple layers and varying the shades a little each time, some very impressive results can be obtained.

MIG weathering powders are aimed at military modellers, but the shades translate equally well to railway subjects and this pot of 'Black Smoke' creates a suitably dusty environment to the cab of this filthy SR 'Light Pacific', plus a little 'Rust' to the tender running plate, applied with a soft-bristled brush.

MIG powders are also perfect for areas of ash staining, such as around the smokebox and 'Industrial City Dust' is just the job. Apply only a little powder at a time, working into any corners before brushing away the excess. Don't be tempted to blow away the dust with your breath, as any moisture will stain the model. Grinding up artist's pastels creates a similar pigment to these powders and offers a wide range of shades for specific tasks.

Leaks of limescale were common on steam locomotives, particularly when working in hard-water areas. Some regions added softening chemicals to the supplies and these could lead to even worse frothing and staining from injection points and wash-out plugs. Tensocrom agents are perfect for recreating this effect, a White Oxide pigment being part of the range.

With the help of some small patches of diluted PVA glue, finely ground coal dust has been applied to the rear of this tender. Using real coal dust and ash, in the same way as weathering powders, can provide some interesting results.

Tamiya offers various packs of weathering pigments, packaged in plastic containers that resemble make-up compacts, each containing three different shades. A twin-ended applicator is included, but I find that a set of cosmetic sponges and foam applicators is better suited to applying the pigments. Used carefully, these applicators can offer similar results to an airbrush in terms of creating streaks and dust deposits.

Areas of flaking paint were common on neglected steam locomotives, particularly around the smokebox, as excessive heat would scorch the paint and cause it to blister. The bare metal would then be prone to rusting and create further loose paint. This effect has been achieved here by painting parts of the smokebox with a mix of rust-coloured paints, with a little talc added for texture. After applying patches of Maskol fluid, the smokebox was painted black and the weathering applied. The Maskol was then peeled off to reveal the 'rust' beneath and some further misting with dirty paint shades tone it all down.

The technique of 'dry brushing' is another important step in the weathering process, serving to highlight any areas of raised or delicate detail. After wiping all but the faintest traces of paint, a shade lighter than the livery colour, from a flat brush (testing on a piece of tissue), lightly brush over the model's surface so that just a hint of the paint is deposited on corners, rivet heads, panel edges and pipes. Particularly effective for bringing out detail on a flat black surface, Humbrol No.53 'Gunmetal' also imparts the look of bare metal, ideal for surfaces that suffer chipped paint such as handrails and footsteps, while using a rust shade is also effective for suggesting where paint has been damaged.

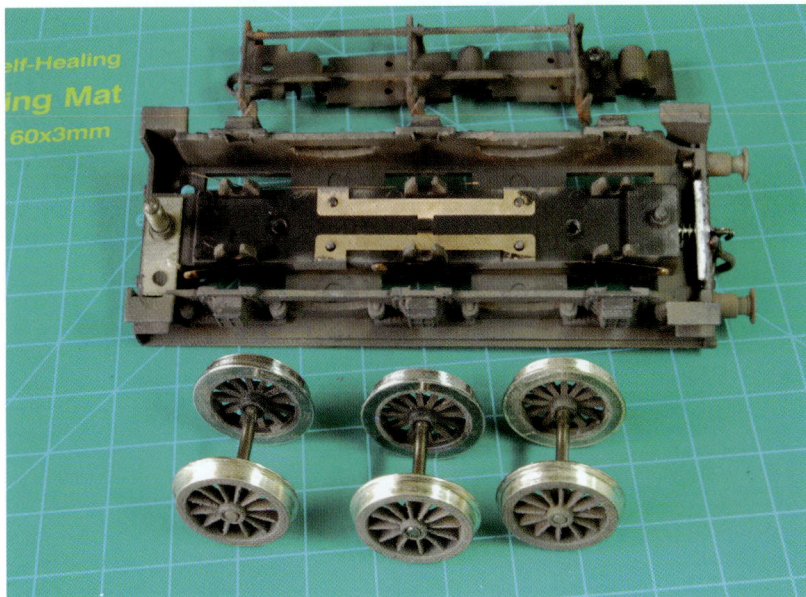

Weathering, especially when applied in quantity, means that all wheels and electric contacts must be thoroughly cleaned before the model can be run. Sometimes it's easier to dismantle a chassis to be able to reach the various parts, such as this Hornby tender underframe. Use fine abrasive paper to clean the surfaces, brushing away all traces of dust before refitting. Some new lubricant may also be needed for the various moving parts and bearing surfaces.

Outlined in this section are a few suggested techniques and materials to obtain a variety of finishes and, while some of them are achieved more easily with an airbrush, it is by no means essential to own one. Weathering has become synonymous with airbrushes in some quarters, but this need not be the case. Although they can be an important part of a modeller's tool kit, they do not offer the only route to obtaining convincing results.

Weathering is a fundamental aspect of all branches of railway modelling and can prove to be the crowning glory of any model, whether it is the only significant modification made to a r-t-r locomotive, or the culmination of a comprehensive detailing job. It may be just a case of adding a little soot and coal dust or creating a filthy, neglected freight machine; either way the processes form a route to creating a more realistic scale model.

Most of the techniques demonstrated (along with those in previous chapters) have been refined over the years through trial and error. Indeed, there are some items of rolling stock in my collection that cause me to wince and, as skills and experience have improved, I've found myself looking back and reworking some of these projects. We're all on a continual learning curve and practice is the only way to achieve competence in anything, so testing out new products and techniques can be done on an old model, or something salvaged from a bargain bin, until you feel confident enough to apply them to a prized locomotive.

Don't forget to clean the tender coupling contacts too.

BELOW: Creating the look of a well-presented, but hardworking, engine can often prove just as time-consuming as portraying a filthy freight mover. This Hornby 'A4' has received an all-over spray of enamel 'dirt' before most of it was removed with a spirit-soaked bud, leaving just enough grime in the creases, corners and crannies of the body panels. T-Cut and some physical buffing gives the paintwork a well-burnished and greasy shine that looks like a cleaner's oily rag has been hard at work, while fresh misting of soot, track dirt and brake dust have accumulated in the hours (and miles) since the engine left its home shed, running cross-country through all weathers.

ABOVE: This 'Grange' may have been supplied with a factory-weathered finish, but a little fine-tuning with T-cut, cotton buds and varying shades of enamels, weathering powders and Tamiya pigments has brought a more bespoke and convincing appearance.

BELOW: For an extreme weathering job, it is important to layer the dirt and build up streaks and runs. After all, the real engine would have taken years to accumulate all this filth. Unless fresh from the works, locomotives such as this War Department 'Austerity' 2-8-0 would never enjoy the attentions of a cleaning gang, especially towards the final years of steam. Enamels, acrylics and Tensocrom paints have been used in various stages and in subtly different shades, applied by hand and airbrush, along with plenty of talcum powder, in order to achieve the 'crusty' appearance of trapped soot, ash, rust and coal dust. As the running numbers became impossible to discern, shed staff often resorted either to painting new numerals on top of the muck, or chalking them on the cab sides and smokebox.

CHAPTER 15

What Next?

Throughout the previous fourteen chapters, a great many of the skills and techniques required in the detailing and modifying of ready-to-run steam locomotives have been covered. Each of the tasks demonstrated has aimed to get the most out of the essential fabric of every model. However, there will always be room for stretching yourself further, not least in terms of improving mechanical performance.

MECHANICAL MATTERS

A quick, convenient and high-performance solution to upgrading older, tender-driven Hornby models is to fit a purpose-built replacement as offered by the Hollywood Foundry. Known as a BullAnt unit, this chassis consists of a powerful, high-quality motor, large brass flywheel and drive to all three axles. The unit featured here has been designed to be an easy (but not direct) fit into the tender of the Hornby LMS '2P' 4-4-0 or '4F' 0-6-0, although there are a number of other options available, either as off-the-peg repowering solutions, or as bespoke units, built to any specification (within certain parameters).

As it replaces a motor unit with plastic wheels and rubber traction tyres, fitting the BullAnt also adds six extra power collection surfaces and

The Hornby LMS '2P', along with other tender-driven models, is beginning to show its age when set against the latest releases, not least in terms of its plastic driving wheels. Although my example is not a bad runner, the performance can be vastly improved by fitting a replacement motor unit. Custom-built in Australia, this BullAnt drive unit features power collection on all wheels, plus drive to each axle and a hefty brass flywheel to promote smooth operation – and all for around £50 (at 2009 prices).

the whole package offers superior performance. Installation is straightforward and the tender chassis can be improved further by the addition of brake gear and rigging, secured to the inside of the plastic chassis frame and independent of the new motor assembly. Indeed, with other modifications and enhancements, the elderly '2P' can be made into an impressive model; not bad for something that was designed by Airfix back in 1981.

The BullAnt unit is designed to be a straightforward fit into the tender of the Hornby '2P' or '4F'. After removing the Hornby motor, the chassis requires some minor modifications to allow the new unit to fit, each end of the aperture being opened-out until the BullAnt's frame can slip inside from below.

Insert the new power unit, fixing the twin wing brackets onto the plastic chassis. Orient the drive shaft end towards the locomotive or the tender body will not be able to be re-fitted. Ensure that the wheel centres align with the axleboxes.

Don't forget to solder the power lines from the locomotive to the BullAnt, checking that the polarity of each is correct and, after thorough testing, the motor can be run in for a period, according to the instructions. If all is satisfactory, the tender body can be refitted. To provide sufficient ballast, one of the original steel weights can be refitted to the rear and I also took the opportunity to squeeze in some extra weight to the underside of the moulded coal load, ensuring that it did not foul the motor or flywheel.

The lack of any brake gear is a glaring omission from the '2P', so adding at least a representation of what should be there will greatly enhance the underframe. Etched components from the Mainly Trains range, as featured in earlier chapters, have been utilized here, fixed to the plastic frames and not the BullAnt chassis.

The finished '2P' – new front bogie wheels, buffers, chimney, handrails, couplings, cab doors and fallplate are some of the improvements made. Along with the new drive unit, this model can now sit alongside the best of the modern products without looking out of place.

GLAZING

A small number of the models featured in these pages are produced with either a cursory amount of cab glazing, or none at all. Additionally, more recent releases contain clear plastic in only some of the cab-side apertures, so being able to fill these voids with a convincing representation of glass is important.

Clear plastic card, cut and fixed in place, is the most convincing solution, although it takes time to get the new parts to fit properly. Fixing can also be tricky, although, if used with care, liquid glazing products can provide excellent results when used as adhesives, setting to a completely transparent finish. Naturally, the liquid glazing is a viable option for use in its own right, particularly for areas such as front or rear spectacle plates and other areas of a model that are likely to receive little handling. Although looking exceptional when set, liquid glazing compounds remain very fragile and susceptible to damage.

Where they were fitted, wooden window surrounds are a nice feature to capture in miniature, using fine strips of wood veneer around a piece of clear plastic. These panels often sat in channels inside the cab, allowing the window to be slid open and fitting some representation of this also adds a little something extra.

Liquid glazing offers the answer to filling empty cab window apertures, saving the hassle of cutting individual pieces of clear plastic. By adding a thin bead of Glue 'n' Glaze, or a similar product, around the edge of the opening, the material can be drawn across with a clean cocktail stick, being careful to avoid introducing any air bubbles.

Once dry, the glazing becomes completely transparent. While this can look great, handling the model carelessly can damage the glazing.

Adding the distinctive wood surround to a sliding cab window is a simple but highly effective upgrade. Check that your prototype carried such a feature, although they were very common. This LNER 'J39' is a typical example.

FINAL THOUGHTS

Modern models certainly offer a level of detail far superior to what was offered ten years ago and we can only dream of the advances that may be made during the next decade. However, the notion that the consumer is constantly being offered more choice is only true up to a point. In 1959, the Western Region of BR had more than one hundred different classes of steam locomotive. Compare this number to the combined output of Hornby and Bachmann, which offer a choice of just over sixty types, spread over the various regions. I mentioned earlier about r-t-r makers now looking further back into the past to find suitable subjects for new models and, as I pen this last chapter, I've just heard that Bachmann is planning to include the GCR Robinson 2-8-0 in its range, something that modellers have been dreaming of for years.

However, the Big Two brands in OO gauge steam locomotives are also aware that they need to keep upgrading existing products, so the amount of virgin territory that is likely to be entered over the coming years may be limited. Therefore, the route to obtaining anything out of the mainstream is likely to involve kit-building, kit-bashing, or converting a vaguely similar r-t-r model. Smaller companies, such as OO Works, have been offering short runs of hand-built but fully r-t-r model steam locomotives for some time now and these are not as expensive as might be supposed. The proliferation of limited-edition products, such as those commissioned by some of the larger model shops, has been an interesting development in the hobby. In addition, Dapol is now treading carefully back into the OO r-t-r market and who knows when this company may announce a steam-outline model to complement its impressive N gauge selection.

Undeniably, there have been a number of quantum steps made in the model railway world during my time in the trade and it's clear that the hobby is changing. This is not only a reflection of the rise in the production quality of r-t-r stock, buildings, scenery and modular track systems, but also in a potential depletion of practical skills and, just as importantly, of inclination, particularly in generational terms. It's probably unusual now to have woodwork teachers promoting model railways as viable projects for GCSE coursework, encompassing so many materials and techniques, as my own teachers did. I wouldn't class myself as being particularly old, but plenty of my contemporaries, being destined for office work rather than a trade, did not develop the craft or DIY aptitudes offered in the school system that my father's generation did.

A shift in perceived forms of leisure and the pressures of work also play their part in dictating modelling trends and, however buoyant the present market may be, encouraging the next generation of modellers is a responsibility that we must all shoulder. Otherwise, without long-term potential markets, how much choice will remain in the r-t-r marketplace fifty years down the line?

Whatever the future may hold for this rewarding hobby, I hope that readers have found some useful information here and, more so, that some degree of inspiration has been taken that can be transferred into your own ideas and projects.

Appendix

USEFUL ADDRESSES

TRADE

247 Developments
Seven Acres
Meltham Road
Marsden
West Yorkshire
HD7 6JZ
Tel: 07872 823 017
www.247developments.co.uk
Etched nameplates and locomotive detailing
components

Aidan Campbell
22 Queens Road
Hoylake
Wirral
CH47 2AH
www.aidan-campbell.co.uk
OO gauge figures, including locomotive crew

The Airbrush Company Ltd
Unit 7
Marlborough Road
Lancing Business Park
Lancing
West Sussex
BN15 8UF
Tel: 08700 660 445
www.airbrushes.com
Lifecolor paints, Iwata airbrushes, painting
equipment, Expo Tools and much more

Alan Gibson
(Workshop)
P.O. Box 597
Oldham
Lancashire
OL1 9FQ
Tel: 0161 678 1607
Detailing components, wheels and handrail
wire

Alexander Models
37 Glanton Road
North Shields
Tyne & Wear
NE29 8LJ
Tel: 0191 257 6716
Email: alexandermodels@fsmail.net
Locomotive and tender kits and components

Axminster Power Tool Centre Ltd
Unit 10
Weycroft Avenue
Axminster
Devon
EX13 5PH
www.axminster.co.uk
Craft and hobby tools

Brassmasters
P.O. Box 1137
Sutton Coldfield
West Midlands
B76 1FU
www.brassmasters.co.uk
Locomotive and tender kits and detailing
components

Cammett Ltd
Unit 5
Greenfield Industrial Estate
Forest Road
Hay-on-Wye
HR3 5FA
Tel: 01497 822757
www.cammett.co.uk
Modelling tools (including Hold 'n' Fold and
the Nutter), accessories and materials

Chris Leigh
Model Rail
Media House
Lynchwood
Peterborough
PE2 6EA
'Golden Arrow' locomotive and carriage
adornments

Comet Models
105 Mossfield Road
Kings Heath
Birmingham
B14 7JE
Tel: 0121 242 1740
www.cometmodels.co.uk
Kits, components, accessories and tools

Crafty Computer Paper
Woodhall
Barrasford
Hexham
Northumberland
NE48 4DB
Tel: 01434 689 153
www.craftycomputerpaper.co.uk
Materials for DIY water-slide transfers

Dart Castings
17 Hurst Close
Staplehurst
Tonbridge
Kent
TN12 0BX
www.dartcastings.co.uk
Cast figures including locomotive crews

Deluxe Materials
Unit 13
Cufaude Business Park
Bramley
Hampshire
RG26 5DL
Tel: 01529 455034
www.deluxematerials.com
Adhesives, fillers, applicators and scenics

East Kent Models
89 High Street
Whitstable
Kent
CT5 1AY
Tel: 01227 770777
Hornby and Lima spare parts

First Class Trains
221 Galmington Road
Taunton
Somerset
TA1 4ST
Tel: 01823 337460
Working oil lamps for locomotives
www.ukmodelshops.co.uk/catalogue/firstclass

Fox Transfers
4 Hill Lane Close
Markfield Industrial Estate
Markfield
Leicestershire
LE67 9PN
Tel: 01530 242801
www.fox-transfers.co.uk
Transfers, etched plates and paints

Hatton's of Liverpool
364–368 Smithdown Road
Liverpool
L15 5AN
Tel: 0151 733 3655
www.hattons.co.uk
R-t-r models at discount prices

Howes Models ltd
12 Banbury Road
Kidlington
Oxon
OX5 2BT
Tel: 01865 848000
www.howesmodels.co.uk
Railmatch paints and detailing components

Mainly Trains
Unit C
South Road Workshops
Watchet
Somerset
TA23 0HF
Tel: 01984 634543
www.mainlytrains.co.uk
Tools (including the Bill Bedford handrail
bending jig), materials, paints and own range of
detailing components

Markits
P.O. Box 40
Watford
Hertfordshire
WD24 6TN
Tel: 01923 249711
Email: markits@btinternet.com
Detailing components and wheel sets

MG Sharp Models
712 Attercliffe Road
Sheffield
South Yorkshire
S9 3RP
Tel: 0114 244 0851
www.mgsharp.com
R-t-r models, A1 Models detailing components
and Kadee couplings

Modelmaster Decals
31 Crown Street
Ayr
KA8 8AG
Scotland
Tel: 01292 289770
www.modelmasterdecals.com
Transfers and etched plates, including the
former Jackson Evans range

Motorbogies.com
www.motorbogies.com
Custom-built or ready made remotoring
solutions (BullAnts) from the Hollywood
Foundry

Phoenix Precision Paints
P.O. Box 8238
Chelmsford
Essex
CM1 7WY
Tel: 01245 494050
www.phoenix-paints.co.uk
Paints, varnishes and thinners

Precision Labels
www.precisionlabels.com
Also available from Frizinghall Models, Tel:
01274 747447
Transfers and headcode panels

Robert Humm & Co.
Transport booksellers
Station House,
Stamford
Lincolnshire
PE9 2JN
01780 766266
www.roberthumm.co.uk

Sarik Vacform
www.sarik-vacform.com
Model locomotive servicing stations that
include a foam cradle and tool store

Shawplan Model Products
2 Upper Dunstead Road
Langley Mill
Notts
NG16 4GR
Tel: 01773 718648
www.shawplan.com
Although catering for diesel and electric
modellers, the packs of lamp bracket strip are
suitable for steam locomotives

Slater's Plastikard Ltd
Temple Road
Matlock Bath
Derbyshire
DE4 3PG
Tel: 01629 583993
www.slatersplastikard.com
Modelling materials, sprung locomotive buffers,
adhesives

Squires Model and Craft Tools
100 London Road
Bognor Regis
West Sussex
PO21 1DD
Tel: 01243 842424
www.squires.com
Tools, equipment and materials

Wizard Models
P.O. Box 70
Barton upon Humber
DN18 5XY
Tel: 01652 635885
www.wizardmodels.co.uk
www.51l.co.uk
Sprat & Winkle couplings and detailing
components

MANUFACTURERS

Bachmann Europe plc
Moat Way
Barwell
Leics
LE9 8EY
Tel: 0870 751 9990
www.bachmann.co.uk

Hornby Hobbies ltd
Westwood
Margate
Kent
CT9 4JX
www.hornby.com

SOURCES OF INFORMATION

A1 Steam Trust
www.a1steam.com

Historical Model Railway Society
www.hmrs.org.uk

Kadee Couplers
www.kadee.com

National Model Railroad Association (British Region)
www.nmrabr.org.uk

National Railway Museum
www.nrm.org.uk
Tel: 08448 153 139

The Terrier Trust
www.terriertrust.org.uk

UK Model Shop Directory
www.ukmodelshops.co.uk

UK Steam Information
www.uksteam.info

REFERENCE MATERIAL SOURCES

Bauer Consumer Media
Media House
Lynchwood
Peterborough
PE2 6EA
Tel: 0845 120 4600
www.model-rail.com
Publishers of:
Model Rail
Four-weekly magazine covering all aspects
of railway modelling, including all eras and
worldwide subjects
And:
Steam Railway
Monthly magazine charting the current
happenings within the British and international
steam preservation movement

Ian Allan Publishing Ltd
Hersham
Surrey
KT12 4RG
www.ianallan.co.uk
Publishers of:
Hornby Magazine
Monthly railway modelling magazine,
favouring the early BR period
www.hornbymagazine.com
Also publishers of countless books on railway
and transport history

Irwell Press Ltd
59A High Street Clophill
Bedfordshire
MK45 4BE
Tel: 01707 876713
www.irwellpress.co.uk
Publishers of:
British Railways Illustrated
Monthly historical magazine of the BR steam
era

And:
Railway Bylines
Monthly magazine devoted to branch lines,
industrial railways, narrow gauge, light railways
and Irish railways
Also publishers of books on railway and
transport history

Midland Counties Publications
4 Watling Drive
Hinckley
Leics
LE10 3EY
Tel: 01455 233747
www.midlandcountiessuperstore.com
Publishers of an extensive range of railway-
related titles.

Peco Publications and Publicity Ltd
Beer
Seaton
Devon
EX12 3NA
Tel: 01297 20580
www.peco-uk.com
Publishers of:
Railway Modeller
A long-standing monthly magazine dealing
with all aspects of British-based railway
modelling

Pendragon Publications
Michael Blakemore
Tel: 01347 824397
Publisher of:
Back Track
A quality historical monthly magazine dealing
with all aspects and eras of Britain's railways

Redgauntlet Publications
P.O. Box 2471
Bournemouth
Hants
BH7 7WF
Tel: 01202 304849
Publisher of:
Steam Days
Monthly, generously illustrated magazine,
concentrating on the history of British steam,
particularly in BR days

Warners Group Publications plc
The Maltings
West Street
Bourne
Lincs
PE10 9PH
Publishers of:
British Railway Modelling
Monthly modelling magazine covering all
aspects of the hobby
www.britishrailwaymodelling.co.uk

Wild Swan Publications Ltd
1–3 Hagbourne Road
Didcot
Oxon
OX11 8DP
Tel: 01235 816478
Publishers of:
Model Railway Journal
Bimonthly journal aimed at the finescale
modeller (mainly British outline), across all
periods; also publishers of a range of books,
concerning both the 'real' railways and railway
modelling

Bibliography

BOOKS

The ABC of British Railways Locomotives, Combined Volume, Summer 1959 and 1963 editions (Ian Allan Ltd)

Atkins, C.P., *The BR Standard 9F 2-10-0s* (Irwell Press, 1993)

Banks, C., *British Railways Locomotives 1962* (OPC, 2005)

Burridge, F., *Nameplates of the Big Four* (OPC, 2006)

Clarke, D., *Locomotives in Profile No.5: Riddles Class 6/7 Standard Pacifics* (Ian Allan, 2006)

Doherty, D., *The LMS Duchesses* (MAP, 1973)

Essery, R.J. and Jenkinson, D., *Illustrated History of LMS locomotives, Volume 5: The Post-Grouping Standard Engines* (Silverlink, 1989)

Hunt, D., Essery, R. and James, F., *LMS Locomotive Profiles, No.5 The Mixed Traffic Class 5s – Nos.5000–5224* (Wild Swan, 2003)

Hunt, D., Essery, R. and James, F., *LMS Locomotive Profiles, No.6 The Mixed Traffic Class 5s – Nos.5225–5499 and 4658-4999* (Wild Swan, 2004)

Hunt, D., Jennison, J., Essery, R. and James, F., *LMS Locomotive Profiles, No.8 The Class 8F 2-8-0s* (Wild Swan, 2005)

Hunt, D., Essery, R. and James, F., *Midland Engines, No.3 The Class 2 Superheated 4-4-0s* (Wild Swan, 2000)

Jenkinson, D., *The Power of the Duchesses* (OPC, 1982)

Kardas, H., *Portrait of the Terriers* (Ian Allan, 1999)

Leigh, C. (ed.), *Model Railway Constructor, Annual 1987* (Ian Allan, 1986)

Lloyd, R., *The Fascination of Railways* (Allen & Unwin, 1951)

Lovett, D. and Wood, L. (Cade, R. and Gallafent, B., eds), *Cade's Locomotive Guide* (Marwain Publishing, 2007)

Molyneaux, T. and Robertson, K., *Pacifics on the South Western* (Ian Allan, 2006)

Morrison, G., *The Power of the BR Standard 4-6-0s* (OPC, 2003)

Morrison, G., *Rebuilt Royal Scots* (Ian Allan, 2002)

Morrison, G., *The Power of the Austerities* (OPC, 2006)

Peel, D., *Locomotive Headboards, the Complete Story* (Sutton, 2006)

Rowledge, J.W.P. and Reed, B., *The Stanier 4-6-0s of the LMS* (David & Charles, 1977)

Ryan, J., McIntosh, D. and Moon, G., *The Power of the 8Fs* (OPC, 2006)

Semmens, W.B. and Goldfinch, A.J., *How Steam Locomotives Really Work* (Oxford University Press, 2003)

Swinger, P., *The Power of the B1s* (OPC, 1994)

Tyler, K., Bond, J. and Wilkinson, A. (eds), *Stanier 8F 2-8-0* (Bradford Barton, 1979)

Welch, M., *The Art of Weathering* (Wild Swan, 1993)

Whiteley, J.S. and Morrison, G., *The Power of the BR Standard Pacifics* (OPC, 1984)

Wilkinson, A., *Stanier 8Fs at Work* (Ian Allan, 1986)

Wragg, D., *The Southern Railway Handbook 1923–1947* (Sutton, 2003)

ARTICLES

Allen, C.J., 'The LNER B1 4-6-0s in Retrospect', *Railway World* (April 1968, pp150–4)

Anon., 'British Railways Heavy Freight Locomotives', *The Railway Gazette* (29 January 1954, pp124–6)

Beattie, I., 'The BR Standard Class 5', *Railway Modeller* (September 1989, pp420–2)

Beattie, I., 'Gresley Class J39', *Railway Modeller* (January 1995, pp12–13)

Blakemore, M. (ed.), '"Granges" on the Great Western', *Back Track* (October 2003, pp570–1)

Blakemore, M. (ed.), 'Parade of the Panniers', *Back Track* (August 2007, pp482–5)

Brodrick, N., '"Small is Beautiful" (Improving the Hornby "Terrier")', *Model Rail* (November 2006, pp40–1)

Cross, D., 'King Arthurs of the Southern Railway', *Locomotives Illustrated* (No.7, 1976, pp4–5)

Kaazmierczak, P., 'BR Standard Tenders', *Model Railway Constructor* (May 1981, pp354–61)

Leigh, C., '120 Years and Still a Winner: "Brighton Terrier" Masterclass', *Model Rail* (February 2002, pp34–42)

Leigh, C., 'Stanier's "Duchess"', *Model Rail* (September 1999, pp18–23)

Leigh, C., 'The Stuff of Legend: "King Arthur" Masterclass', *Model Rail* (May 2008, pp52–7)

Percival, D., 'Masterclass: Gresley's "A3" 4-6-2s', *Model Rail* (March 2000, pp42–51)

Rixon, G., 'The LMS "Jinty" Class 3F 0-6-0T', *Steam World* (January 1994, pp22–3)

Romans, M., 'Masterclass: GWR Pannier Tanks', *Model Rail* (Christmas 2007, pp22–9)

Shackleton, T., 'Building a Better "Jinty"', *Model Railway Journal* (No.160, 2005, pp163–72)

Shackleton, T., 'The Perfect Choice? – Modelling a Pair of BR Standard Class 5s', *Model Railway Journal* (No.144, 2003, pp185–93)

Wright, T., 'Great "Scots"', *Model Rail* (June 2003, pp20–7)

Wright, T., 'WD Austerity Masterclass: Riddles' Rugged Workhorses', *Model Rail* (September 2002, pp42–9)

Index